Model-based Software Engineering

Model-based Software Engineering

G. Bruno

Dipartimento di Automatica e Informatica
Politecnico di Torino
Torino
Italy

CHAPMAN & HALL

London · Glasgow · Weinheim · New York · Tokyo · Melbourne · Madras

Published by Chapman & Hall, 2-6 Boundary Row, London SE1 8HN, UK

Chapman & Hall, 2-6 Boundary Row, London SE1 8HN, UK

Blackie Academic & Professional, Wester Cleddens Road, Bishopbriggs, Glasgow G64 2NZ, UK

Chapman & Hall GmbH, Pappelallee 3, 69469 Weinheim, Germany

Chapman & Hall USA, One Penn Plaza, 41st Floor, New York NY10119, USA

Chapman & Hall Japan, ITP-Japan, Kyowa Building, 3F, 2-2-1 Hirakawacho, Chiyoda-ku, Tokyo 102, Japan

Chapman & Hall Australia, Thomas Nelson Australia, 102 Dodds Street, South Melbourne, Victoria 3205, Australia

Chapman & Hall India, R. Seshadri, 32 Second Main Road, CIT East, Madras 600 035, India

First edition 1995

Printed in Great Britain by T.J. Press, Padstow, Cornwall

ISBN 0 412 48670 9

A catalogue record for this book is available from the British Library

∞ Printed on permanent acid-free text paper, manufactured in accordance with ANSI/NISO Z39.48-1992 and ANSI/NISO Z39.48-1984 (Permanence of Paper).

To Pia, Giulia and Silvia
and to my parents, Cristina and Giovanni

Contents

List of figures   xi

1   Introduction   **1**
   1.1   Aim of the book   2
   1.2   Background   4
   1.3   Contents of the book   6
   1.4   Acknowledgments   6

2   Structured analysis   **9**
   2.1   Functional models   9
       2.1.1   The data dictionary   12
       2.1.2   Merging and branching dataflows   13
   2.2   An example of a functional model   14
   2.3   More about the functional model   20
       2.3.1   Mastering complexity   21
       2.3.2   Top-down or bottom-up analysis   22
       2.3.3   Reusability   23
       2.3.4   Executability   24
   2.4   Information models   25
       2.4.1   Entities and attributes   25
       2.4.2   Relationships   27
       2.4.3   Extensions to the ER formalism   29
   2.5   An example of an information model   30
       2.5.1   Navigation   31
   2.6   Integrating functions and information   33
   2.7   Control models   35
   2.8   Integrating functions and control   40
   2.9   Summary   45

3 Object orientation   **47**
   3.1   Object-oriented programming   47
         3.1.1   The major features of OOP   49
   3.2   Object-oriented analysis   54
   3.3   An example of an OOA model   55
         3.3.1   Class-Relationship models   56
         3.3.2   State and functional models   58
         3.3.3   Event models   61
   3.4   Summary   61

4 Petri nets   **63**
   4.1   Basic concepts   63
   4.2   Modeling with Petri nets   69
   4.3   Properties of Petri nets   74
         4.3.1   Reachability   74
         4.3.2   Boundedness and safeness   75
         4.3.3   Liveness   75
         4.3.4   Reversibility   76
   4.4   Analysis of behavioral properties   76
   4.5   Subclasses of Petri nets   80
         4.5.1   State machines   80
         4.5.2   Marked graphs   81
         4.5.3   Free-choice nets   83
         4.5.4   Extended free-choice nets   84
         4.5.5   Asymmetric-choice nets   84
   4.6   Reduction rules   87
   4.7   Timing constraints   90
         4.7.1   Timed marked graphs   94
   4.8   High-level nets   96
   4.9   Summary   101

5 Protob   **103**
   5.1   Protob nets   103
         5.1.1   Places and tokens   104
         5.1.2   Transitions   105
   5.2   Temporal behavior   109
         5.2.1   Simulation of the model   115
   5.3   Views   116
   5.4   Object orientation   118
         5.4.1   Local variables and parameters   124
         5.4.2   Using local variables   126
   5.5   Building client server models   130
   5.6   Inheritance   134
   5.7   Adding services to net-based objects   135

	5.7.1	Using services and nets	138
5.8	Comparison with structured analysis		138
5.9	Summary		144

6 Quid **147**

6.1	Operational information models		148
	6.1.1	Navigation	151
	6.1.2	Navigating inheritance relationships	155
	6.1.3	Object-oriented navigation	157
	6.1.4	Navigating recursive relationships	159
6.2	Actor models		160
6.3	Summary		166

7 Building models **167**

7.1	Model architecture		167
	7.1.1	Actors and object models	172
	7.1.2	Navigational statements in transitions	178
7.2	Modeling simple behaviors		181
7.3	Combining behaviors		190
	7.3.1	An example of synchronous transitions	194
7.4	Summary		197

8 Model-based software engineering **199**

8.1	Basic development chain		200
8.2	Simulation process		201
	8.2.1	Animation of models	202
8.3	Application generation process		207
8.4	Operational life cycle		208
	8.4.1	System modeling	210
	8.4.2	Software modeling	210
	8.4.3	Software production and maintenance	211
	8.4.4	Comparison with other life cycles	212
8.5	Program generation		213
8.6	Tools		218
8.7	Summary		224

9 Applications **225**

9.1	CIM systems		225
	9.1.1	Shop-floor design	226
	9.1.2	Supervisor design and development	232
9.2	Telecommunications systems		239
9.3	Summary		243

10 Epilogue   **245**
   10.1 Results of model-based software engineering   245
   10.2 Future trends   247
   10.3 Conclusion   249

References   **251**

Index   **255**

List of figures

2.1   The models used in structured analysis   10
2.2   A dataflow diagram   11
2.3   The simplified layout of the manufacturing cell   15
2.4   An example of production data   16
2.5   A fragment of the supervisor data dictionary   17
2.6   The context diagram of the cell supervisor   18
2.7   The major functions of the cell supervisor   19
2.8   The expansion of process Assign_Mission   20
2.9   The description of process Issue_Mission_2   21
2.10 The description of process Send_W_Cmd   22
2.11 The process tree of the cell supervisor model   23
2.12 The entities of the company database   26
2.13 The entities and relationships of the company database   28
2.14 A case of inheritance   30
2.15 Two cases of composition   31
2.16 The information model of the cell supervisor: view A   32
2.17 The information model of the cell supervisor: view B   33
2.18 An instance graph related to the supervisor information
      model   34
2.19 The control model of the lighting of a room   36
2.20 The control model of a simple cell   37
2.21 The state-transition diagram of process Control_Cart   38
2.22 The state-transition diagram of process Control_Warehouse   39
2.23 The control model of the cart motion   42
2.24 A fragment of the cell control system   44

3.1   The graphical representation of an object   48
3.2   A case of inheritance   53
3.3   A case of polymorphism   54
3.4   Models used in object-oriented analysis   56

3.5   The Class-Relationship model of the manufacturing cell   57
3.6   The Class-Relationship model contained in the supervisor   58
3.7   The state model of the supervisor   59
3.8   The functional model of the supervisor   60
3.9   The event model of the manufacturing cell   61

4.1   A Petri net   65
4.2   The firing rule   66
4.3   The graph of the markings for the net shown in Figure 4.1   67
4.4   The actual reachability graph for the net shown in Figure 4.1   68
4.5   Interactions between a producer and a consumer   69
4.6   Interactions between a sender and a receiver   70
4.7   The model of the workstation   71
4.8   Interactions between the workstation and its environment   72
4.9   The state-transition diagrams of the workstation   73
4.10 The reachability tree for the net given in Figure 4.1   78
4.11 The coverability graph for the net given in Figure 4.5   79
4.12 The marked directed graph for the net given in Figure 4.6   82
4.13 The modified sender/receiver model exhibiting a deadlock   82
4.14 The marked directed graph for the net given in Figure 4.13   83
4.15 A safe FC net   85
4.16 An FC net which is not live   86
4.17 Transformation of an EFC net into an equivalent FC net   87
4.18 Symmetric and asymmetric confusion   88
4.19 Reduction rules   89
4.20 The reduction of the net shown in Figure 4.1   91
4.21 A net with timing constraints   93
4.22 Temporal diagram for the net given in Figure 4.21   94
4.23 Temporal diagram for the net given in Figure 4.21 with two tokens in place Idle   95
4.24 A Colored Petri net   98
4.25 The CP-net for the five dining philosophers problem   100

5.1   Places, place types and initial tokens   104
5.2   A transition that propagates tokens and modifies their contents   107
5.3   A transition with a predicate   110
5.4   Transitions with different priorities   111
5.5   Delayed-release transitions   112
5.6   The evolution over time of the model shown in Figure 5.5   113
5.7   A net including a delayed-firing transition   114
5.8   The decomposition into views of the model shown in Figure 5.5   117

5.9   The model of the workstation decomposed into views   119
5.10 Objects based on nets   120
5.11 Classes and objects   121
5.12 A compound class   123
5.13 Types of links   124
5.14 Compound links and compound ports   125
5.15 Parameters and local variables   127
5.16 The first model of the timer   128
5.17 The second model of the timer   130
5.18 How a server replies to the right client when there are many
      clients and one server   131
5.19 How to make several clients interact with several servers   133
5.20 Inheritance of nets   135
5.21 Symbols and connections used in the net model and in the
      service model   136
5.22 The third model of the timer   139
5.23 The fourth model of the timer   140
5.24 Transformation rules from DFDs into Protob nets   141
5.25 Transformation rules from DFDs into Protob nets (contin-
      ued)   143

6.1   A Quid model   149
6.2   An object graph related to the model shown in Figure 6.1   150
6.3   The order in which an object graph is traversed   152
6.4   A model featuring inheritance   156
6.5   A fragment of the information model related to a Petri net
      editor   158
6.6   A recursive relationship   159
6.7   An actor model   161
6.8   The Protob net describing client actors   162
6.9   The Protob net describing server actors   163
6.10 The Protob net describing router actors   164
6.11 A Protob class that includes an actor model   165

7.1   The actor model of the manufacturing system   169
7.2   A class that includes an actor model   170
7.3   A class that includes an actor diagram   171
7.4   The main view of class Supervisor   172
7.5   The object model included in the supervisor   174
7.6   The views of class Supervisor   175
7.7   The views of class Supervisor (continued)   177
7.8   A transition that acts on an object graph   179
7.9   The state-transition diagram of the cart   183
7.10 The state net of a single cart   185

7.11 The multiple-state net that handles four carts   187
7.12 The state net of the warehouse   188
7.13 The standard forms of interaction between actors   191
7.14 The actors forming the cell supervisor   193
7.15 The actors of the production system   195
7.16 A compound actor obtained by merging two simple actors   197

8.1   The basic development chain   200
8.2   The simulation process   201
8.3   The animation of a net during simulation   203
8.4   Browsing an information structure during simulation   206
8.5   The application generation process   207
8.6   The simulation and application generation processes inte-
      grated   209
8.7   Implementation models   214
8.8   The model of the simulation workbench   217
8.9   The model of the application workbench   219
8.10 A fragment of the behavior of the Protob editor   220
8.11 Part of the information model of the Protob editor   222

9.1   The simplified layout of a gearbox assembly plant   227
9.2   The shop-floor model of the gearbox assembly plant   229
9.3   The model of the line   230
9.4   The model of the marking station   231
9.5   The model of the plant management system   233
9.6   The extended model of the marking station   235
9.7   The new model of the line   236
9.8   Part of the model of the line supervisor   237
9.9   Distributed code generation for the plant management
      system   238
9.10 An example of the animation of a line supervisor   239
9.11 A call from a ground operator to a train operator   241
9.12 A simplified model of the call   242
9.13 An example of the animation of the model of the call   243

1

Introduction

The realization of a software system can be hindered by several troubles which originate from three major causes: the intrinsic complexity of the system, the difficulty of mastering the underlying technology and the poor organization of the development process.

Intrinsic complexity makes it difficult first to transform an often vague idea of the system to be developed into a set of clear and consistent requirements and then to check that what is being developed matches all the functional and non-functional requirements.

Mastering the underlying technology, such as programming languages, operating systems, network facilities and graphical interfaces, requires considerable effort as well as skills that are costly to develop. Distributed real-time applications are probably the greatest challenge because they need all the above-mentioned skills, and, what is more, if such skills are not available, the time and cost of providing them often account for a large part of the budget of the project.

Process improvement is a hot topic in all industrial sectors. In fact, the emphasis placed on the quality of the process comes from a firm belief that the quality of the final product very much depends on the quality of the production process itself. Growing interest is being shown in finding ways that help managers understand and control the software process effectively (Humphrey, 1989), but there is still a long way to go.

The above-mentioned obstacles can be overcome by taking action in three major directions: understanding, tools and organization.

The thesis of this book is that ideas should be formalized using models that are based on operational modeling languages. Models can be simulated and animated in order to generate behavioral traces which can then be compared with what was originally expected. Understanding is thus improved, since analysts can actually work out exactly how the system functions by observing its behavioral traces; in particular, they can validate the behavior and assess the performance of the system.

Further, support tools can be built to automatically transform models into applications so that developers can avoid going deeply into the technical details of the underlying technology, just as programmers who use a third-generation programming language ignore all issues related to the operation of the processor and to the management of devices.

Finally, using models makes the production process more transparent, improves the possibility of reuse and facilitates maintenance.

The approach presented in this book is referred to as *model-based software engineering* in order to emphasize the key role played by models. Software development consists, therefore, in building, testing and refining models within a seamless process that leads the analyst/developer from analysis to design and finally to the implementation of the system. Operational models can be executed and tested during each phase so that quality control is spread throughout the whole development cycle.

1.1 Aim of the book

Using models to study the properties of complex systems is common to all disciplines. Models can be scaled physical systems, mathematical equations or functional representations.

In general, a model is an abstract, rigorous representation of a system, which enables the user to reason about a well-defined set of its properties.

If attention is focused on software development, models are used during analysis to specify the functions and the behavior of the system being considered and during design to define the architecture of the implementation.

The definition of requirements, which is the aim of the analysis phase, is a critical activity. In fact, requirements which are not clear often lead to the development of inappropriate products, thus causing disputes to arise between the purchaser and the supplier. Therefore, if the analyst builds a model that formalizes the requirements, he or she can get an insight into the behavior of the system being developed and work out whether there are any possible inconsistencies or whether any information is missing, before the actual development takes place.

However, the study of a model yields only limited results if it is based solely on inspection, whereas if the model can be executed so that traces of the system's behavior are obtained, then a thorough analysis can be performed and the risk of delivering an unsatisfactory product is minimized.

Growing interest is being shown in operational models (Zave, 1984), i.e. models that can be executed using a suitable support environment. Most operational models are graphical and can be considered as high-level programs which are developed using high-level modeling languages.

An operational model can be modified and tuned until the behavioral traces it generates match those expected. In this way, the model is a reference point for the development of the system and, what is more, the purchaser feels confident that the system, being developed according to the model, will behave properly.

Operational models often allow timing constraints to be expressed and, consequently, a discrete-event simulation of the model can be performed. In this way, statistical estimates of the system's parameters can be collected in order to support decision making. When a formal proof would be too expensive, such statistics can confidently be used to determine some properties of the system.

Operational and evolutionary principles can be brought together to form a powerful software development paradigm. In fact, what characterizes software development with respect to the other disciplines, such as the design and manufacture of mechanical parts, is that the model and the final system have a common origin since they are both computer programs.

For this reason, the final system can be seen as the final step of an evolutionary transformation which enriches the initial abstract model with details and progressively turns it into the deliverable system.

This approach provides important benefits, such as

1. minimizing the risk of finding out that information is missing or inconsistent at the time the system is brought into operation;

2. maximizing the reuse of software modules (this is because their corresponding models are reused and reusing models is much easier than reusing programs);

3. improving productivity, because the final code can be generated from the model automatically.

There are two key factors in the model-based life cycle described in this book.

The rigorous modeling language. The same language can be used at different levels (e.g. specification and design) and by different people (e.g. analysts, implementors and end-users) with unambiguous semantics. Since the language is operational, the model can always be validated.

The technology. Several advanced support tools are needed to put this approach into practice. The most important tools are graphical editors, code generators and simulation and application workbenches. Such tools enhance productivity as the complete application can be produced from its model automatically.

This book presents *model-based software engineering* in terms of two modeling languages, Protob and Quid: the former covers functional and control issues while the latter addresses informational aspects.

The major aims of Protob are illustrated below.

Expressivity. By combining the most important features of high-level timed Petri nets with those of extended dataflows, Protob provides an integrated view of both functional and control aspects. Protob is an object-oriented modeling language which supports the *software chip* metaphore. Protob objects are parameterized building blocks which can easily be put together to form more powerful objects or even final applications. Such a capability enables the developer to effectively reuse ideas, and not only pieces of code.

Executability. Protob models can be simulated and animated and such features are essential to understand complex requirements, to evaluate alternatives rapidly, to get performance figures early and, in general, to control the quality of models.

Productivity. According to the operational paradigm, an executable program can be generated from the model. However, such a program is generally conceived only as a prototype of the final system, and is suitable for exploring and evaluating some of its features but is not intended to become the actual implementation. Instead, the technology associated with Protob makes it possible to generate automatically an efficient implementation for a variety of target architectures, including both embedded systems and distributed ones. The code generation feature of Protob, which is, in principle, similar to that of an optimizing compiler, supplements the operational paradigm with the possibility of dramatically increasing productivity.

Protob models can automatically be translated into distributed programs, therefore the designer can focus his or her attention on conceptual issues, since the management of concurrent processes and of inter-process communications is performed implicitly according to the behavior expressed by the model.

Quid supports Entity-Relationship models as well as Class-Relationship models. It provides linguistic constructs to manage objects and associations between them and also to navigate the object base. Navigation enables the analyst to move from a given object to all the objects that are associated with it by virtue of a given relationship. It is possible to act on the objects that are met during navigation.

Protob models and Quid models can be integrated, therefore all the issues of a complex system are handled within a coherent, conceptual and operational framework.

1.2 Background

A pioneer operational language for embedded systems is Paisley, which was developed by Zave (1982). It is a textual language based on functional programming and on communicating concurrent processes and calls for a considerable programming skill.

Graphical models have been used for a long time for specification and design purposes: dataflows (De Marco, 1979 and Gane and Sarson, 1979), extended dataflows for real-time systems (Ward and Mellor, 1985 and Hatley and Pirbhai, 1987), structure charts (Yourdon and Constantine, 1978) and Entity-Relationship diagrams (Chen, 1976) are well known formalisms. For a survey of requirements specification techniques the reader is referred to the recent book by Davis (1993).

Dataflows are well-known models aimed at describing the functions that the system being considered must perform. They do not exhibit operational features because of the restrictions imposed by the technology at the time they were designed.

Several developers of CASE tools have recently tried to overcome the limitations of traditional dataflows by enabling analysts to specify functions using an executable language and by introducing rules for scheduling the execution of functions. However, the lack of effective structuring features makes it difficult to use dataflows when complex systems, which are made up of several interacting components, have to be modeled.

The object-oriented approach offer superior features with regard to the architecture of models. Several techniques have been proposed, such as OMT (Rumbaugh *et al.*, 1991), Fusion (Coleman *et al.*, 1994), OOA by Coad and Yourdon (1991) and by Shlaer and Mellor (1988 and 1992), OOD (Booch, 1986 and 1991) and responsibility-driven design (Wirfs-Brock, Wilkerson and Wiener, 1990). Such techniques, being based on the notions of classification, inheritance, composition and relationship, facilitate the decomposition of models into building blocks, the objects, which are easier to understand and to reuse. However, they are still descriptive approaches, since models based on them cannot be executed, and this is mainly due to the fact that their attention is focused on architectural issues rather than on the rigorous definition of the behavior of the building blocks.

On the other hand, classical control models, such as those based on finite-state automata, state charts and Petri nets, are by their very nature operational models. In fact, such modeling languages have intrinsic execution mechanisms, but they can only be used to represent the control aspects of a system.

Petri nets (Murata, 1989), which express concurrency and synchronization in a very elegant way, have been extended to handle functional aspects and timing constraints as well. However, most languages derived from Petri nets are system modeling tools rather than software development ones; further, they are not suitable for building very complex models.

The need to combine the best features of the above-mentioned approaches led to the development of Protob (Baldassari and Bruno, 1991), a graphical language which is amenable to different kinds of execution. In fact, the possibility of using Protob as both a system modeling language and a software development tool is what characterizes the integration that has been pursued in our work.

The same goal, i.e. providing operational models, has been pursued with regard to information structures; thus another modeling language, Quid (Bruno, Grammatica and Macario, 1992), has been developed.

1.3 Contents of the book

Chapters 2-4 survey the best known modeling techniques. Chapter 2 focuses on the structured approach and illustrates its three dimensions, i.e. functions, information structure and control. Chapter 3 discusses the principles of object orientation and emphasizes object-oriented modeling. Chapter 4 presents traditional Petri nets, surveys the major subclasses and gives a short description of Colored Petri nets as well as of the meaning of timing constraints.

Chapters 5 and 6 illustrate the Protob and Quid modeling languages. Chapter 5 describes the basic features of Protob nets, the object-oriented decomposition of Protob nets, the metaphore of software chips and the transformation of dataflows into Protob nets. Chapter 6 illustrates operational information models as well as actor models whose classes are Protob classes; the features of Quid and, especially, the notion of navigation are presented.

Chapter 7 explains how models built with Protob and Quid can be integrated and what the resulting architecture is. It is shown how complex Protob models can be made up of simple actors which interact with each other using standard interaction mechanisms.

Chapter 8 illustrates the operational life cycle that is based on Protob and Quid. It is explained how models can be simulated and animated and how distributed programs can automatically be generated from Protob models. The development of the support tools according to such a life cycle is discussed as well.

Chapter 9 describes the modeling and development of two complex applications in the domains of computer-integrating manufacturing systems and of telecommunications systems.

1.4 Acknowledgments

The ideas expressed in this book were developed over a long period of time during which I have had the opportunity of working with several talented people, colleagues, students and users, each of whom made an important contribution. It would be too long to mention all of them, further there is the risk of leaving someone out, so I would like everyone who has worked with me to know that I am grateful for their help.

I also wish to thank all the people of the Artis company who, by developing and marketing the Protob and Quid support tools, have turned *model-based software engineering* into a reality.

Finally, my thanks to the referees and to the editor for their suggestions.

2

Structured analysis

Structured analysis (SA) is a part of the structured paradigm, which encompasses different techniques to be used in analysis, design and coding.

SA is a technique which helps the analyst build a model of the system being considered in terms of functions, information structure and control. Modern SA integrates three well-known formalisms, namely dataflows, Entity-Relationship and state-transition diagrams, which address functional issues, information issues and control issues, respectively. The resulting models are called functional models, information models and control models.

As will be discussed later, the architecture of the integration of such models, shown in Figure 2.1, means that the functional model is very tightly coupled with the control one; furthermore, the control model is contained in the functional one.

Early publications on structured analysis (De Marco, 1979 and Gane and Sarson, 1979) mainly focused on functional models. The control model was subsequently added in order to provide a more adequate description of discrete-event systems. Pioneer texts on the integration between the functional model and the control one are those by Ward and Mellor (1985) and by Hatley and Pirbhai (1987). Recent contributions on modern SA are those by Peters (1988), Yourdon (1989) and Edwards (1993).

This chapter provides a synthesis of the formalisms that support the three above-mentioned models and discusses their limitations.

2.1 Functional models

The functional model points out what the system has to do, without showing how and when it is done.

Basically, the functional model consists of a network of processing units, called processes or functions. Each process transforms input data into output data and an output of one process can be an input of another process.

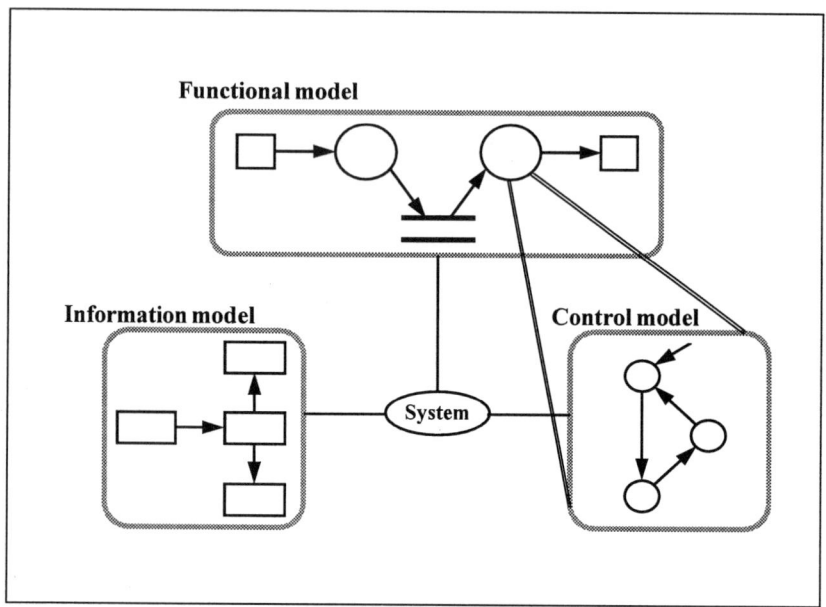

Figure 2.1 *The models used in structured analysis*

Dataflow diagrams are used to provide the functional model with a graphical representation. More precisely, the structure of a dataflow diagram (DFD) is a directed graph with three kinds of nodes: processes, agents and datastores. An example of a DFD is shown in Figure 2.2.

Oriented arcs, called dataflows, connect pairs of nodes and each arc represents a flow of information from the source node to the destination node. Information flows in discrete units called tokens; the tokens moving in a given dataflow are homogeneous.

Each dataflow has a label which describes the nature of the tokens moving in it; the label is a noun, e.g. Order, Invoice and Command. Tokens can contain simple values, such as integer numbers or characters, but they are often made up of complex structures. For example, an Order usually contains several items, such as the order date, its number, the address and the name of the customer, the information about the products ordered and payment details.

The content of tokens can formally be defined in a complementary (to the DFD) textual structure, called data dictionary. The data dictionary, which is illustrated later in this section, is based on the notation of regular expressions (Hopcroft and Ullman, 1969).

Processes, which are usually depicted as circles, are abstract computations that transform tokens taken from incoming dataflows into tokens delivered to outgoing dataflows. Since processes model actions, their labels

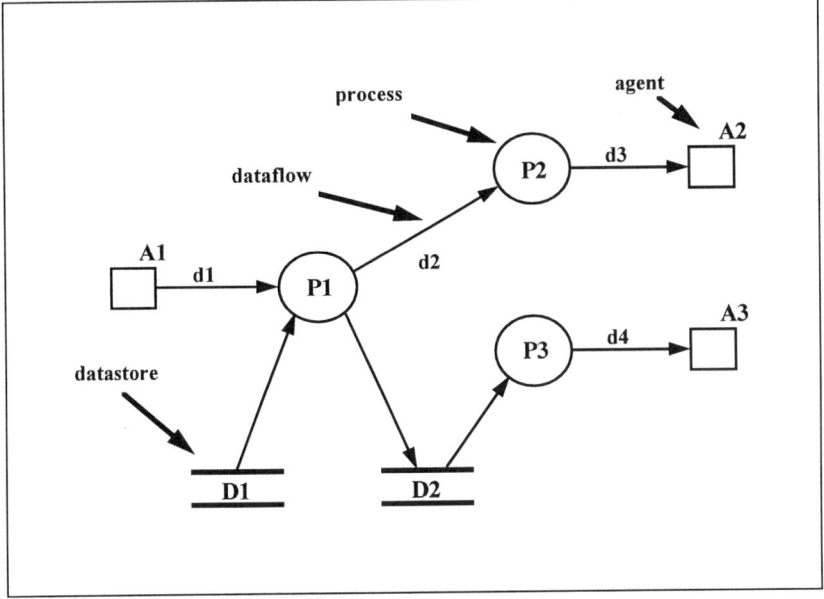

Figure 2.2 *A dataflow diagram*

are formed by an action verb followed by an object noun, e.g. Update_-
Orders and Assign_Mission.

From a modeling point of view, a process is an atomic computation step
which takes zero time to execute; it is stateless, just like a mathematical
function, because its action exclusively depends on input data. The action
of a process can be specified by means of a formal or semi-formal algorithm
or it can simply be written in English (or in a natural language). Actions
are contained in the data dictionary.

Agents, usually depicted as squares, model external entities (with respect
to the system being considered) and can only send tokens to processes
or receive tokens from processes. Each agent is labelled by a noun, e.g.
Customer and Control_Computer.

The collection of agents forms the environment of the system being considered; their role is to identify the external inputs and outputs (called
environment dataflows) of the system.

Datastores, usually depicted as pairs of parallel horizontal segments, are
facilities which store tokens for later use. They allow tokens to be retrieved
in an order which can be different from the one they had when they were
introduced.

The labels of datastores have the same meaning as the labels of dataflows.

Datastores are only connected to processes. In fact, when a process, P, is
linked to a datastore, D, e.g. P1 and D2 in Figure 2.2, P is an input process

for D and it can introduce tokens or modify tokens in D. If the dataflow connecting P to D has no label, then P is assumed to have a complete view of the structure of the tokens contained in D; otherwise (if the dataflow has a label) P has a partial view. In the latter case, as will be discussed later, the data structure associated with the dataflow must be a component of the data structure associated with the datastore.

Likewise, when a datastore, D, is linked to a process, P, e.g. P3 and D2 in Figure 2.2, P is an output process for D and it can read tokens (without removing them) or extract tokens from D. The meaning of the dataflow label is the same as in the above case.

The precise nature (insertion or modification) of the action performed on a datastore, D, by an input process, P, as well as that (extraction or reading) of the action performed on D by an output process, Q, are not apparent from the DFD and must be described in the textual information associated with the processes, such as P and Q, that act on the datastores.

The interrelationships between processes can be classified into two categories:

1. Strong coupling. When a process, A, is connected to another process, B, the dataflow between them acts as a pipeline, so tokens are received by B in the same order as they are produced by A. In Figure 2.2, processes P1 and P2 are strongly coupled.

2. Loose coupling. If a process, A, is an input process for a datastore, D, and if another process, B (B $\neq$ A), is an output process for D, then tokens are read or extracted from D in the order established by B and this order can be different from the order in which tokens were introduced by A. In Figure 2.2, processes P1 and P3 are loosely coupled.

2.1.1 The data dictionary

The data dictionary contains the definitions of data and processes.

For each dataflow and for each datastore there is a definition which either maps it onto a predefined type (such as integer, real or string) or describes its structure as the composition of several items, each item being defined with the same technique.

The definition A = B C D indicates that A consists of three items, B, C and D. The definition B = `integer` states that B is an integer number.

In order to support more complex structures, three other notions are introduced, namely repetition, optionality and choice. They are expressed by specific operators, as illustrated below.

Repetition. The items enclosed within curly brackets {} can be repeated several times (also zero times). The definition of Orders, given in Figure 2.5, shows that this term denotes a collection of data structures, each data structure consisting of three items, Order, Quantity and Wip.

If a positive number precedes the left curly bracket and/or follows the right curly bracket, a lower limit and/or an upper limit are set to the repetition. The definition of Operations, given in Figure 2.5, shows that repetitions can be nested. In fact, Operations denotes a collection of data structures, each data structure consisting of three items. The first two items are Part_Code and Op_Number, the third item is a non-empty collection of data structures made up of two items. The first such item is Op_Code and the second is a non-empty collection of Wst_Code items.

Optionality. The items enclosed within square brackets [] can be present or absent. In the definition of Workstation given in Figure 2.5, a group of three items (Order_Code, Part_Code and Current_Op_Number) is optional.

Choice. An item can often be one of several alternatives. In the definitions given in Figure 2.5, Event can be either Op_Done or Mission_Done, and Mission can be one of Mission_1, Mission_2 or Mission_3. Alternatives are listed within parentheses () and separated from each other by \ (the backslash operator). An alternative can also be a constant value, i.e. a string enclosed within " "; for example, Wst_State denotes one of three values, Idle, Working and Finished_Working.

The data dictionary can be checked in order to ensure that definitions are complete and consistent. Completeness implies that each item appearing in the definition of some term must be defined in turn; consistency requires each term to be defined only once. The definitions given in Figure 2.5 are incomplete because some terms, such as Wst_Cmd and Op_Done, are undefined.

The major entries of the data dictionary are those related to dataflows and datastores. The items that appear in such definitions and are not major entries are called secondary items. Secondary items can have a local scope or a global scope. In the former case, a secondary item, such as Mission_1, Mission_2 or Mission_3, appears in just one major definition, so it is defined after the major term it refers to and, what is more, it is shown indented with respect to the major entry. Secondary items having a global scope are defined in the section called Common Definitions.

2.1.2 Merging and branching dataflows

If a process P receives similar tokens *t* from two or more source processes, then, instead of drawing a dataflow *t* from each of them to P, we can use a merge node, which receives all the outgoing dataflows *t* from the source processes and produces only one incoming dataflow *t* for P. An example is shown in Figure 2.8, where three processes, namely Issue_Mission_1, Issue_Mission_2 and Issue_Mission_3, send similar tokens (Cart_Info) to process Send_Cart_Cmd.

The label of each incoming dataflow and the label of the outgoing dataflow of a merge node need not be the same, and if they are not, the label of the former must be one of the alternatives contained in the choice structure denoted by the label of the latter. This is the case of the merge node shown at the bottom of Figure 2.8; in fact, dataflows Wst_Cmd, Cart_Cmd and W_Cmd are merged into dataflow Command. When labels are identical, for the sake of simplicity, only the one associated with the outgoing dataflow is written.

Similar rules also hold for branch nodes. An example is shown in Figure 2.7: if Event is Op_Done, it is sent to process Notice_Op_Completion, otherwise (if it is Mission_Done) it is sent to process Notice_Mission_-Completion.

If the labels of all the outgoing dataflows of a branch node are identical to the one of the incoming dataflow, then incoming tokens are copied into all the outgoing dataflows. In this case, to simplify matters, only the label associated with the incoming dataflow is written.

2.2 An example of a functional model

In order to get an insight into functional models, we present a non-trivial case study concerning the specification of the supervisor of a manufacturing cell for mechanical parts.

Modern flexible production is based on self-contained production units, called cells, which are made up of several devices (called shop-floor devices). A group of interrelated cells forms a larger production unit, called a plant.

The production cell shown in Figure 2.3 contains four general-purpose workstations (Wst1, Wst2, Wst3, Wst4) capable of performing several operations on different parts, a warehouse (W), which stores raw materials, intermediate products and finished parts, and a cart which moves the parts.

The cart is able to perform missions and a mission consists in taking a part from one device and carrying it to another device.

Raw materials (and finished parts) are moved to (and extracted from) the cell through the warehouse using mechanisms that, for the sake of simplicity, are not considered here. We assume that raw materials are available in the warehouse; further, the warehouse has sufficient space to store intermediate products and finished parts.

The goal of this case study is to specify the cell supervisor, which is a software system responsible for managing production in the cell according to directives received from the plant management system (in short, the plant supervisor).

The following requirements illustrate the activities to be performed by the cell supervisor.

The cell supervisor acts between the shop-floor devices and the plant supervisor. It receives orders for parts to be produced by the cell. As shown

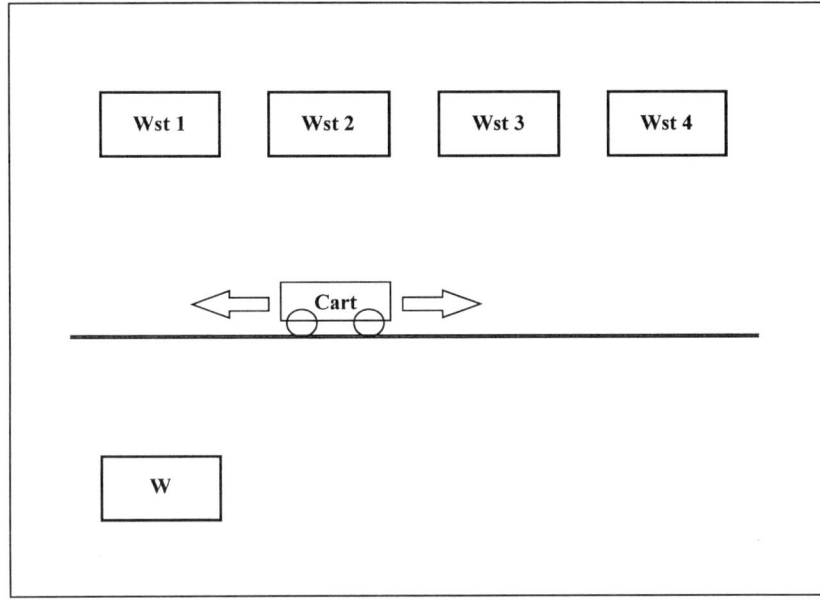

Figure 2.3 *The simplified layout of the manufacturing cell*

in Figure 2.4, each order contains the order code, the part code, the quantity of parts to be produced and the maximum number of parts (`wip`) that can form the work in process for the order. The wip value indicates what is the maximum number of parts that are allowed to circulate in the cell at any given time for that order. Wip values determine the mix of parts to be produced; as shown in Figure 2.4, in a given period the cell will produce the same quantity x of parts P1 and P3 and a double quantity, i.e. $2x$, of parts P2.

Each part requires a sequence of operations and each operation can be carried out by one of a number of equivalent (for that operation) workstations.

As shown in Figure 2.4, the operations for each type of part are defined by a structure containing the part code, the number of operations and the sequence of operations. Each operation contains the operation code and the set of the workstations that are capable of performing it.

The supervisor manages production by issuing appropriate cart missions. The major missions carried out by the cart consist in:

1. Moving a raw part from the warehouse to a workstation that is able to perform the first operation on the part.

2. Moving a part from a workstation, after the current operation has been completed, to another workstation that is able to perform the next oper-

The Structure of Orders :

Order_Code	Part_Code	Quantity	Wip

Example of Orders:

O1	P1	100	1
O2	· P2	200	2
O3	P3	100	1

The structure of Operations on Parts :

Part_Code	Op_Number
	Op_code Set of Workstations

Example of Operations on Parts :

P1	3		
	Op1	Wst1	Wst2
	Op2	Wst3	
	Op3	Wst4	
P2	3		
	Op1	Wst1	Wst2
	Op3	Wst4	
	Op4	Wst1	
P3	2		
	Op3	Wst4	
	Op4	Wst1	

Figure 2.4 *An example of production data*

ation. This mission is feasible only if the operation which has just been performed is not the final one for that part.

3. Moving a part from a workstation that has finished performing the last operation on it to the warehouse.

Additional missions could be carried out to move intermediate products into the warehouse and to retrieve them later on. In fact, it could be necessary to move a part from a workstation to the warehouse in order not to block this workstation, if there is no free workstation that is able to perform the next operation. For the sake of simplicity, such missions are not considered.

The supervisor issues commands to the shop-floor devices. These commands specify the mission to be carried out by the cart, or the operation to be performed by the workstation to which the command is addressed, or the action (storing or retrieving a part) to be executed by the warehouse.

Shop-floor devices inform the supervisor when commands have been completed by sending it appropriate events. Events can also be unsolicited, as in the case of alarms raised when mechanical failures or malfunctions are detected. For the sake of simplicity, alarms are not considered.

Periodically, the supervisor sends production reports to the plant supervisor.

The model of the cell supervisor is presented in top-down hierarchical order, from the most general view to the most detailed processes. Top-down decomposition is discussed in the next section.

Some definitions of dataflows and datastores are shown in Figure 2.5.

DATAFLOWS
Order = Order_Code Part_Code Quantity Wip
Command = (Wst_Cmd \ W_Cmd \ Cart_Cmd)
Event = (Op_Done \ Mission_Done)

DATASTORES
Orders = {Order Quantity Wip}
Operations = {Part_Code Op_Number 1{Op_Code 1{Wst_Code}}}
    Op_Code = string
    Op_Number = integer
Workstations = {Wst_Code Wst_State [Order_Code Part_Code
                                    Current_Op_Number]}
    Wst_State = ("Idle" \ "Working" \ "Finished_Working")
    Current_Op_Number = integer
Mission = (Mission_1 \ Mission_2 \ Mission_3)
    Mission_1 = Part_Code Destination
    Mission_2 = Source Destination
    Mission_3 = Source Part_Code
    Source = Wst_Code
    Destination = Wst_Code

COMMON DEFINITIONS
Quantity = integer
Wip = integer
Wst_Code = string
Part_Code = string
Order_Code = string

Figure 2.5 *A fragment of the supervisor data dictionary*

The first DFD of the model, called the context diagram, is shown in Figure 2.6. It contains only one process, Supervise_Cell, which represents the system to be specified, all the agents forming the system's environment and all the environment dataflows.

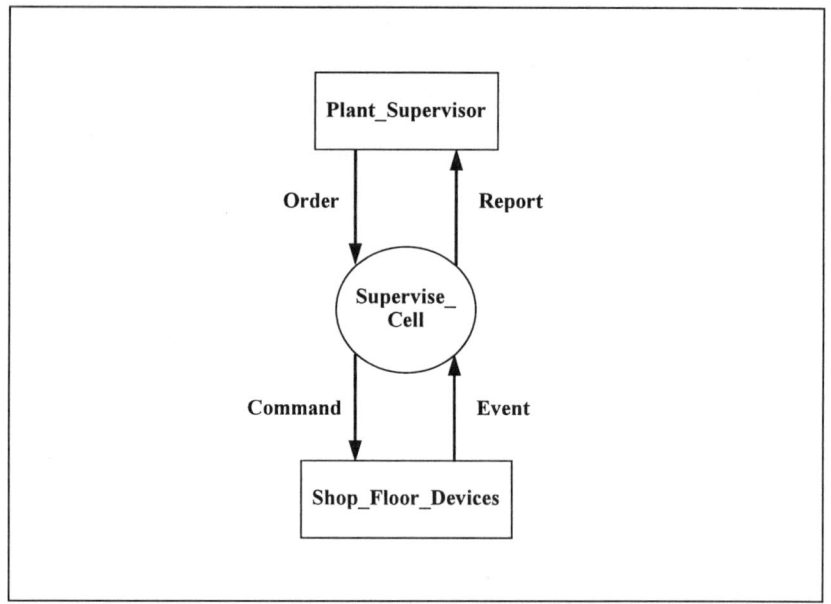

Figure 2.6 *The context diagram of the cell supervisor*

If we expand process Supervise_Cell, we obtain the DFD shown in Figure 2.7.

Communication between the cell supervisor and the plant supervisor is modeled by two processes, namely Update_Orders and Send_Report. The former receives new orders and writes them into datastore Orders, the latter periodically sends the plant supervisor information on current orders and on workstations.

Datastore Orders contains the orders received from the plant supervisor as well as current information on each order, such as the number of parts that have been produced so far and the current wip.

Datastore Workstations keeps the current state (Idle, Working or Finished_Working) of each workstation and, when a workstation is not idle, it also contains the information regarding the part that is being worked on or has just been processed by that workstation. Such information consists of the order code, the part code and the current operation number.

Events coming from shop-floor devices are managed by processes Notice_Op_Completion and Notice_Mission_Completion, which are described below.

1. On receiving an event Op_Done from a workstation, Notice_Op_Completion changes the state of this workstation to Finished_Working.

2. On receiving an event Mission_Done from the cart, Notice_Mission_Completion updates the states of the workstations involved according

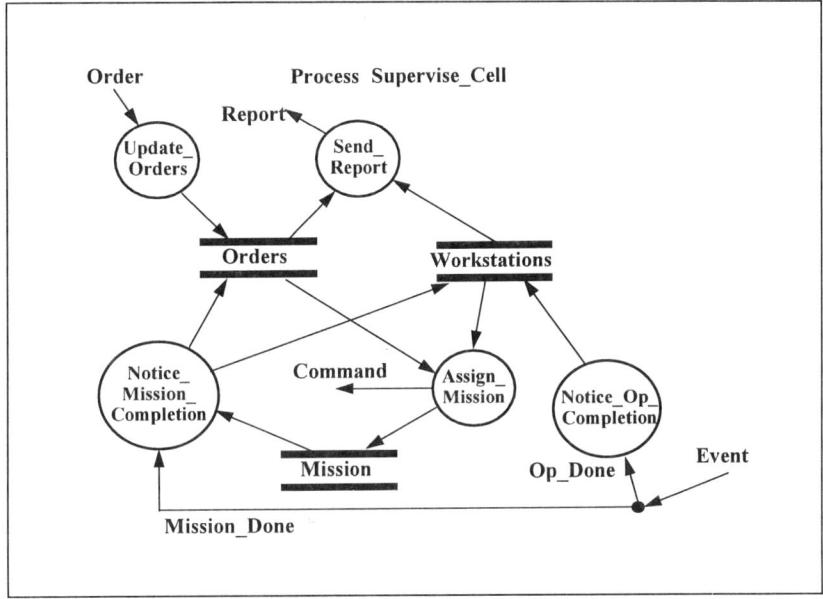

Figure 2.7 *The major functions of the cell supervisor*

to the type of the mission, and cancels the mission by clearing datastore Mission. For example, in the case of mission type 2, it changes the state of the source workstation to Idle and the state of the destination workstation to Working; further, the order code, the part code and the current operation number of the part that has been delivered to the destination workstation are associated with this workstation.

Datastore Mission contains the information about the current mission, if there is one. If there is no mission, the cart is assumed to be idle.

The decision regarding the next mission to be performed is up to process Assign_Mission. It takes the current situation of orders and the state of workstations into account and issues the appropriate commands to the shop-floor devices involved. This process encompasses a complex activity which needs to be refined, therefore it is expanded into another DFD, shown in Figure 2.8.

Each type of mission is handled by one of three different processes, namely Issue_Mission_1, Issue_Mission_2 or Issue_Mission_3. Similarly, communication with shop-floor devices is managed by specific processes, depending on the device.

Mission-handling processes look up datastore Operations, which contains the operations to be performed on each kind of part. It is assumed that the supervisor has the knowledge of all the types of the parts that can be manufactured in the cell, so this datastore is read-only.

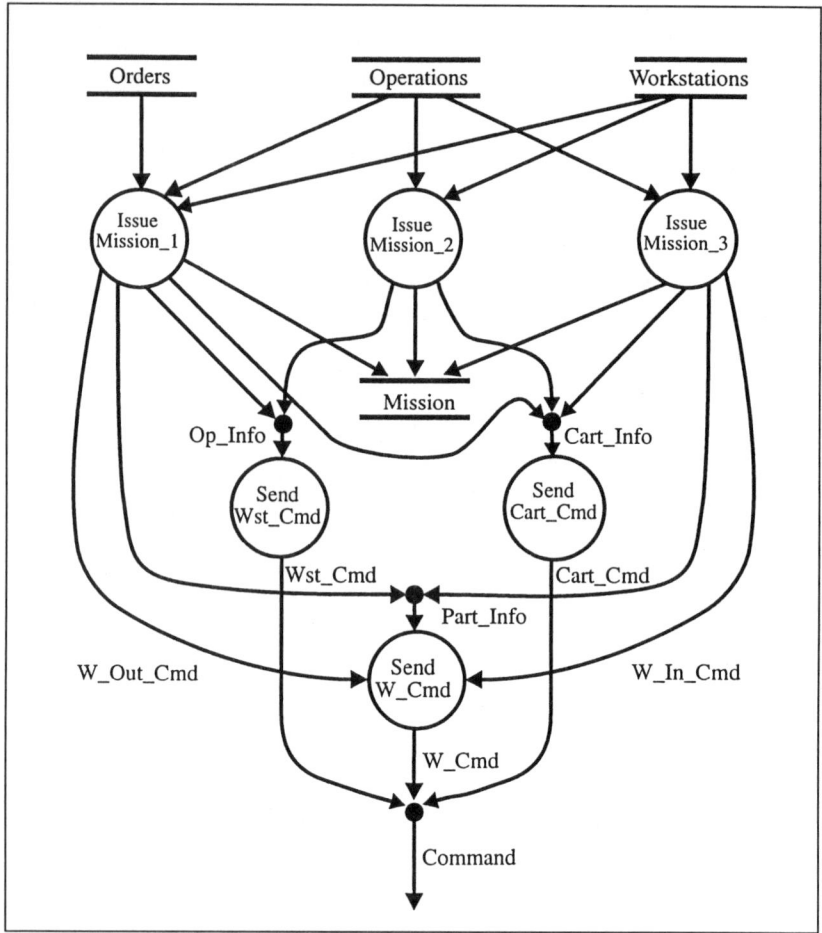

Figure 2.8 *The expansion of process Assign_Mission*

The descriptions of processes Issue_Mission_2 and Send_W_Cmd are given in Figures 2.9 and 2.10, respectively. The structure of process descriptions is illustrated in the next section.

2.3 More about the functional model

We are now in a position to complete the presentation of the functional approach and to discuss some open issues.

process Issue_Mission_2 is

precondition on Operations, Workstations, Mission is

there is no current mission (i.e. datastore Mission is empty)
and there is a workstation, A, that has finished
performing an operation, j, on a part, P,
and j is not the last operation to be performed on P and
there is a workstation, B, which is idle and
able to perform the next operation on P;
=>
action on Mission, Op_Info, Cart_Info is

generate a mission of type 2 from workstation A
to workstation B
(i.e. fill in datastore Mission with the appropriate information);
send a command to the cart and
a command to the destination workstation;

end process;

Figure 2.9 *The description of process Issue_Mission_2*

2.3.1 Mastering complexity

Hierarchical decomposition is the technique which is provided to structure
a complex model. A process can be simple or compound. In the former case,
it has a description in the data dictionary; in the latter case, it is expanded
into another DFD, whose processes, in turn, can be simple or compound.
The resulting process structure is a tree, as depicted in Figure 2.11 for the
model of the cell supervisor.

In general, hierarchical models must observe some syntactical rules which
guarantee consistency between a compound element and the model into
which it is expanded. For DFDs, there is the following rule, called flow
balancing: all the input and output dataflows of a compound process must
match the external dataflows of the DFD into which it is expanded. The
external dataflows of a given DFD are all those dataflows that have either no
source (such dataflows are called external input dataflows) or no destination
(when they are called external output dataflows) in the DFD. The missing

```
process Send_W_Cmd is

precondition on W_Out_Cmd, Part_Info;
=>
action on W_Cmd is
send an Unload command to the warehouse for the part
indicated in Part_Info;

precondition on W_In_Cmd, Part _Info;
=>
action on W_Cmd is
send a Load command to the warehouse for the part
indicated in  Part_Info;

end_process;
```

Figure 2.10 *The description of process Send_W_Cmd*

elements can be found in another DFD, the one containing the compound process.

As shown in Figure 2.6, process Supervise_Cell has two input flows, Order and Event, and two output flows, Report and Command, which match the external flows of its DFD, presented in Figure 2.7.

The same datastore can appear in several DFDs. In fact, if a datastore, D, is used by two processes, P1 and P2, in a given DFD and if P1 is compound, then D will also appear in the DFD associated with P1 and, possibly, in the DFDs of some compound processes belonging to the subtree of processes which originates from P1.

A datastore, D, is said to be local to a compound process, P, if it is used only by the processes contained in P. In the cell supervisor model, datastore Operations is local to process Assign_Mission.

Agents only appear in the context diagram.

2.3.2 Top-down or bottom-up analysis

We avoid discussing whether top-down modeling is or is not better than bottom-up modeling, because, in practice, a mix of the two is used. The pre-

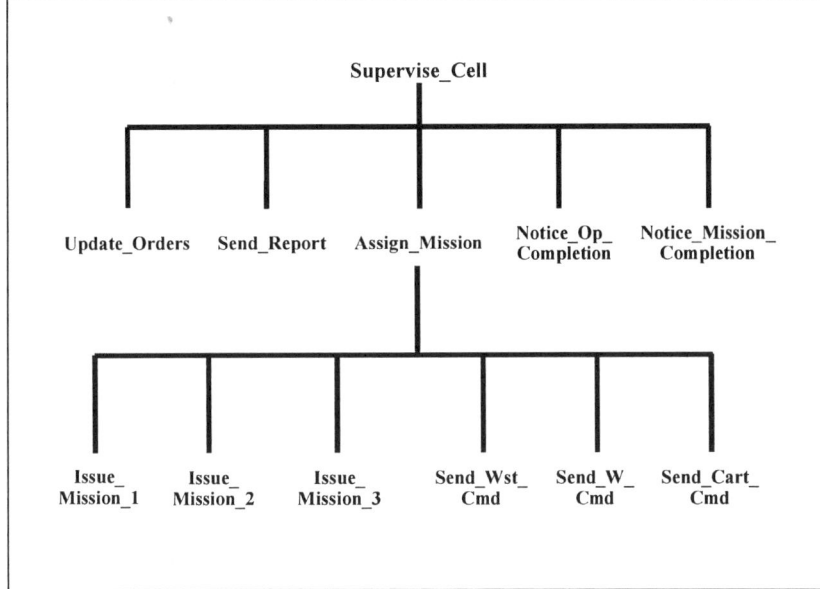

Figure 2.11 *The process tree of the cell supervisor model*

sentation of a model takes place top-down, because it is easier to explain a system from the most general concepts to the most detailed ones. However, there is no preference for one direction or the other during analysis.

If the problem is unknown, the analyst will work out a rather large network of processes which cover all the major functions, then he or she will reconstruct the missing hierarchy (this technique is called upward repartitioning). However, if the analyst is familiar with the problem or with a part of it, he or she will probably start by identifying the major subsystems top-down and then proceed bottom-up with the unknown portions.

2.3.3 Reusability

Top-down decomposition, which yields a tree structure of processes, may prevent the analyst from reusing a portion of the model. In fact, if two subsystems happen to be identical, it would be more convenient to model them using two compound processes which are expanded into the same DFD; however, this is not possible, since it would lead to a process structure which is a graph and no longer a tree.

If two independent systems have an identical subsystem, S, and the model of the first system has already been developed, the compound process (and its associated DFD) that represents S can be reused in the model of the second system only if the names of the corresponding input and output dataflows of S and of the corresponding non-local datastores of S are identical in both models. Moreover, the reuse of S is obtained by copying it from the first model to the second one.

Reusability can be greatly enhanced by means of the object-oriented approach, as will be illustrated in Chapter 3.

2.3.4 Executability

As pointed out by research on operational languages (Zave, 1984), executing a model gives us a better insight into its behavior than a simple inspection.

Three major obstacles, in the form of inaccurate information flow, informal description of processes and missing execution policy, must be overcome in order to make a functional model operational.

Inaccurate information flow. From a DFD alone it is not possible to know exactly from which input dataflows a given process, P, takes tokens and to which output dataflows it delivers tokens during a specific execution. In fact, the DFD shows what potential information is needed and produced by P, disregarding any specific execution of P. Therefore, P could require input data from dataflows (or deliver output data to dataflows) which are different from one activation to another. For example, process Send_W_Cmd has two input dataflows, W_Out_Cmd and W_In_Cmd, but it is executed whenever a token is received from either dataflow.

In order to specify the behavior of simple processes, textual descriptions are introduced into the data dictionary. The textual description of a process consists of a sequence of pairs `precondition` => `action`, where each pair defines a different mode of execution of the process. In particular, the precondition defines which input dataflows and input datastores are involved in the execution mode being considered; if the execution of the process depends on the contents of the input datastores, the precondition specifies which condition must be satisfied by the input datastores so that the process can be executed. The action indicates which output dataflows and output datastores are involved in the execution mode being considered, and describes the activity of the process.

Two examples of process descriptions are given in Figures 2.9 and 2.10.

Process Issue_Mission_2 has only one mode of execution, so it has one pair `precondition` => `action`. The precondition states that:

1. the cart must be idle (i.e. datastore Mission must be empty);

2. there must be a workstation that has finished working on a part;

3. there must be another workstation which is both idle and able to perform the next operation on that part.

The action consists in writing information on the mission into datastore Mission and in sending appropriate commands to the cart and to the workstation that will receive the part.

Process Send_W_Cmd has two modes of execution, depending on which command, W_Out_Cmd or W_In_Cmd, it receives.

Informal description of processes. The contents of preconditions and actions are often expressed in an informal language, which is not executable. As an alternative, we could use some kind of higher-level programming language and execute it by means of an interpreter.

Missing execution policy. Executing a functional model implies:

1. detecting the (simple) processes whose preconditions are satisfied (they are called enabled processes);

2. choosing the process to be executed, when two or more processes are simultaneously enabled;

3. executing the process; this means removing tokens from input data-flows and input datastores, executing the action and delivering tokens to output dataflows and output datastores.

The second step could involve the user who is asked to select the process to be executed, or can be done automatically, provided that a policy of choice has been given. A simple solution is to assign a statical priority to the processes that can simultaneously be enabled. In the example of the cell supervisor, processes Issue_Mission_1, Issue_Mission_2 and Issue_Mission_3, shown in Figure 2.8, can be enabled at the same time, so a choice has to be made: if the highest priority is given to process Issue_Mission_2, the criterion of maximizing the utilization of workstations is pursued.

In any case, external inputs, i.e. input data coming from external agents, have to be introduced manually, because the environment's behavior is not modeled by the agents.

2.4 Information models

The data dictionary illustrated in the functional model offers limited features for structuring information and is not intuitive. On the other hand, research on database systems has yielded a powerful and expressive formalism, called Entity-Relationship (ER) (Chen, 1976), which helps the analyst build conceptual data models. Such models are also suitable for software specification, so modern structured analysis incorporates the ER formalism.

The Entity-Relationship formalism is based on three concepts, namely entity, attribute and relationship.

2.4.1 Entities and attributes

An entity represents a class of individuals, all having the same features. For example, let us consider, from a logical point of view, a fragment of the database of a large company. This fragment is made up of records that refer to employees, departments and projects. Each record is the aggregation of simpler elements, called fields. There is one record for each employee, one record for each department and one record for each project.

Employee records are similar, as all of them have the same structure of fields, each field containing a value that is specific to the employee to whom the record refers. Examples of fields are: the name of the employee, the date of birth, the address, and the salary. Likewise, all department records are similar and contain the name of the department and its address. Project records contain the name of the project and its budget.

If we abstract the common features of the company database, we obtain three entities, Employee, Department and Project, which are graphically represented in Figure 2.12. Each element of the domain being considered is represented by a specific instance of an entity.

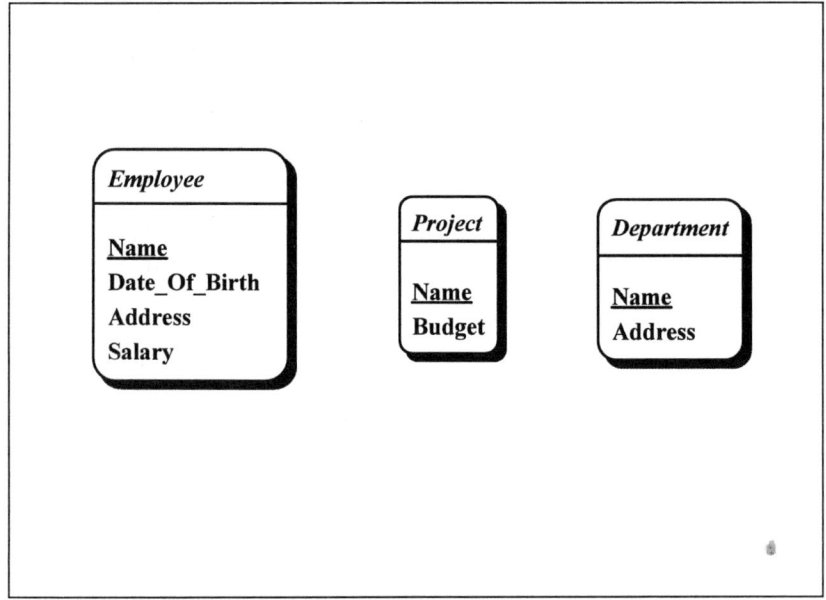

Figure 2.12 *The entities of the company database*

Each entity is depicted as a box, in which the upper name is the entity name and the other names denote the entity attributes.

The attributes of an entity indicate which attributes make up the instances belonging to the entity.

Each attribute contains a value which can be simple, such as an integer number or a character string, or composite. For the sake of simplicity, we assume values to be simple. The interested reader can find further details in the book by Elmasri and Navathe (1989).

Some attributes, or just one, of a given entity can be defined to be key attributes; this constraint implies that any pair of instances of such an entity cannot have the same combination of values in their key attributes. In the example given in Figure 2.12, Name is the key attribute of all the entities. Key attributes are underlined.

2.4.2 Relationships

The key feature of the ER formalism is the emphasis placed on the associations which exist between instances of entities. Such associations are represented in the conceptual model by relationships, which are now illustrated.

Many associations exist between the elements of the domain being considered: for example, each employee is related to the department he or she belongs to and to the project he or she works on and each project is related to the department that manages it.

Such associations between individuals can be represented, in the conceptual model, by relationships between entities. Therefore, each association between individuals is an instance of a relationship which exists between the corresponding entities.

The ER model of the company database is shown in Figure 2.13. It contains three relationships: Belongs_to which exists between employees and departments, Works_on which exists between employees and projects, and Manages which exists between departments and projects.

For the sake of simplicity, entities are depicted as rectangles and attributes are not shown. ER models are also called ER schemata or simply schemata.

The relationships that involve two entities, like those in Figure 2.13, are called binary. Relationships of a higher order (e.g. ternary) are allowed as well, but, for the sake of simplicity, we restrict our attention to binary ones.

Relationships are inherently bidirectional, i.e. they can be followed in either direction. For example, we can follow relationship Works_on from a given employee to each project he/she is involved in, or, alternatively, we can follow the same relationship from a given project to each employee assigned to it.

Relationships are drawn as oriented arcs so that the direction in which the name of the relationship must be read is indicated. In fact, if we read the names of entities and relationships in the order *Source-Entity Relationship Destination-Entity*, e.g. *Employee Works_on Project, Department Manages Project* and *Employee Belongs_to Department*, we obtain meaningful sentences.

Since relationships are drawn as oriented arcs, we often speak of source entities (or source instances) and of destination entities (or destination instances), keeping in mind that it is a convention and that entities and instances are symmetric with respect to relationships and associations.

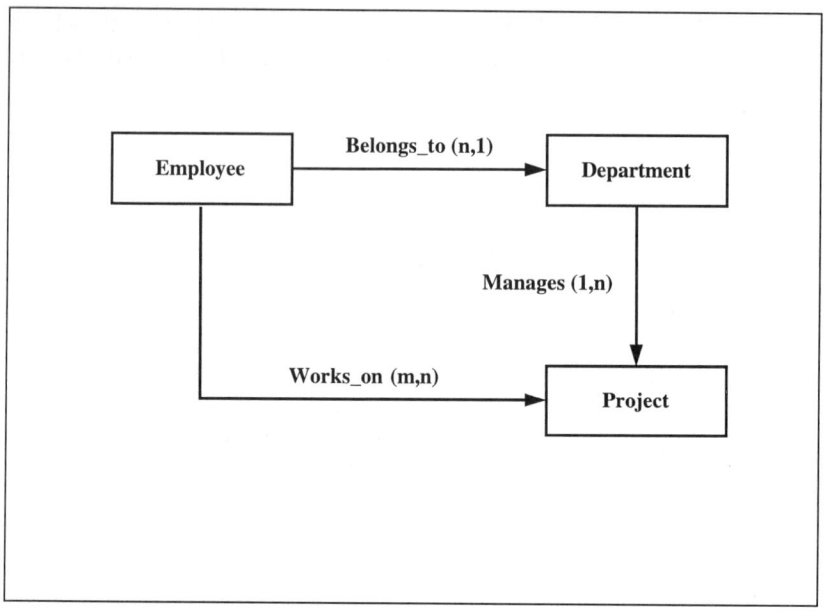

Figure 2.13 *The entities and relationships of the company database*

Relationships can also have attributes; for example, an attribute of rela-tionship Works_on could be the date of the assignment of the employee to the project.

Each relationship features a constraint, called cardinality, on the number of associations in which source instances and destination instances can be involved. Cardinalities can be one-to-one $(1,1)$, one-to-many $(1,n)$, many-to-one $(n,1)$ or many-to-many (m,n). In the example shown in Figure 2.13, relationship Works_on has a many-to-many cardinality because any em-ployee can be involved in several projects and several employees can be assigned to the same project. Relationship Belongs_to has a many-to-one cardinality because each employee belongs to just one department, but each department can have several employees. Relationship Manages is one-to-many because each department can manage several projects, but each project is managed by only one department.

In other words, the cardinality of a given relationship is a constraint on the number of associations that can enter any destination instance and leave any source instance. In fact, if a relationship, R, from an entity, A, to another entity, B, has a one-to-many cardinality, then an instance of A can be connected to several instances of B and an instance of B can be connected to at most one instance of A; therefore, there can be several associations leaving an instance of A, but at most one association entering an instance of B.

When an instance of an entity, A, can be connected to several instances of another entity, B, by virtue of a relationship, R, we can introduce the following additional constraint to enhance the descriptive power of the schema: we can order the associations leaving a source instance or those entering a destination instance. In fact, if an instance, a, of A is connected to several instances of B, say b_1, b_2 and b_3, a possible order is $a \rightarrow b_1$, $a \rightarrow b_3$, $a \rightarrow b_2$. If a relationship is ordered, we can introduce two operators, Next and Previous, which act as follows: if Next is applied to the association between a and b_1, it returns the association between a and b_3, whilst, if Previous is applied to the association between a and b_2, it returns the association between a and b_3.

In the same way, if several instances, say, a_1, a_2 and a_3, of an entity, A, are connected to an instance, b, of another entity, B, then, we can order such associations so as to obtain, for example, $a_1 \rightarrow b$, $a_3 \rightarrow b$, $a_2 \rightarrow b$. In this case, if the Previous operator is applied to the association $a_3 \rightarrow b$, it returns the association $a_1 \rightarrow b$.

We adopt the following convention to indicate the ordering of associations: if the associations leaving (entering) the source (destination) instances are ordered, then, the first (second) constraint of the cardinality of the corresponding relationship is enclosed within angular brackets.

An example of an ordered relationship is given in Figure 2.16; in fact, relationship Shaped_by associates, with each part, the sequence of operations to be performed on that part, as will be illustrated in the next section.

Many other features, such as participation constraints, can characterize relationships. For additional details, the reader is referred to the books by Elmasri and Navathe (1989) and by Batini, Ceri and Navathe (1992).

2.4.3 Extensions to the ER formalism

The basic Entity-Relationship formalism has been extended to provide more descriptive power, but, unfortunately, no standardization of the notation has been achieved so far.

The major features we present here are single inheritance and composition. Other extensions are described by Elmasri and Navathe (1989) and Batini, Ceri and Navathe (1992).

Inheritance is a special kind of relationship, called is-a, which can be used to connect a more specific entity, B, to a more generic one, A. Inheritance means that all the features (attributes and relationships) of A also become features of B. A is called a superclass of B and B is called a subclass of A.

An example is given in Figure 2.14, where Car and Truck are subclasses of Vehicle and Vehicle is a superclass of Car and Truck.

Inheritance is introduced through specialization or generalization actions. Specialization means that a given entity, such as Vehicle, can orig-

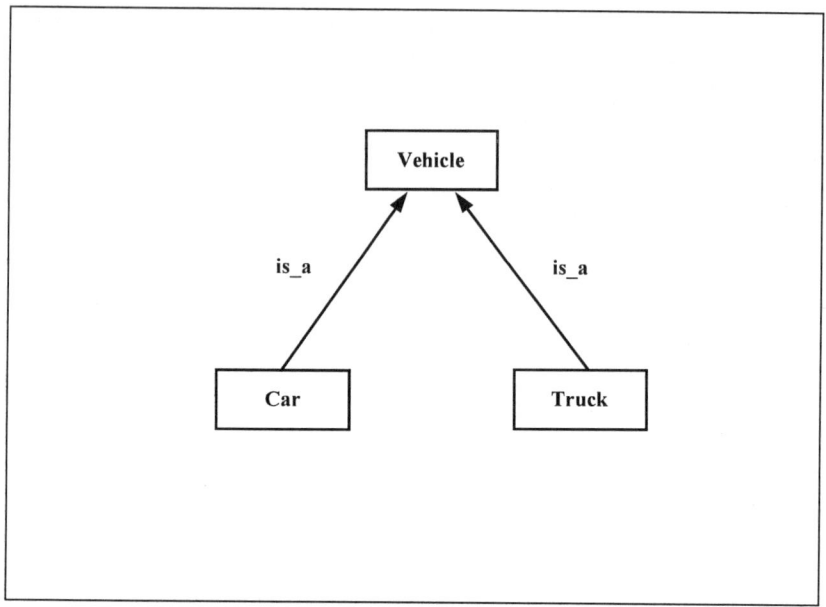

Figure 2.14 *A case of inheritance*

inate more specific entities, such as Car and Truck, while generalization
means that, if two or more entities have common features, it is possible to
abstract these features into a common superclass entity.

Composition is another special relationship, which captures a common
reality consisting of compound objects made up of component objects. This
relationship is called `is-part-of` and can be used to connect a component
entity, B, to a compound entity, A. As a consequence, each instance of A
will contain one instance of B (with all its attributes and associations).

In addition, relationship `is-part-of` has a cardinality which can be a
natural number, in the case of fixed composition, or m, when the number
of components is not known a priori. When the cardinality is 1, it can be
omitted for the sake of simplicity.

Two examples of composition are given in Figure 2.15. The first example
shows that a stool contains four legs and one seat, and that a seat is made
up of one frame and one cushion. The second example models a bill of
materials, each part of which can be the result of the assembly of several
simpler parts.

2.5 An example of an information model

Using the Entity-Relationship formalism, we can build a more expressive
information model for the cell supervisor, as compared to the data dictio-

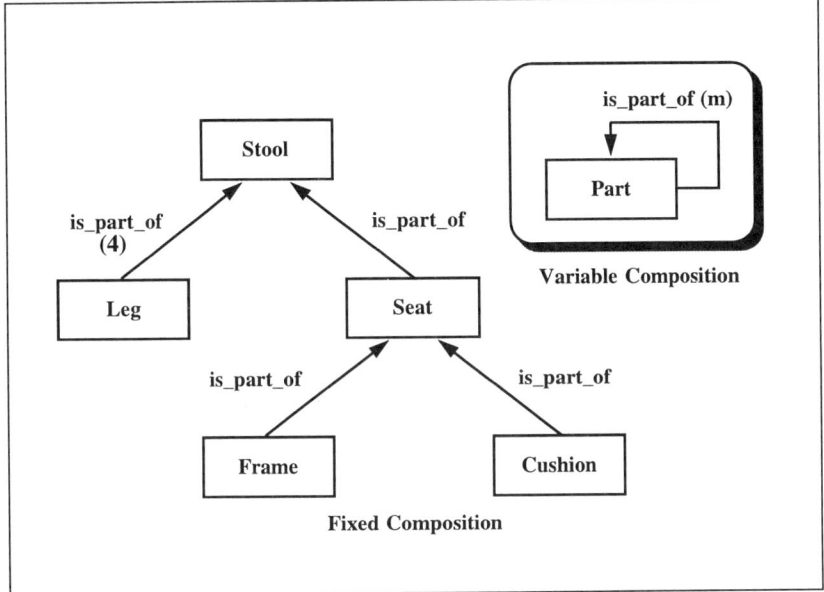

Figure 2.15 *Two cases of composition*

nary definitions shown in Figure 2.5. The information model of the cell supervisor is shown in Figures 2.16 and 2.17.

The schema given in Figure 2.16 indicates that:

1. each order refers to a particular part type;

2. each part type is shaped by a sequence of operations;

3. each operation is performed by a set of workstations;

4. each instance of entity Wip, which models a part present in the cell (i.e. a component of the work in process), is related to a particular order, is located at a particular workstation, and is currently being shaped by (or has just been shaped by) a particular operation.

The schema shown in Figure 2.17 describes the structure of missions, according to the three kinds of mission defined previously.

The ER formalism provides for horizontal decomposition. In fact, a complex schema can be decomposed into portions, called views. The same entity can appear in several views, but each relationship appears in just one view.

2.5.1 Navigation

An ER model represents a real structure, which is made up of instances of entities and relationships. Such a structure is called instance graph. An

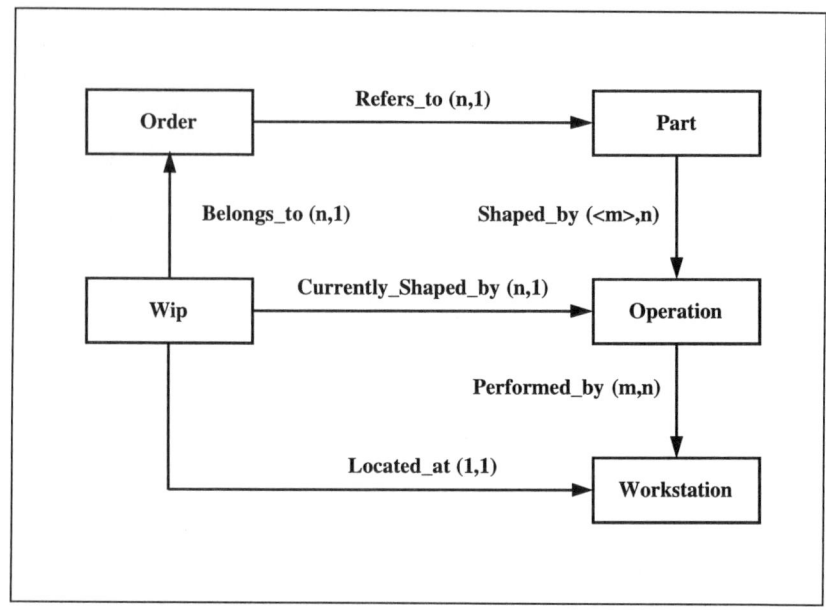

Figure 2.16 *The information model of the cell supervisor: view A*

instance graph evolves over time, since instances can be added or removed and attributes can be modified.

The instance graph that contains the supervisor data given in Figure 2.4 is shown in Figure 2.18. Each entity instance is indicated by a dot and a label is used as a reference to it. Associations are represented by oriented arcs between instances of entities, entities are depicted as sets of instances, and relationships are depicted as groups of associations.

Navigation refers to the possibility of moving from one entity instance to another, provided that an association which belongs to a given relationship exists between those instances. Using navigation we can easily answer complex questions, e.g. which are all the operations to be performed on the part represented by instance W1 of entity Wip.

In order to answer such a question, we follow association Belongs_to from W1 to O3, which represents the order to which W1 belongs; then we follow association Refers_to from O3 to P3, P3 being the part type of W1. Finally, by following the two Shaped_by associations leaving P3, we obtain operations Op3 and Op4, which give the answer to the original question.

Navigation should be supported by a suitable language so that the previous ideas can formally be expressed. An example of a navigational language is Quid, which will be presented in Chapter 6.

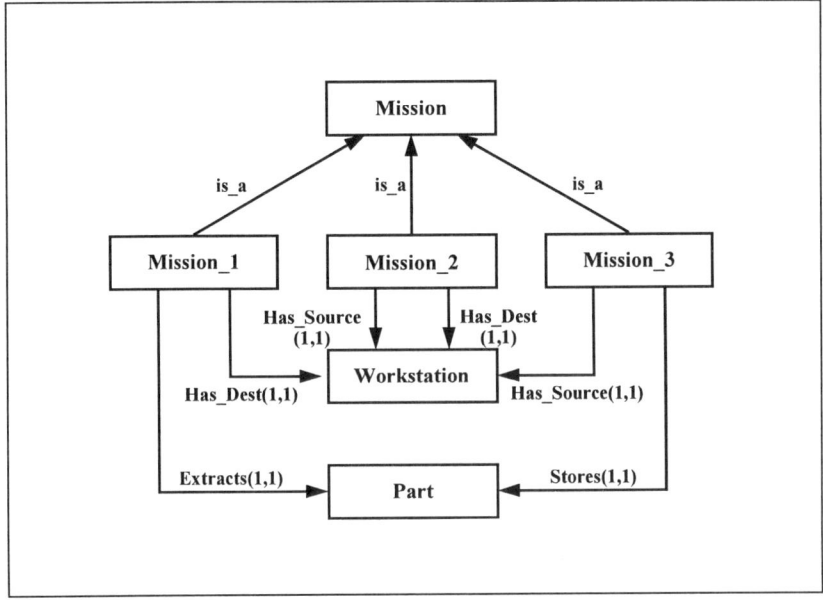

Figure 2.17 *The information model of the cell supervisor: view B*

2.6 Integrating functions and information

In general, datastores are mapped onto the entities of the information model. If we compare the functional model of the cell supervisor with the information one, we notice that datastores Orders and Workstations correspond to entities Order and Workstation, respectively, that entity Mission and its subclasses represent datastore Mission, and that datastore Operation is transformed into entities Part and Operation. On the other hand, entity Wip has no corresponding datastore, as it has been introduced after a careful analysis so that immediate information can be provided on the parts which are located at the workstations. The original functional model should be reworked in order to maintain a one-to-one mapping between datastores and entities; this exercise is left to the reader.

In addition, the ER formalism facilitates a rigorous description of functional processes in terms of navigations and operations to be performed on the underlying information model. This allows a more precise specification to be produced.

As an example of the link between the functional model and the information one, we present the precondition and the action of process Issue_Mission_2; the conditions and the navigations that are guided by the ER schema given in Figures 2.16 and 2.17 are written in italics. The instances mentioned in navigations are shown in Figure 2.18.

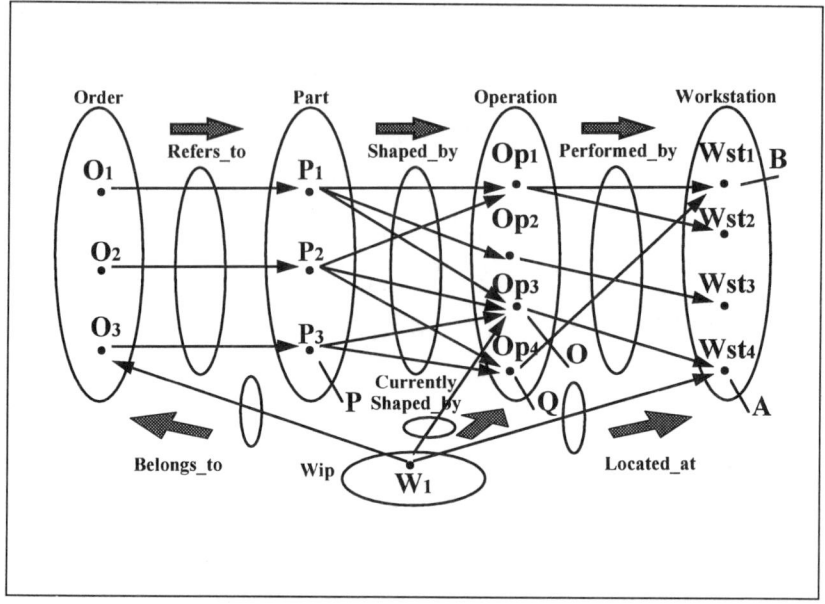

Figure 2.18 *An instance graph related to the supervisor information model*

Precondition of process Issue_Mission_2. There is no current mission (*no instance of any subclass of Mission*) and there is a workstation, A, that has finished (*A is an instance of Workstation and its state is Finished_Working*) performing an operation, O, on a part, W, which belongs to a part type, P (*W is obtained by following association Located_at from A; O is reached from W by following association Currently_Shaped_by; P is reached from W by following first association Belongs_to and then association Refers_to*), and O is not the last operation to be carried out on P (*the association from P to O is followed by another association, and Q is the next operation*) and there is a workstation, B, that is both idle and able to perform the next operation (Q) on P (*B is an instance of Workstation and its state is Idle, and there is an association Performed_by from Q to B*).

Action of process Issue_Mission_2. A mission of type 2 from workstation A to workstation B is generated (*an instance of Mission_2 is generated and it is connected to the workstation instances denoted by A and B with associations Has_Source and Has_Destination, respectively*). A command is sent to the cart and information on the next operation is sent to the destination workstation.

2.7 Control models

Since the functional model is based on data-driven processes, it is quite reasonable for pure data-processing systems, but it is inadequate when the system is reactive: a reactive system must respond to external events by executing specific functions under timing constraints and its reaction can change over time.

A new model, called control model, which is based on the notions of state, state-transition and event, provides a better representation of reactive systems.

Reactive systems often consist of several subsystems, called actors, which act concurrently and occasionally communicate and synchronize with each other. An actor is characterized by a control model which is based on a set of states, as each state defines a mode of operation of the actor. At any time, an actor is in one state, called the current state. An actor changes its state, e.g. it moves from state S_i to state S_j which becomes the current state, when it receives a particular stimulus or event.

As will be explained later in this section, if an actor has both a functional model and a control model, the latter controls the former; therefore, when the state is changed from a state, S_i, to another state, S_j, some of the functional processes that were running in S_i will be stopped, while some of the processes that were inactive in S_i will be started.

The control model is based on state-transition diagrams (STDs). A state-transition diagram is a directed graph whose nodes represent the states of the control model and whose directed arcs represent the state-transitions. States are drawn as boxes. There is one particular state, called initial state, which is indicated by just one entering arc (called initial transition), and this arc has no source state.

Each transition is labeled by an event name and all the transitions leaving a state must have different labels. Further, actions can be associated with transitions. An action, for the moment, is a sequence of events to be emitted when the transition is performed. The initial transition has no label, but it can have an action.

The STD is given the following interpretation: if a transition, T, with a label, E, and an action, A, links state S_i to state S_j, when the actor is in state S_i and event E is received, then the actor goes into state S_j, while performing action A. Events are assumed to occur at different points (instants) of time. If an event, E, is received when the actor is in a certain state and if there is no outgoing transition of this state whose label matches E, the event is lost. A transition is carried out in zero-time, thus the execution of its action is atomic and instantaneous.

An STD is built as follows. First, the analyst determines the initial state, then looking at the initial state, he or she tries to answer the following questions. Which are the next states? Which are the events causing the transitions to the next states? Which are the actions to be performed during those transitions?

In answering such questions, he or she may introduce new states that will have to be examined in a similar way. When all the states have been examined, the STD is complete.

The STD is an operational device, as it defines feasible event sequences and it shows which actions will be performed at any change of state. A feasible event sequence is a sequence of events corresponding to a path in the STD. Every path starts from the initial state (which is the first current state) and can be obtained by repeating the following steps: choose one of the transitions leaving the current state and set the current state to the one that is the destination of this transition.

An example of an STD is given in Figure 2.19(a). It shows how to control the lighting of a room by means of a push-button. At the beginning, the room is dark; each time the button is pressed (event S), the lamp is alternately switched on or off (events On and Off) to lighten or darken the room, respectively.

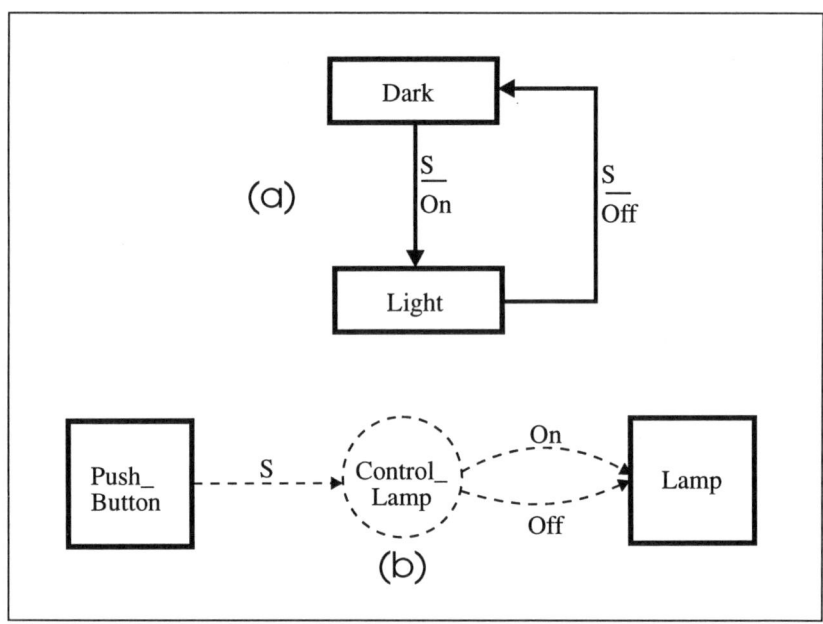

Figure 2.19 *The control model of the lighting of a room*

Events often have the meaning of commands, especially when they are directed to an agent, as is the case of On and Off in the control model shown in Figure 2.19.

A control model is made up of STDs, agents and events. As shown in

Figure 2.19(b), an STD is represented by a symbol, called control process, drawn as a dashed circle. Events flowing into/out of a control process are shown as dashed arcs and their labels match the labels associated with the transitions of the corresponding STD.

A more complex example is shown in Figures 2.20, 2.21 and 2.22. It refers to the manufacturing cell introduced previously and presents the detailed management of the cart and the warehouse. For the sake of simplicity, we assume that the cell contains only one workstation.

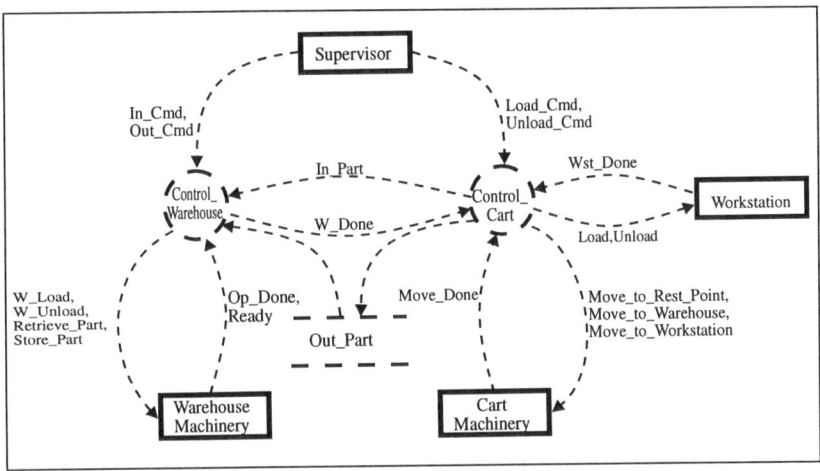

Figure 2.20 *The control model of a simple cell*

Each device is managed by a control process which interacts, by sending commands and receiving replies, with the actual machinery (made up of suitable sensors and actuators).

The control model given in Figure 2.20 contains two control processes, Control_Cart and Control_Warehouse. In general, a control model can contain several control processes.

Process Control_Cart is illustrated in Figure 2.21.

Initially, the cart is assumed to be located at a rest point between the workstation and the warehouse. The initial state of the cart is Idle; in this state, it can receive, from the supervisor, either command Load_Cmd to carry a raw part to the workstation, or command Unload_Cmd to take a finished part from the workstation. If the cart receives Load_Cmd, then it has to move to the warehouse to get a part. The cart control process starts the motion by sending command Move_to_Warehouse to the machinery which actually governs the cart. The new state is Moving_from_Rest_Point_to_-Warehouse and the control process remains in this state until it receives event Move_Done, which notifies the completion of the motion, from the machinery. Then, command Out_Part is sent to the warehouse so that it

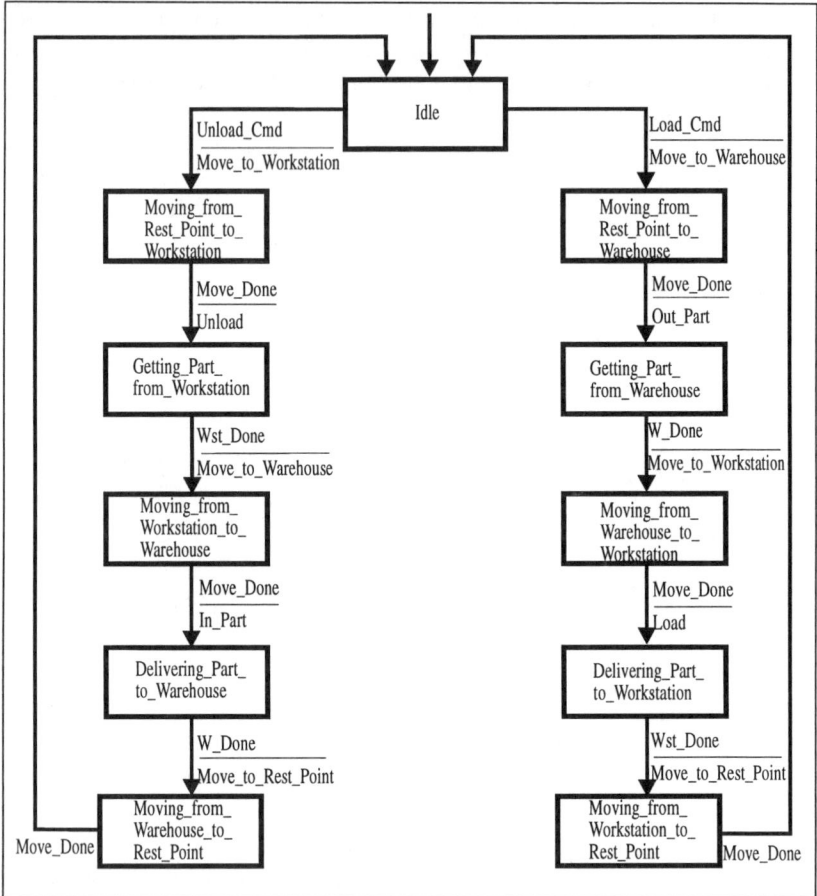

Figure 2.21 *The state-transition diagram of process Control_Cart*

delivers the part to the cart and the state becomes Getting_Part_from_-Warehouse. Delivering the part is the responsibility of the machinery of the warehouse and, when it is done, the cart receives event W_Done. This event causes the cart to move to the workstation; in fact, command Move_-to_Workstation is sent to the cart machinery and the new state is Moving_from_Warehouse_to_Workstation. When event Move_Done is received, the cart sends command Load to the workstation so that it takes the part. The workstation, after taking the part, informs the cart by sending it event Wst_Done. Finally, the cart comes back to the rest point by issuing command Move_to_Rest_Point. When the motion is done, the state of the cart control process is the initial one.

The behavior of the cart in response to command Unload_Cmd can easily be followed on Figure 2.21, so its description is omitted.

Control process Control_Warehouse, given in Figure 2.22, has a similar behavior. In fact, it has to handle two commands coming from the supervisor: Out_Cmd, when the warehouse has to deliver a raw part to the cart, and In_Cmd, when the warehouse must get ready to take a finished part from the cart and to store it.

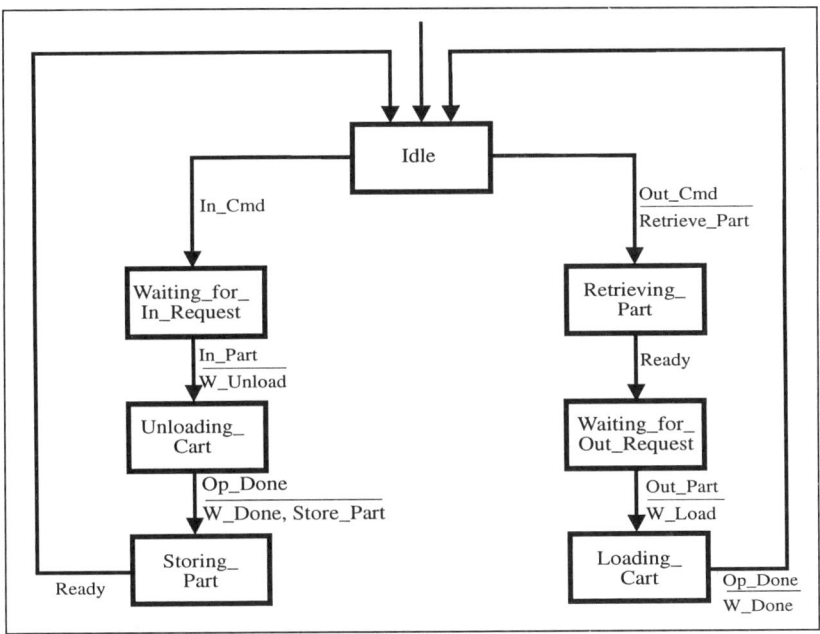

Figure 2.22 *The state-transition diagram of process Control_Warehouse*

When command Out_Cmd is received, the warehouse control process sends command Retrieve_Part to the machinery which actually governs the warehouse. The machinery responds with event Ready when the part has been retrieved and is available at the I/O port of the warehouse. At this point, the control process is able to accept command Out_Part and, when Out_Part is received, it issues command W_Load so that the machinery carries the part from the I/O port to the cart. The new state is Loading_Cart and the control process remains in this state until it receives event Op_Done, which notifies that the part has been delivered to the cart, from the machinery. As a consequence of that event, the warehouse control process sends event W_Done to the cart control process and, then, the new state is the initial one. The behavior of the warehouse in response to command In_Cmd is omitted.

A new feature of the formalism, i.e. the control store, appears in Figure 2.20. A control store is used to keep an event that must not be lost. In fact, according to the semantics of STDs, if an event, E, is received by a control process when it is in a state from which E does not cause a transition, E is lost. If the loss has to be avoided, a control store must be introduced. A control store is similar to a datastore, but it is drawn with dashed segments. It is connected only to control processes. A control store remembers the event that has been written into it by an input control process until an output control process is in a state from which there is a transition whose label matches the event.

Control store Out_Part, which appears between processes Control_Cart and Control_Warehouse in Figure 2.20, is needed because the cart could reach the warehouse (and send command Out_Part) before the warehouse has retrieved the part (i.e. the warehouse is still in state Retrieving_Part).

2.8 Integrating functions and control

The functional model shows what input data are needed by the functional processes and what output data they produce, but it does not indicate when the functional processes that are not purely data-driven must be executed. Instead, the control model, as has been illustrated so far, is able to describe an event-driven behavior, but it is not able to represent the activities that must be executed in the various states. In fact, the control model only shows the emission of commands and events.

The integration between the functional model and the control one combines two complementary views of the system. Basically, the interaction between control processes and functional processes takes place as follows: control processes can use special commands, called control flows, to start and stop the execution of functional processes, whilst functional processes can send events to control processes; therefore, control flows are directed from control processes to functional processes and events are directed from functional processes to control processes. Like event flows, control flows are drawn as dashed arcs.

From an architectural point of view, the above-mentioned integration is achieved by introducing control processes into dataflow diagrams, thus top-down decomposition is enforced.

Such an approach emphasizes the functional view of the system, because when we look at a model, first we see the functional processes, and only after zooming into a control process can we see a state-transition diagram. For this reason, the resulting formalism is known as *extended dataflows* and it is often associated with real-time systems. Well-known extended dataflow techniques are presented by Ward and Mellor (1985) and by Hatley and Pirbhai (1987). We prefer to describe their similarities, here, rather than point out their differences.

Functional processes fall into two categories: uncontrolled, or strictly data-driven, and controlled. The former are not influenced by control processes, since their execution exclusively depends on input data. The execution of the latter depends on control flows, which can be subdivided, on the basis of their labels, into the three groups listed below.

Enable. If an Enable control flow connects a control process, C, to a functional process, P, then P is started when an action of C that includes the statement `Enable P` is executed. If P is compound, all the uncontrolled processes that it contains are started.

Disable. If a Disable control flow connects a control process, C, to a functional process, P, then P is stopped when an action of C that includes the statement `Disable P` is executed. Input data received by P when it is disabled is lost. If P is compound, all the processes that it contains are stopped.

Trigger. If a Trigger control flow connects a control process, C, to a functional process, P, then P is executed once; this takes place when an action of C that includes the statement `Trigger P` is executed. The destination of a Trigger control flow is a simple functional process.

Initially, all controlled processes are assumed to be disabled, while the other processes are automatically started.

When a functional process, P, sends an event to a control process, C, then the behavior of C depends on a condition that P must check on its input data.

The example shown in Figure 2.23 details the control of the motion of the cart. We assume that the cart follows a linear route, that the warehouse is located at the origin of the reference system, and that the rest point and the workstation are located at positions x and y, respectively $(x, y > 0, y > x)$.

The machinery of the cart governs the motion step-by-step; it sends the current position of the cart to the control process and receives the following commands from it: forwards, to move the cart one step opposite to the origin, backwards, to move the cart one step towards the origin, and stop, to stop the cart at the current position. Positions are given in integer numbers.

Functional process Control_Motion is controlled by control process Control_Cart and, when it is enabled, it moves the cart on the basis of its current position (contained in dataflow Current_Position which is received from the cart machinery) and of the destination (contained in datastore Set_Point). The destination has been previously set by one of three processes, Set_Warehouse_as_Target, Set_Rest_Point_as_Target and Set_Workstation_as_Target. Each of them is controlled and copies the position of a specific destination into datastore Set_Point; the positions of the three possible destinations of the cart are contained in datastores Warehouse_Position, Rest_Point_Position and Workstation_Position.

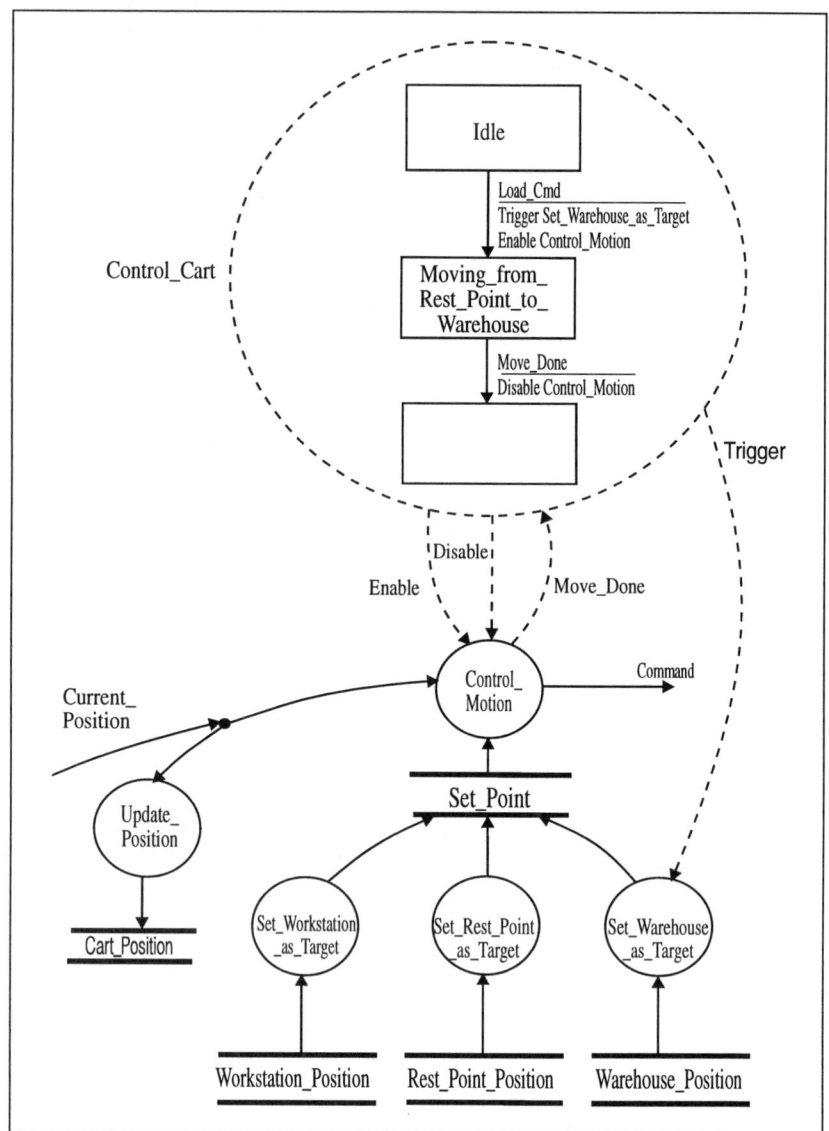

Figure 2.23 *The control model of the cart motion*

The action of process Control_Motion can be sketched as follows:

```
if Current_Position < Set_Point then
  issue Command Forwards;
else if Current_Position > Set_Point then
  issue Command Backwards;
else
  issue Command Stop and Event Move_Done;
end if;
```

Dataflow Command contains a value specifying the command to be performed.

Process Update_Position is uncontrolled and it is used to write the current position of the cart into datastore Cart_Position. An additional process which displays the current position and the speed of the cart could easily be connected to that datastore.

The fragment of STD shown in Figure 2.23 details the control of the cart during the motion from the rest point to the warehouse. Unlike the STD given in Figure 2.21, where it is assumed that the machinery is able to carry out high-level commands such as Move_to_Warehouse, in this case the machinery is driven by simpler commands. Therefore, when the control process of the cart receives command Load_Cmd from the supervisor, it updates the destination of the motion by executing process Set_Warehouse_as_Target, then it enables process Control_Motion and, finally, it enters state Moving_from_Rest_Point_to_Warehouse. In this state, it waits for the motion completion to be signalled by event Move_Done which comes from process Control_Motion.

The remainder of this section is dedicated to illustrating the interactions between control processes and those between control processes and compound functional processes.

A DFD can contain two or more control processes. If two control processes appear in a DFD, they can be peers or one can be controlled by the other. In the second case, the control process which is being controlled receives Enable and Disable control flows from the control process which is exercising the control.

Control processes can be started and stopped, just like functional processes. When a control process is started, its initial action is executed and its initial state becomes its current state. When a control process is stopped, its state becomes undefined.

As an example, a fragment of the cell control system is presented in Figure 2.24.

For the sake of simplicity, top-level process Control_Cell shows its contents transparently. It contains two compound functional processes (Manage_Cart and Manage_Warehouse) and one control process. The latter, Activate_Device_Controllers, which is automatically started, has a very simple

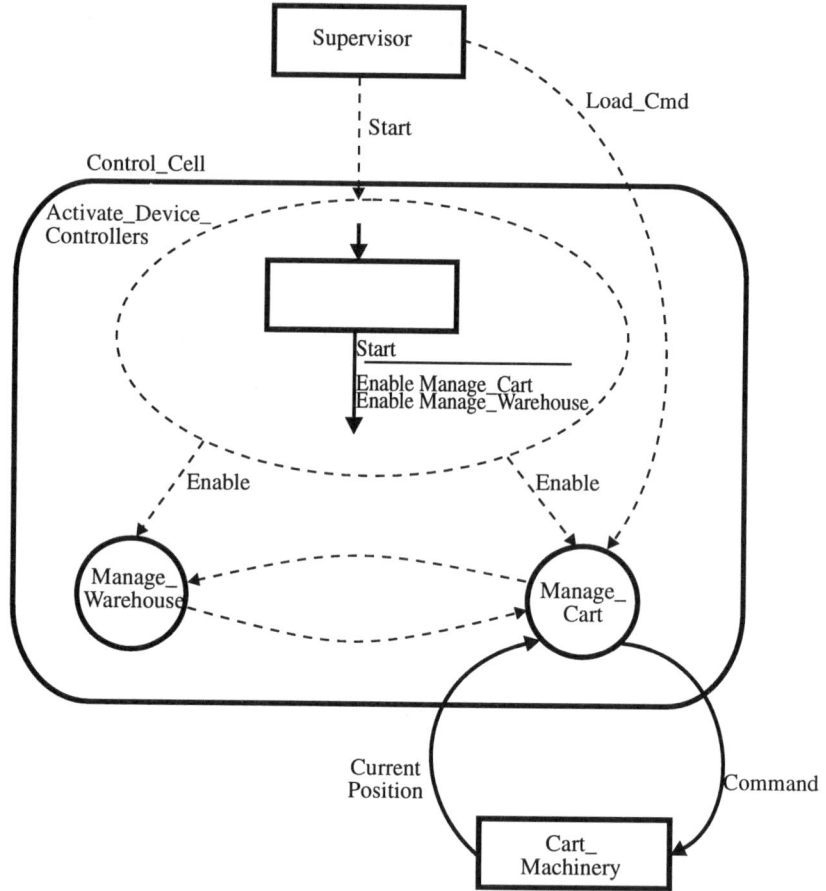

Figure 2.24 *A fragment of the cell control system*

STD: after receiving command Start from the supervisor, it starts the compound functional processes. Manage_Cart has been detailed in Figure 2.23.

Syntactical rules concerning event flows and control flows are summarized below.

1. A compound functional process can send dataflows or events but not control commands.

2. An Enable or Disable control flow can connect a control process to another control process, to a simple functional process, or to a compound functional process.

3. A Trigger control flow can only be directed to a simple functional process.

4. An event that is not directed to an agent must eventually reach a control process whose STD has a transition which depends on that event.

5. Events can be produced by agents, control processes and simple functional processes.

Although the integration of functions and control increases the modeling power of structured analysis, it is hard to understand a complex model with several levels of nested state-transition diagrams and to follow an intricate grouping of events going up and down the hierarchy.

Furthermore, if a model that contains one control process and several functional processes is too large to fit a single DFD, it must be decomposed into a hierarchy of nested DFDs. Consequently, it is possible that the original control process, too, has to be decomposed into several nested control processes which, in turn, will require additional events so as to synchronize their actions. In this case, top-down decomposition is too rigid and some kind of horizontal decomposition, such as the views of the Entity-Relationship formalism, would be more convenient.

2.9 Summary

This chapter has surveyed the three formalisms, i.e. dataflows, Entity-Relationship and state-transition diagrams, which are used in modern structured analysis. It has also discussed which extensions are required so that these formalisms can be made operational. In particular, with reference to functional models, it is necessary for the preconditions and the actions of processes to be written in an executable language; further, the rules for scheduling the execution of processes must be defined as well.

The nature of Entity-Relationship models is descriptive, but if the notion of navigation is supported by a formal language, then it is possible to rigorously specify the operations that processes have to perform on the underlying information structure.

The integration of functions and control yields a more powerful descriptive model, but the notation becomes more complicated and it is more difficult to introduce execution rules, as many additional issues, such as the propagation of events and control commands as well as the scheduling of control processes, must be taken into account.

3

Object orientation

Object orientation is gaining wider and wider acceptance at the programming level, because it offers superior features for managing software complexity and for enhancing understanding, robustness and reusability.

Similar benefits are expected to be obtained if this approach is extended to the early phases, analysis and design, of software development. The overall aim is to provide an integrated life cycle whose phases are tightly connected, because they operate on the same kind of items: objects. An interesting model for the object-oriented software life cycle is presented by Henderson-Sellers and Edwards (1990).

However, while object-oriented programming (OOP) is based on a set of consolidated concepts, the same is not true for object-oriented design (OOD) and object-oriented analysis (OOA).

This chapter first surveys the notions of OOP, then focuses on the models on which OOA is based.

3.1 Object-oriented programming

According to object-oriented programming (OOP), an application consists of a collection of interacting objects. An object groups a data structure (made up of attributes) and all the services, also called operations, that can be performed on this data structure. An object can be depicted as shown in Figure 3.1.

Alpha, the object shown in Figure 3.1, has an internal structure and an interface. Its internal structure is made up of four attributes, A1, A2, A3 and A4, and of three services, S1, S2 and S3. Its interface indicates which services can be invoked by other objects. The objects that invoke the services provided by Alpha are called the clients of Alpha. Services are similar to the procedures and functions of conventional programming languages and can have parameters. Since S3 does not appear in Alpha's

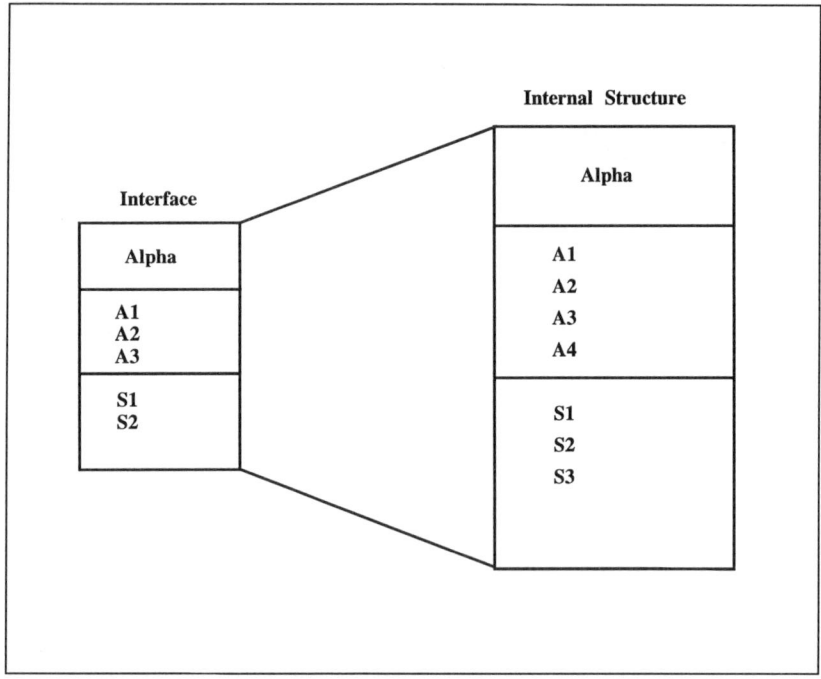

Figure 3.1 *The graphical representation of an object*

interface, it is assumed to be local to Alpha. Therefore, it cannot be called by Alpha's clients, but can be invoked by the other services of Alpha.

Some attributes can appear in the interface of an object, just as A1, A2 and A3 appear in the interface of Alpha. Such attributes can be read by the object's clients, but they cannot be modified directly. Listing the visible attributes of an object in its interface is a short-cut to writing specific functions which return the attribute values when invoked. The attributes that do not appear in the object's interface are called local attributes.

The term feature of an object will henceforth be used to denote any attribute or service of the object. Visible features are those listed in the object's interface.

Objects are building blocks that effectively help the programmer manage the complexity of software systems and, at the same time, improve understanding, reusability and robustness.

Understanding is improved for two important reasons.

1. Realism. An object refers to an entity that has a precise meaning in the problem domain or in the solution domain and collects all the useful knowledge about this entity. For example, the problem domain concerning an order entry system will probably include objects associated with

Orders and Customers, while the solution domain will probably include objects related to Stacks and Queues. To sum up, objects represent entities which either really exist or have a logical existence.

2. Well-defined interaction. Objects interact with each other through a clear mechanism, i.e. service invocation; thus side-effects, which derive from the uncontrolled use of global variables and cause frequent trouble in procedural programming, are avoided.

Reusability depends directly on understanding. In fact, if an entity is well understood, it will probably be reused in other similar applications. Reusability also implies extending the features of the reused entity without duplicating it. As will be illustrated later, this can be obtained by means of a powerful mechanism, called inheritance, which enables the programmer to build a more specific entity incrementally by adding new features to an existing entity.

Robustness is a quality that concerns both the architecture of the program and the possibility of restricting the effects of run-time errors.

A program made up of objects is less sensitive to modifications than a procedural program. In fact, each object observes the well-known information hiding principle (Parnas, 1972), so local attributes and local services are completely hidden from the other objects. In this way, the impact of a modification is limited; in fact, if an object is modified, but the modification does not affect its interface, its client objects need not be modified. In addition, since objects are larger-grain entities than functions, when the system's functionality is modified, a program made up of objects is more stable than an equivalent procedural program, even if the interfaces of objects have to be modified.

Thanks to the absence of side-effects, run-time errors in object-oriented programs are easier to isolate and to relate to the defective objects than in procedural programs.

3.1.1 The major features of OOP

A well-known classification schema proposed by Wegner (1987) helps the software developer determine to what extent a programming language supports the concepts of object orientation. A language is

1. object-based, if it has specific constructs to manage objects;
2. class-based, if it is object-based and each object belongs to a class;
3. object-oriented, if it is class-based and classes can share features by means of inheritance;
4. strongly-typed object-oriented, if it is both object-oriented and strongly typed.

According to the above schema, Ada (US Dept. of Defense, 1983) is object-based, CLU (Liskov *et al.*, 1977) is class-based, Simula (Birtwistle *et al.*, 1979) and Smalltalk (Goldberg and Robson, 1983) are object-oriented, and Eiffel (Meyer, 1988) and C++ (Stroustrup, 1986) are strongly-typed object-oriented.

We will now illustrate the major features of OOP, namely identity, classification, inheritance and polymorphism, adopting a strongly-typed object-oriented language. An in-depth analysis of these features is presented by Korson and McGregor (1990).

Identity. Each object is unique; therefore, two objects are distinct even if the values of all their attributes are identical.

Classification. Objects, like animals and plants, can have similarities in their features and behavior. Therefore, if we have a group of similar objects, instead of repeating a similar description for each of them, we can define a class that represents all of them as well as any other object having the same features. Each object is, in this way, an instance of a class.

The generation of an object (called instantiation) is explicit. When an object is generated, it is given a handle which can be stored in a variable for later use. Therefore, variables can contain either handles to objects (they are called object variables) or values that belong to predefined types.

Two graphical classes, Point and Rectangle (Rectangle is a client of Point), are shown below. They are written in an imaginary language drawing on Eiffel (Meyer, 1988).

```
class Point provides
   {The names of the visible features of the class
    are listed after the provides keyword}
   X, Y, Create, Translate, Draw_Segment;
attributes
   X,Y: integer; {the coordinates of the point}
services
   procedure Create (A,B: integer);
   begin
      X := A; Y := B;
   end;
   procedure Translate (A,B: integer);
   begin
      X := X+A; Y := Y+B;
   end;
   procedure Draw_Segment (P: Point);
   begin
      Draw_Line(X,Y,P.X,P.Y);
      {Draw_Line is a graphical primitive}
   end;
end class;
```

```
class Rectangle provides
  {This class handles rectangles whose sides are parallel
   to the axes of the coordinate system}
  V1, Lx, Ly, Create, Translate, Draw;
attributes
  V1: Point; {upper left vertex}
  V2,V3,V4: Point; {other vertices from V1 clockwise;}
  Lx: integer; {length of the horizontal side}
  Ly: integer; {length of the vertical side}
services
  procedure Create (X,Y,L1,L2: integer);
  begin
    V1.Create(X,Y); V2.Create(X+L1,Y);
    V3.Create(X+L1,Y-L2); V4.Create(X,Y-L2);
    Lx := L1; Ly := L2;
  end;
  procedure Translate (A,B: integer);
  begin
    V1.Translate(A,B); V2.Translate(A,B);
    V3.Translate(A,B); V4.Translate(A,B);
  end;
  procedure Draw;
  begin
    V1.Draw_Segment(V2); V2.Draw_Segment(V3);
    V3.Draw_Segment(V4); V4.Draw_Segment(V1);
  end;
end class;
```

A class, A, is said to use another class, B, if A contains object variables (or parameters) of class B. In the above example, class Rectangle uses class Point, because it contains object variables V1, V2, V3 and V4 which belong to class Point.

The dot notation *object_variable.service* is used to ask an object variable (more precisely, the object which is referred to by the handle contained in the object variable) to perform a service.

Inheritance. The key feature of OOP is inheritance, a powerful mechanism which enables the programmer to build new classes by extending the existing ones.

A new class can be built on top of one existing class (single inheritance) or on top of several existing classes (multiple inheritance). For the sake of simplicity, we restrict our attention to single inheritance, which is exemplified below.

```
class Colored_Rectangle
inherits from Rectangle redefining Create, Draw;
```

```
provides Change_Color, Color;
  {only the new features are listed after the
  provides keyword}
attributes
  Color: integer;
services
  procedure Create (X,Y,L1,L2,C: integer);
  begin
    V1.Create(X,Y); V2.Create(X+L1,Y);
    V3.Create(X+L1,Y-L2); V4.Create(X,Y-L2);
    Lx := L1; Ly := L2; Color := C;
  end;
  procedure Change_Color (C: integer);
  begin
    Color := C;
  end;
  procedure Draw;
  begin
    Set_Color(Color);
    {Set_Color is a graphical primitive}
    V1.Draw_Segment(V2); V2.Draw_Segment(V3);
    V3.Draw_Segment(V4); V4.Draw_Segment(V1);
    Set_Default_Color;
    {Set_Default_Color is a graphical primitive}
  end;
end class;
```

Inheritance, as shown in Figure 3.2, is indicated by an arc which is directed from the inheriting class to the inherited one; its label is is_a.

All the features of Rectangle, the inherited class, are also features of Colored_Rectangle, the inheriting class, so there is no need to duplicate them. The inheriting class contains only specific features, such as new attributes and new services, and those services that are provided by the inherited class but need to be redefined in the inheriting class (such as service Draw).

If a class, B, inherits from another class, A, then B is said to be a descendant or a subclass of A, while A is said to be an ancestor or a superclass of B.

If we depict all the inheritance relationships between classes, we obtain, in general, a graph which is called inheritance graph. We say that inheritance is direct from a class, A, to another class, B, if there is an arc connecting B to A in the inheritance graph; inheritance is indirect from A to B, if there is a path connecting B to A which consists of two or more arcs.

Polymorphism and dynamic binding. If a declaration states that an object variable, V, belongs to a class, C, then V is said to be statically bound to C.

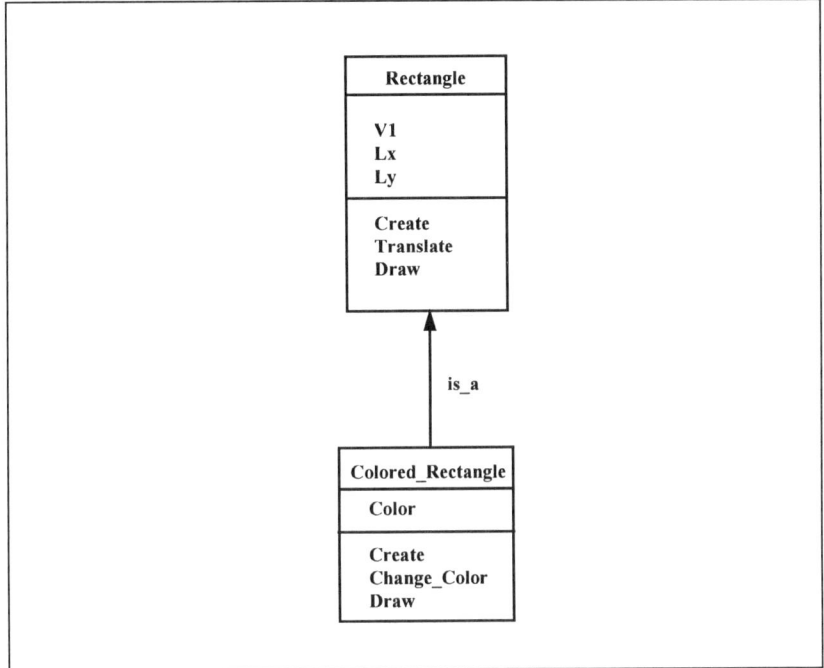

Figure 3.2 *A case of inheritance*

However, if C has subclasses and if, during the execution of the program, V is given a handle to an object that belongs to a subclass, D, of C, then V is also said to be dynamically bound to D.

The client class in Figure 3.3 has three object variables, P, R and T; thus it uses classes Polygon, Rectangle and Triangle. Use is graphically represented by an unlabeled oriented arc from the client class to the used class.

Variable P is statically bound to class Polygon. However, after the first assignment in procedure S, P will be dynamically bound to class Rectangle, so, when P is asked to perform service Draw, the one provided by class Rectangle will be executed. After the second assignment, P will be dynamically bound to class Triangle, so when P is asked to perform service Draw the second time, the service provided by class Triangle will be executed.

When an object variable, such as P, is dynamically bound to different classes at run-time, it is called polymorphic. In fact, P, which is initially a rectangle, becomes a triangle.

When a polymorphic object variable, V, is asked to perform a service, S, the implementation of S is sought in the inheritance graph starting from the class to which V is dynamically bound; therefore, it is not generally

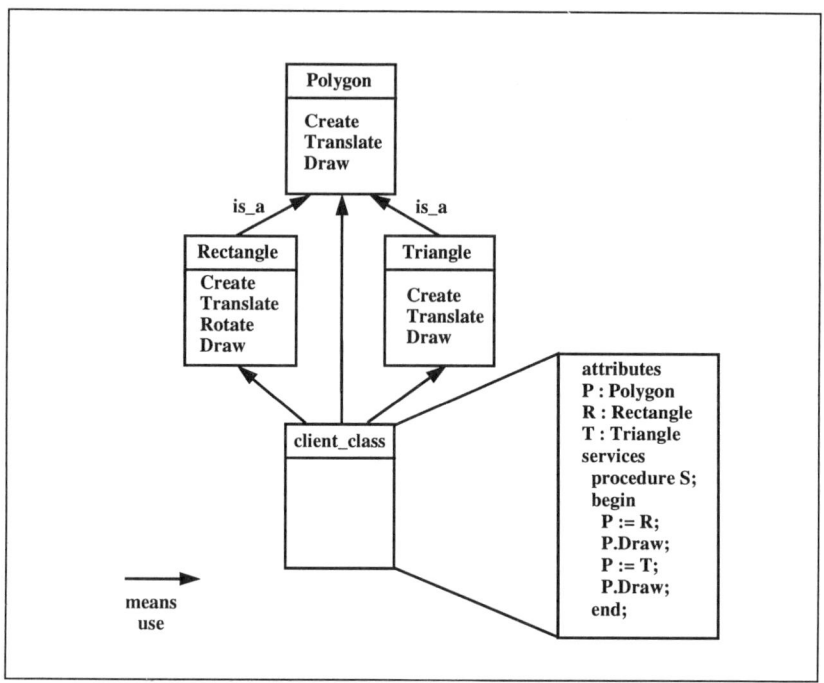

Figure 3.3 *A case of polymorphism*

known at compile-time which class will provide the implementation of S and thus it must be determined at run-time.

Other important features such as abstract classes and generic classes are not addressed here for lack of space but can easily be found in books on object-oriented programming, such as the book written by Meyer (1988).

3.2 Object-oriented analysis

Since there is no doubt that the early phases of software development have a dramatic impact on the overall project, much is expected of the extension of the object-oriented paradigm in analysis and design. We all certainly agree with the statement made by Rumbaugh *et al.* (1991) 'The real payoff comes from addressing front-end conceptual issues, rather than back-end implementation issues'.

In this section, we focus our attention on object-oriented analysis (OOA) because it has a more general scope, while object-oriented design (OOD) can be considered to be a specialization of OOA which tackles design issues concerning specific implementation technologies. A well-known reference book on OOD is the one written by Booch (1991), while a survey on current research in OOD is presented by Wirfs-Brock and Johnson (1990).

Regarding the support formalism of OOA, many approaches have been proposed; however, they often lack a rigorous definition, thus causing non-negligible trouble to the developers of CASE tools.

A recent survey of representations and processes supporting OOA and OOD is presented by Monarchi and Puhr (1992).

Instead of presenting specific formalisms, we will try to illustrate OOA emphasizing the common trend which is emerging from some recent approaches, such as the ones proposed by Rumbaugh *et al.* (1991), Shlaer and Mellor (1988 and 1992), and Coad and Yourdon (1991).

OOA models can be considered from four points of view, as shown in Figure 3.4.

Structure. Classes and relationships are described by a Class-Relationship (CR) model. CR models are similar to ER models presented in Chapter 2. The major difference concerns the boxes that now represent classes instead of entities; thus, each box contains all the visible features, attributes and services of the class it represents. Classes can be subdivided into two categories: active classes, which represent objects that can take decisions and react to external events autonomously, and passive classes, which represent objects that provide services on request. Objects belonging to active (passive) classes are called active (passive) objects. Active objects (also called actors) have their own thread of control, while passive objects have not. If a class is active, it has no textual interface, because its services can be derived from the event model.

Control. A state model, given by a state-transition diagram, is associated with each active class and represents the thread of control of the corresponding objects.

Functions. If an active class performs a complex activity, it also has a functional model, described by a dataflow diagram. The thick arrow in Figure 3.4 emphasizes that the functional model of a class is controlled by its state model.

Communications. The events and the data exchanged between active classes are described by an event model.

Further details are given in the next section, which presents an OOA model.

3.3 An example of an OOA model

This section presents the OOA model of the supervisor illustrated in Chapter 2.

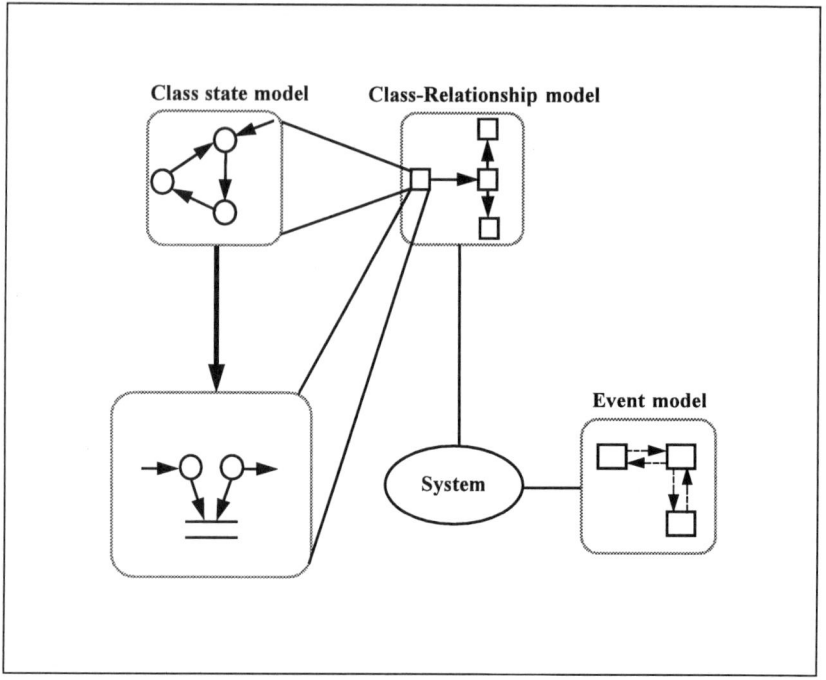

Figure 3.4 *Models used in object-oriented analysis*

3.3.1 *Class-Relationship models*

CR models can contain three kinds of relationships: inheritance, association and composition. Association and composition can be further characterized by an important property that we call communication property.

It should be noted that while in OOP there are two kinds of relationships between classes, i.e. inheritance and use, in OOA the notion of use is refined into the more specific notions of association and composition. Moreover, as pointed out by Rumbaugh (1987), an association between classes represents information that conceptually does not belong to either class, even if we could implement it by introducing into each class an object variable belonging to the other class. Therefore, the notion of association is more abstract and richer (semantically) than the notion of use provided by OOP.

The CR model of the manufacturing cell can be decomposed into two views, as shown in Figures 3.5 and 3.6.

There are four major classes in the system, i.e. the supervisor and three controllers (the cart controller, the workstation controller and the warehouse controller). Controllers carry out the supervisor's directives by governing their corresponding devices.

There are five associations and one composition in Figure 3.5. Compo-

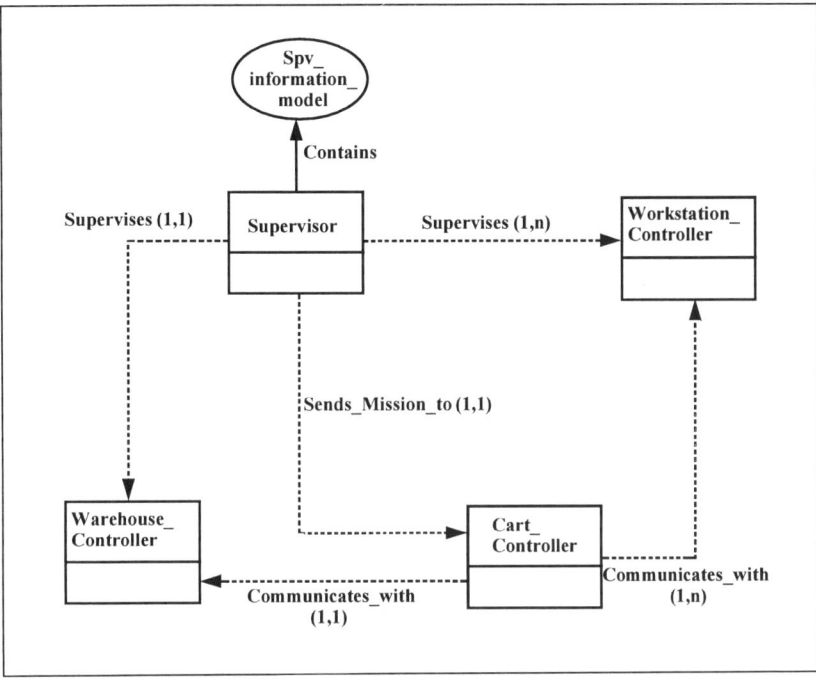

Figure 3.5 *The Class-Relationship model of the manufacturing cell*

sition is represented by an oriented arc whose label is Contains, directed
from the enclosing class to the enclosed classes. When association and composition links also entail communication between the classes they connect
(as takes place in Figure 3.5 for association links), they are drawn as dashed
arcs.

Communicating classes represent objects that send events to each other:
they are characterized by a state model and by a functional model which
together are responsible for managing the events received and for generating
the events to be sent. Details on events are given in the event model.

An association cannot be set between an active class and a passive one,
because it cannot be given clear semantics. An active class can contain
passive classes and this is expressed by a relationship Contains directed
from the enclosing active class to the enclosed passive classes. In fact, class
Supervisor contains the passive classes shown in Figure 3.6. In Figure 3.5,
there is a new symbol, the oval, which corresponds to a view. Such a notation indicates that class Supervisor contains all the classes shown in that
view.

For the sake of simplicity, only the CR model corresponding to the ER model shown in Figure 2.16, is given in Figure 3.6, while the CR model corresponding to the ER model shown in Figure 2.17 is omitted.

Since inheritance between active classes is still a research topic, inheritance will only be allowed between passive classes.

If there is a composition relationship from a class, A, to another class, B, and it entails communication, then both classes must be active. A passive class cannot contain active classes.

The classes shown in Figure 3.6 are passive, thus they have neither state models nor functional ones and their visible features are listed in their interfaces.

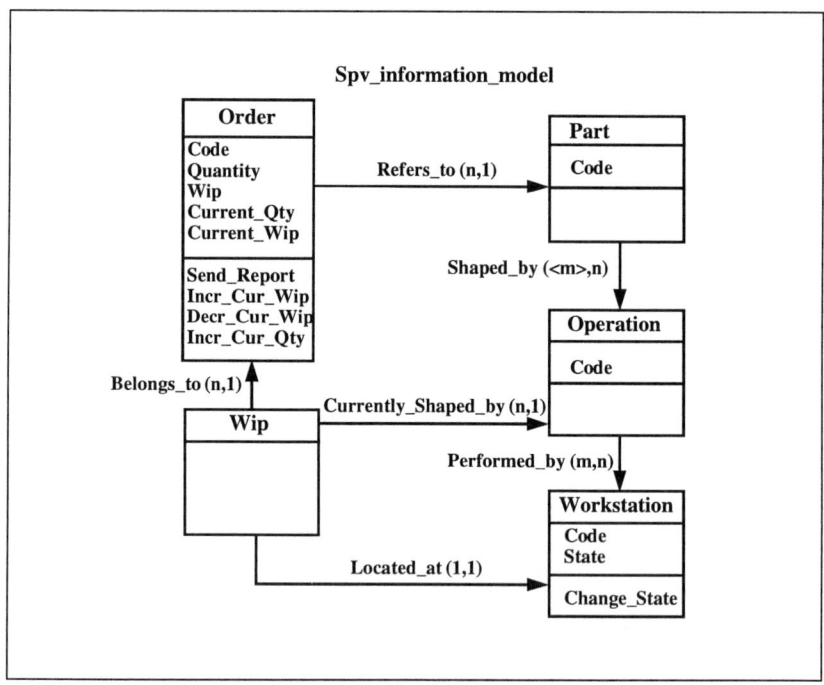

Figure 3.6 *The Class-Relationship model contained in the supervisor*

3.3.2 State and functional models

The classes shown in Figure 3.5 have state and functional models, some of which are similar to those presented in Chapter 2.

Class Supervisor has the state model shown in Figure 3.7 and the functional model shown in Figure 3.8. The latter is very similar to the one presented in Figure 2.7 but, for the sake of simplicity, process Assign_Misssion has not been expanded. The supervisor acts on the objects which belong to the CR model shown in Figure 3.6. These objects appear as datastores in the functional model.

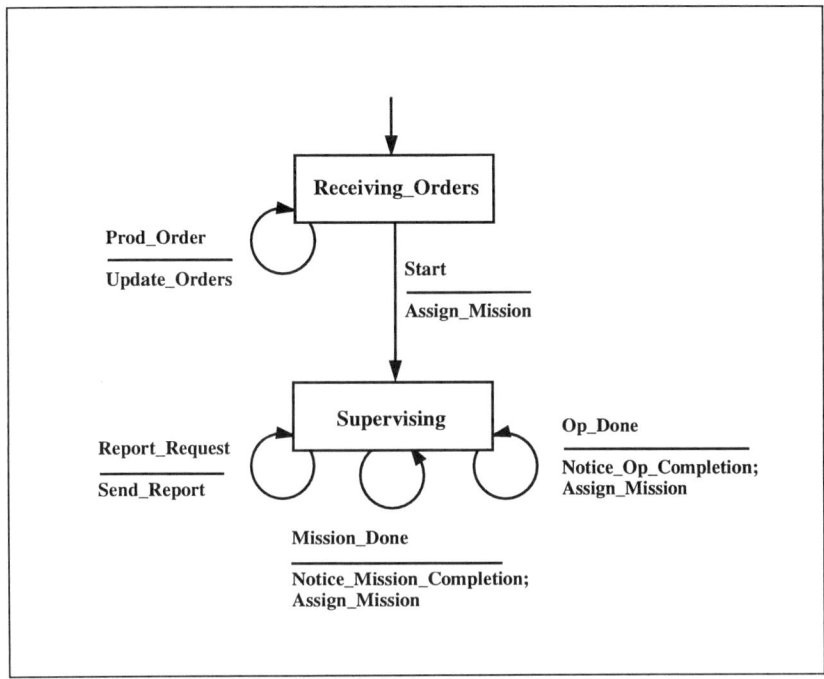

Figure 3.7 *The state model of the supervisor*

The supervisor performs five major functions, corresponding to the processes given in Figure 3.8; they are controlled by the state model shown in Figure 3.7. The state model has two states: Receiving_Orders which is the initial one, and Supervising. In the initial state, the supervisor can receive orders from the plant supervisor. In fact, a Prod_Order event signals the arrival of a new order and the supervisor processes it by executing process Update_Orders.

Whenever an event carries data, there is, in the functional model, a dataflow that has the same name as the event. When the supervisor receives event Start (a pure command), it enters state Supervising and then three events can be received:

1. Report_Request. The supervisor executes process Send_Report, which sends the plant supervisor the information on the current state of orders.

2. Mission_Done. The supervisor updates several objects, as shown in the functional model, by executing process Notice_Mission_Completion, then, since the cart has just become idle and a new mission has to be scheduled, it performs process Assign_Mission.

3. Op_Done. The supervisor, by executing process Notice_Op_Completion, updates the state of its internal object which represents the workstation that has finished working on a part and then, since the cart could already be idle, it performs process Assign_Mission.

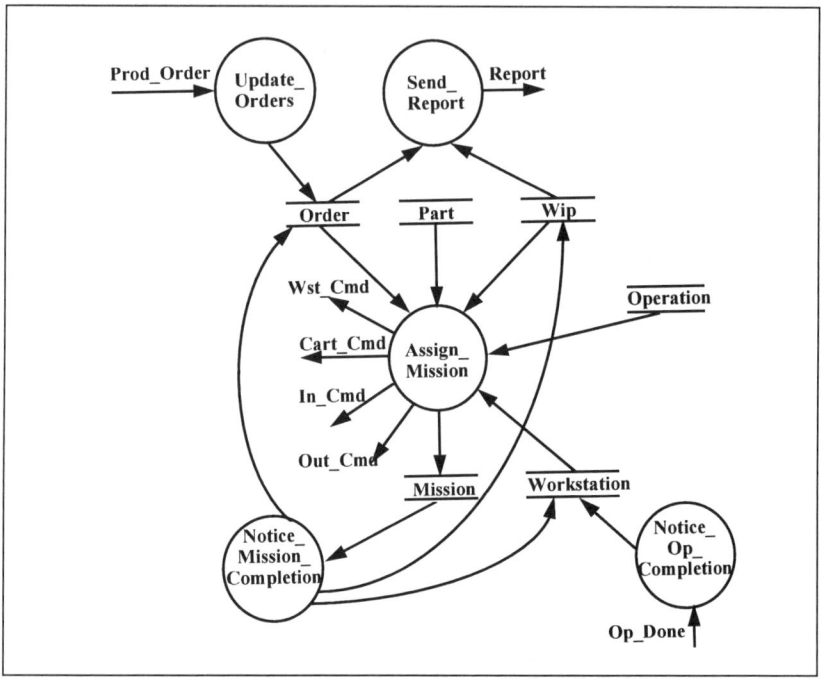

Figure 3.8 *The functional model of the supervisor*

If a class, such as Supervisor, contains passive objects, it has a functional model that shows which processes act on these objects; the descriptions of such processes indicate which services of the passive objects have to be performed. For example, process Notice_Op_Completion asks the object of class Workstation (whose Code attribute matches the workstation code supplied by dataflow Op_Done) to perform service Change_State, while process Send_Report sends the plant supervisor the current information on the orders, by asking each object of class Order to perform service Send_-Report.

The interaction between the state model and the functional one is simpler than in structured analysis. In fact, since functional processes are always controlled and their execution is always triggered, control flows are avoided and it is necessary to write only the name of a process in the action of a transition in order to cause its execution.

State diagrams, as suggested by Rumbaugh *et al.* (1991), can be organized hierarchically into statecharts (Harel *et al.*, 1990), so as to provide a more compact representation.

3.3.3 Event models

The event model shows the events exchanged between active classes, the agents that make up the environment of the system being considered, and the events and the dataflows exchanged between classes and agents.

The event model of the manufacturing cell is given in Figure 3.9. There are four agents, Plant_Supervisor, Warehouse_Machinery, Cart_Machinery and Workstation_Machinery.

Events that contain data are drawn as dataflows.

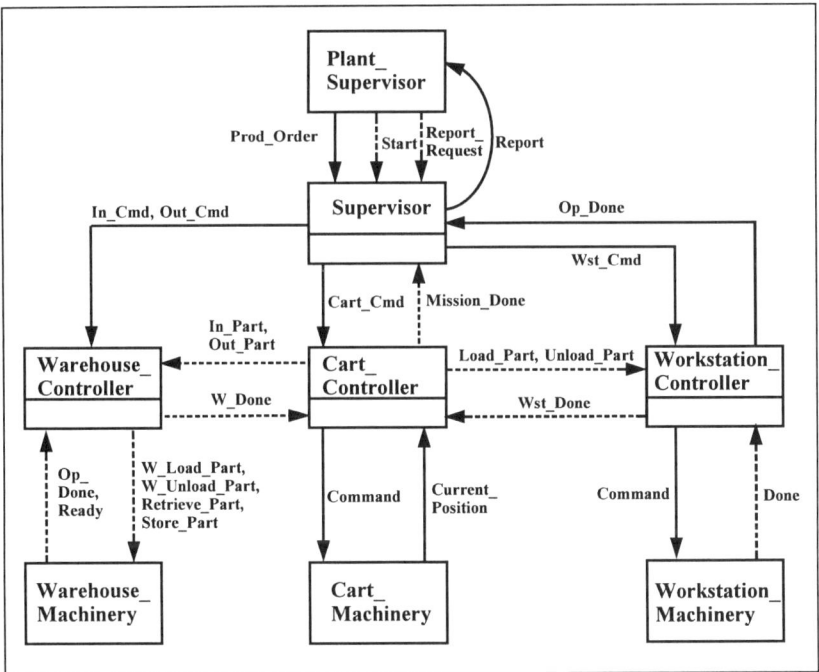

Figure 3.9 *The event model of the manufacturing cell*

Classes Cart, Warehouse and Workstation have behaviors similar to those presented in Chapter 2. Adapting their state models to the approach presented in this section is left as an exercise to the reader.

3.4 Summary

This chapter has presented the basic notions of object-oriented programming and has then discussed the models on which object-oriented analysis is based. Although the formalisms used in OOA are very similar to the ones adopted in structured analysis, there is a substantial difference in the steps of analysis; in fact, in OOA attention is focused first on extracting the classes and their relationships from the problem requirements. The resulting CR model provides the overall OOA model with a stable foundation because modifications are more likely to affect functions (which are within the classes) than the structure of classes itself.

Object orientation places great emphasis on reusability. In fact, the programmer is encouraged to design and develop classes in such a way that they can be applied more widely. Classes can be organized into a library, which is intended to offer a significant reduction in costs and in effort to similar future projects.

As models grow in complexity, executability becomes more and more important in order to ensure that the analysis is consistent and complete. The same considerations made about the execution of functional models also hold in this case; in particular, process descriptions must be written in a rigorous executable language and the scheduling of objects must be defined.

4

Petri nets

Petri nets are both a graphical language and a mathematical tool for modeling and analysing concurrent systems, i.e. systems made up of autonomous components which communicate and synchronize with each other.

Petri nets were introduced by Carl Adam Petri in 1962 (Petri, 1962); since then a lot of work has been done to increase their modeling power, to extend their scope of analysis and to broaden their range of applications.

Research on Petri nets has led to a rich family of languages which can be roughly classified into:

1. Ordinary nets. They focus on concurrency and synchronization, thus providing an essential tool for building control models.

2. High-level (or colored) nets. They make models more compact and represent functional aspects as well.

3. Time-dependent nets. They enable the analyst to set (either deterministic or stochastic) timing constraints and to study their effects.

4. Operational nets. They provide a very high-level language for system simulation and software development.

This chapter reviews the basic notions of Petri nets. An excellent survey is presented by Murata (1989) and a well-known reference book has been written by Peterson (1981).

4.1 Basic concepts

A Petri net is an abstract mathematical entity consisting of a structure and a behavior. The structure is defined as follows:

Definition 1 *A Petri net structure is a 4-tuple, $N = (P, T, F, W)$, where:*

1. $P = \{p_1, p_2, \cdots, p_m\}$ is a non-empty set of places;

2. $T = \{t_1, t_2, \cdots, t_n\}$ is a non-empty set of transitions; P and T are disjoint;

3. $F \subseteq (P \times T) \cup (T \times P)$ *is a non-empty set of arcs;*

4. $W : F \to \mathcal{N}^+$ *is a weight function.*

$\mathcal{N}$ denotes the set of natural numbers; $\mathcal{N}^+$ denotes the set of natural numbers, zero excluded.

For the sake of simplicity, henceforth in this chapter, t denotes a transition $(t \in T)$ and p denotes a place $(p \in P)$ of the Petri net being considered.

If (t, p) denotes an arc belonging to F, we say that p is an output place of t and that t is an input transition of p. If (p, t) denotes an arc belonging to F, we say that p is an input place of t and that t is an output transition of p.

The weight associated with an arc (x, y) is simply indicated as $W(x, y)$.

From the above definition, the structure of a Petri net corresponds to a bipartite directed weighted graph: this means that all the nodes of the graph can be partitioned into two disjoint sets (P and T), such that each arc connects an element of one set to an element of the other. Arcs cannot be duplicated, therefore, given two nodes, x and y, if there is an arc from x to y, it is the only arc from x to y.

The graphical representation of a Petri net structure depends on the above-mentioned correspondence; in fact, we can build a graph from N by drawing a circle for each place of P, a bar for each transition of T and a directed arc for each element of F. Arc weights, different from 1, are written as labels of the arcs. Transitions are often depicted as rectangles.

Places can contain tokens and the arrangement of tokens in places is called marking of the net.

The marking of a net can change over time according to the firing rule given below and it is defined by a vector (M) with m elements (m is the number of places): $M[i]$ contains the number of tokens which are in place p_i. We depict the marking of a net at a given instant by writing the number of tokens contained in each place inside the circle that represents the place. If a place is empty, the number 0 is omitted. Sometimes, tokens are depicted as dots.

The behavior of a Petri net is given by the evolution of its marking over time and is determined by the initial arrangement of its tokens, called initial marking. Therefore, a Petri net, PN, is completely defined by its structure (N) and by its initial marking, called M_0: formally, $PN = (N, M_0)$ or $PN = (P, T, F, W, M_0)$.

An example of a Petri net is given in Figure 4.1. The initial marking consists of one token in place P1.

At any time, the state of a Petri net, PN, is given by the current arrangement of tokens in places, which is called current marking (or simply marking). The state can change as a consequence of the firing of a transition, according to the firing rule given below.

Given a Petri net, $PN = (P, T, F, W, M_0)$, whose current marking is M

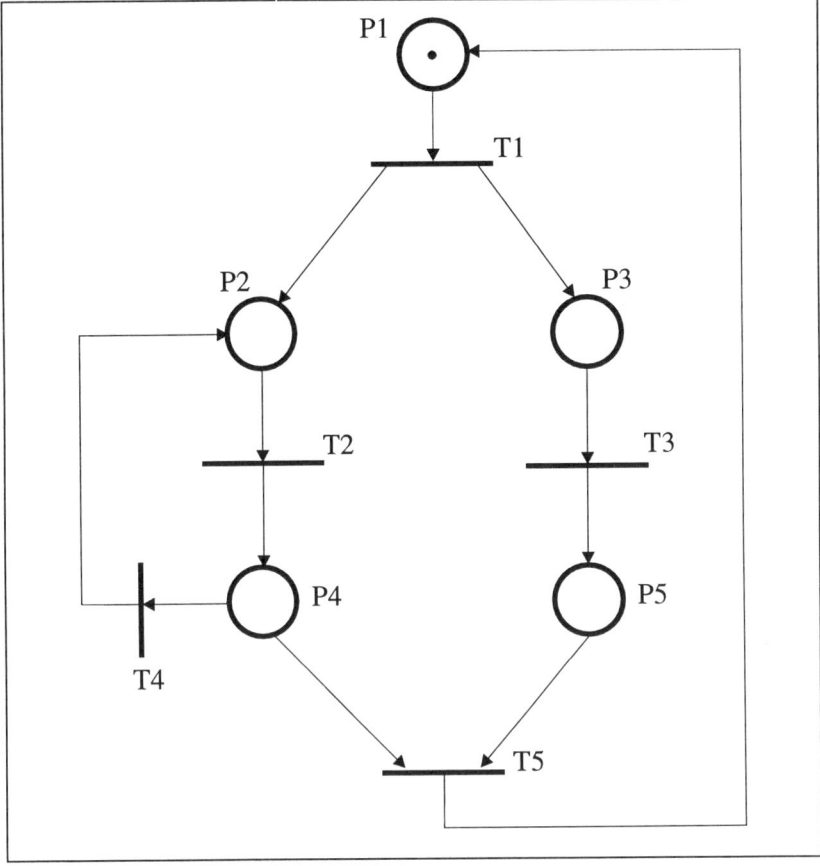

Figure 4.1 *A Petri net*

1. a transition, t, can fire iff it is enabled; t is enabled iff for each input place, p,

$$M(p) \geq W(p, t)$$

2. the firing of t is atomic and leads to a new marking, M', which affects the input places and the output places of t; in particular, for each input place, p,

$$M'(p) = M(p) - W(p, t)$$

and for each output place, q,

$$M'(q) = M(q) + W(t, q)$$

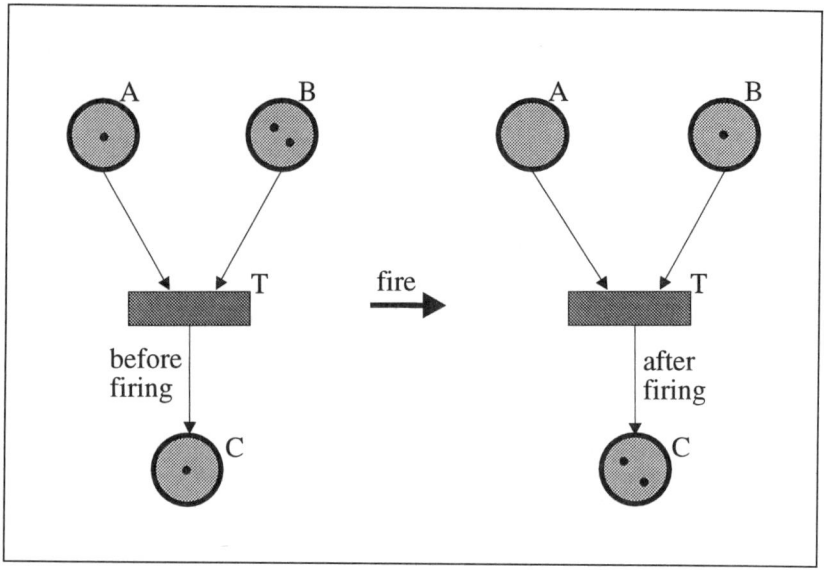

Figure 4.2 *The firing rule*

The firing rule is depicted in Figure 4.2. It states that a transition, t, is enabled if and only if each input place, p, of t contains a number of tokens greater than the weight of the arc connecting p to t. The firing of an enabled transition causes the removal of tokens from its input places and the addition of tokens to its output places in quantities equal to the weights of the corresponding arcs. The tokens that are removed from the input places of t when t fires are referred to as the input tokens of t while the tokens that are delivered to the output places of t when t fires are referred to as the output tokens of t.

The firing rule is non-deterministic, because when two or more transitions happen to be enabled at the same time it does not specify which transition fires first.

If we consider the net shown in Figure 4.1, transition $T1$ is the first to fire and the next marking is M_1, as shown in Figure 4.3. Then, both $T2$ and $T3$ are enabled: if $T2$ fires, the next marking is M_2, otherwise (if $T3$ fires) the next marking is M_3. When the marking is M_2, both $T3$ and $T4$ are enabled: if $T3$ fires, the next marking is M_4, otherwise (if $T4$ fires) the net takes marking M_1 again. In M_4, both $T4$ and $T5$ are enabled; however, the firing of one of them disables the other. When two or more transitions are in this situation, they are said to be in conflict. If $T4$ fires, the next marking is M_3, otherwise (if $T5$ fires) the net assumes the initial marking again. When the marking is M_3, only $T2$ is allowed to fire, then the next marking is M_4.

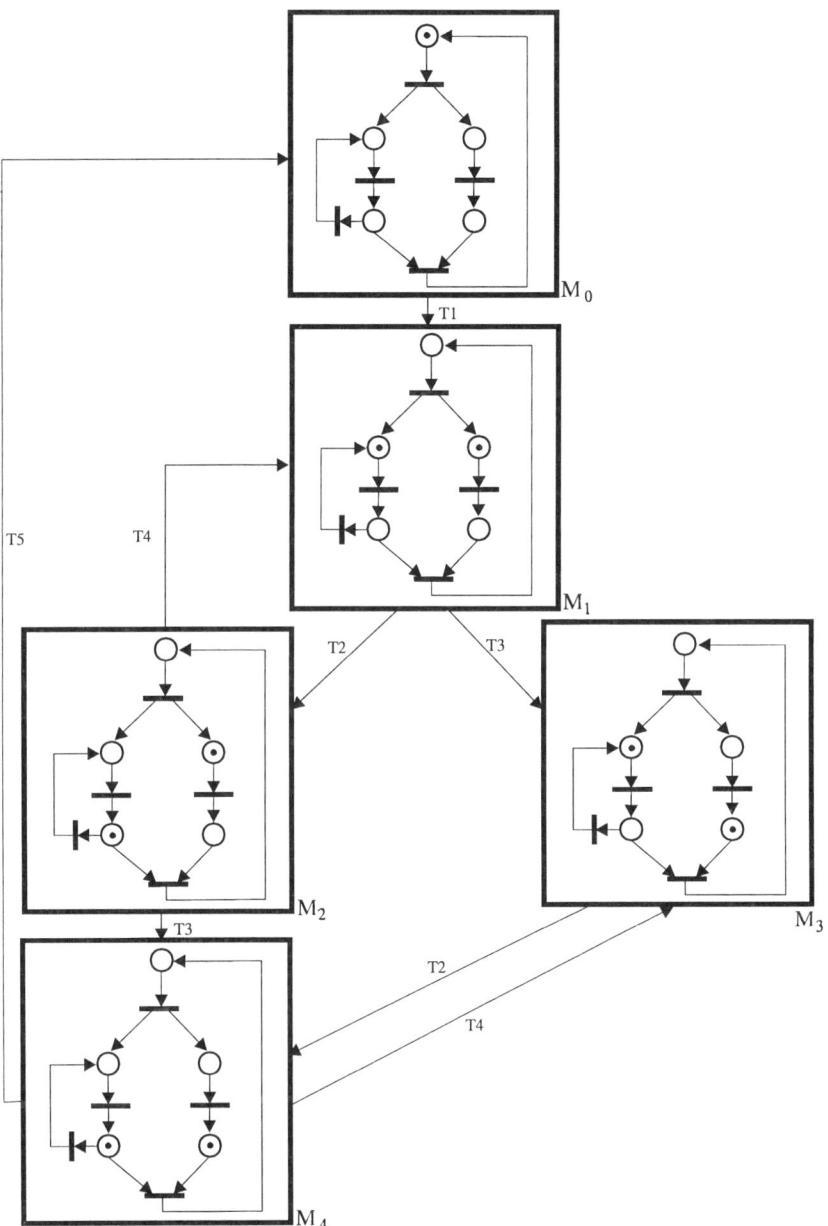

Figure 4.3 *The graph of the markings for the net shown in Figure 4.1*

The structure that shows all the possible markings and all the possible firing sequences is called a reachability graph; as will be explained later, it can be built only for those nets whose places contain a bounded number of tokens. In the Petri net shown in Figure 4.1, each place contains at most one token.

Actually, the reachability graph has as many nodes as the possible different markings and, for each node, it shows the contents of the marking vector. The actual reachability graph for the Petri net shown in Figure 4.1 is illustrated in Figure 4.4.

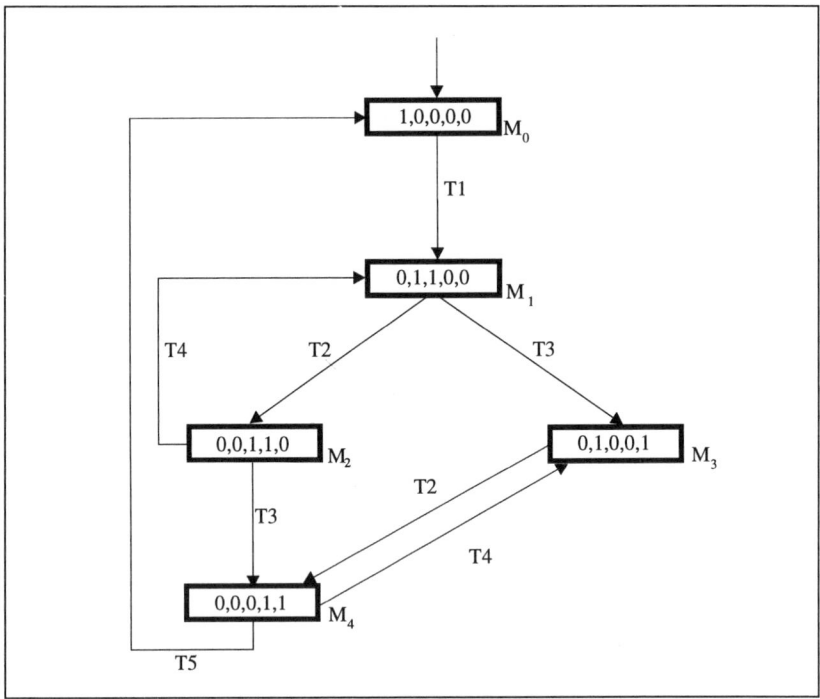

Figure 4.4 *The actual reachability graph for the net shown in Figure 4.1*

Finite capacity Petri nets. So far, no limit has been set to the number of tokens that a place can contain. It is often useful to work with nets whose places have bounded capacities. To obtain this, we extend the previous definition of a Petri net structure, by adding function $K : P \rightarrow \mathcal{N}^+$: it sets a limit, $K(p)$, to the number of the tokens which can be contained in each place, p. Such a limit is also called the capacity of the place. The Petri nets defined in this way are called finite-capacity Petri nets.

The firing rule has to be extended, too, because the firing of a transition is not allowed if it leads to a marking that exceeds the capacities of its output places.

A finite-capacity Petri net can always be transformed into an equivalent (infinite-capacity) Petri net, thus only (infinite-capacity) Petri nets will be considered in the remainder of this chapter.

4.2 Modeling with Petri nets

Petri nets are especially suitable for modeling concurrent activities or subsystems that need to communicate and to synchronize with each other. The paper by Murata (1989) contains several references to papers which illustrate the applications of Petri nets in the areas of communication protocols, distributed and concurrent systems, production systems and VLSI systems.

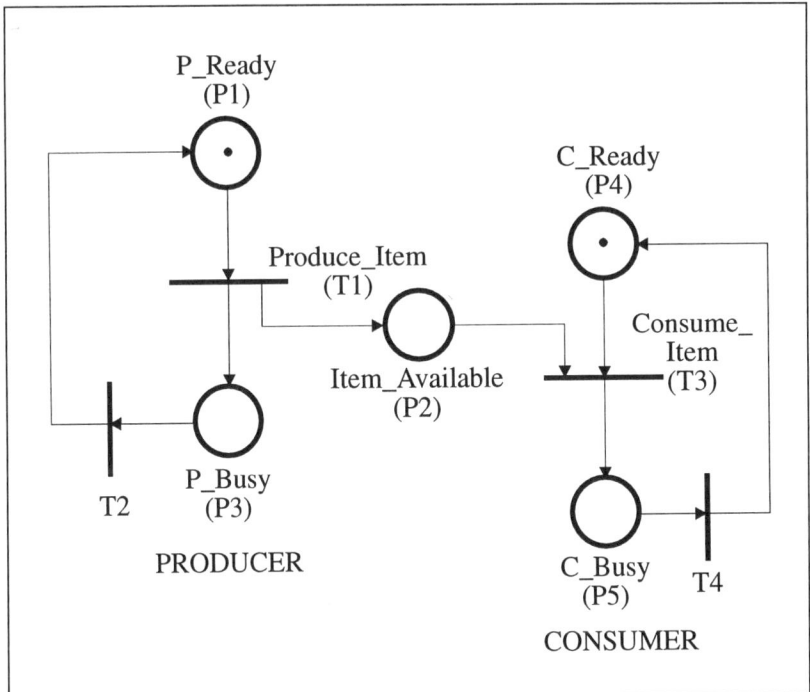

Figure 4.5 *Interactions between a producer and a consumer*

The example given in Figure 4.5 shows the interaction between a producer and a consumer. When the producer is ready (there is a token in place P_Ready), it produces an item (Produce_Item fires and puts a token into place Item_Available). Transition Consume_Item fires when the consumer is ready (there is a token in place C_Ready) and an item is available (there is a token in place Item_Available). If the producer is faster than the consumer, tokens increasingly accumulate in place Item_Available.

A place where the number of tokens can be arbitrarily high is said to be unbounded; if a net contains unbounded places, it is said to be unbounded.

Some elements of the net shown in Figure 4.5, such as P_Ready and Produce_Item, have also been given short names (e.g. P1 and T1): short names will be used later when the analysis of nets is exemplified.

Communication protocols are often modeled using Petri nets. A simple protocol between a sender and a receiver is shown in Figure 4.6.

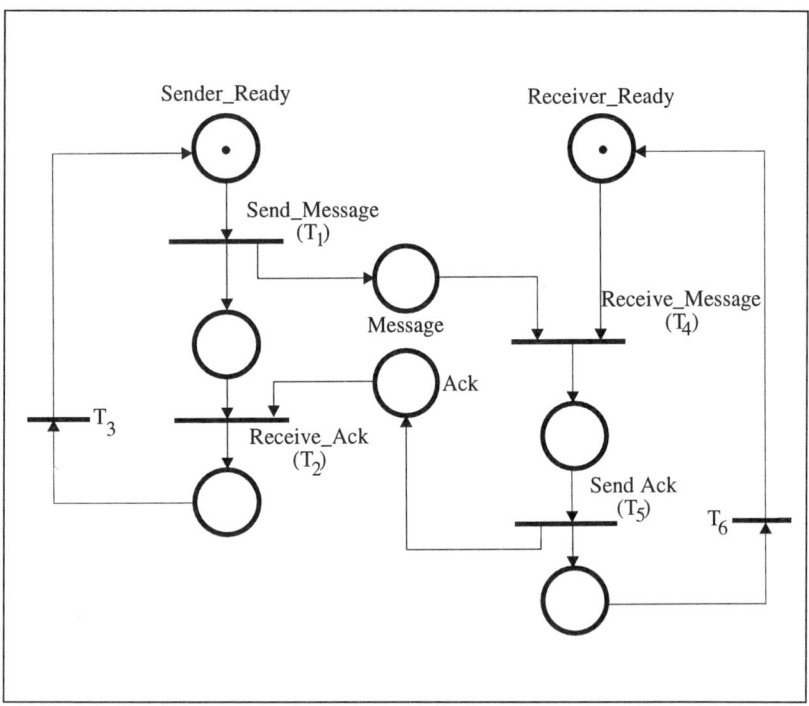

Figure 4.6 *Interactions between a sender and a receiver*

The sender sends a message, then waits for the acknowledgement. The receiver waits for the message, then sends the acknowledgement. The sender, after receiving the acknowledgement, sends a new message. The receiver, after sending the acknowledgement, waits for a new message.

An interesting example of synchronization is given in Figure 4.7. It refers to the simple production system whose requirements are given below.

A mechanical workstation is made up of three subsystems: the input buffer, the output buffer and the machining place. Each of them contains at most one part.

When the input buffer is empty, the workstation sends an input request

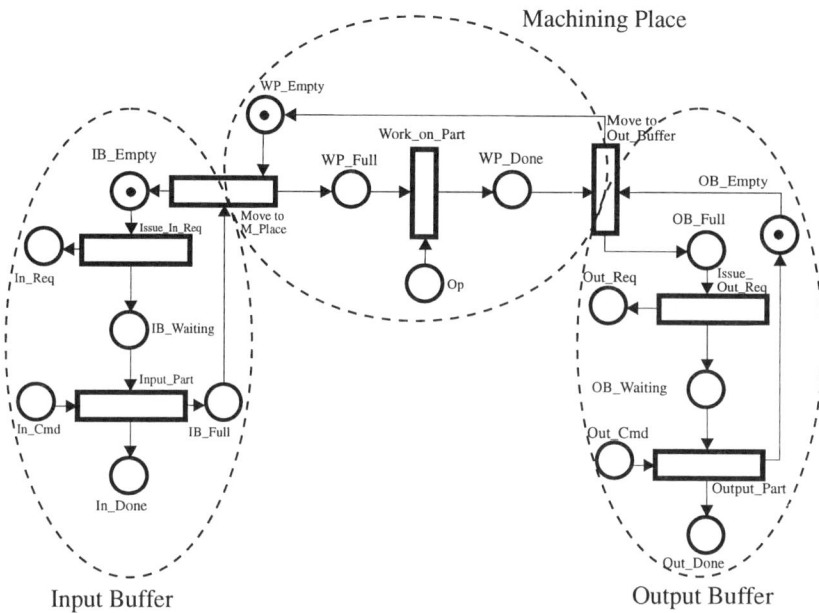

Figure 4.7 *The model of the workstation*

to the supervisor which commands a cart to carry a raw part to the workstation. When the cart is near the input buffer, it sends a signal to the workstation so that the shuttling mechanism of the input buffer can carry the part from the cart to the input buffer. Then, the workstation sends an acknowledgement to the cart so that it can become ready for another mission.

The part is carried by an internal shuttling mechanism from the input buffer to the machining place, when the latter is empty. Machining depends on the type of the part, so the supervisor sends the workstation the information on the operation required when it commands the cart to carry a raw part to the workstation.

After the part has been machined, it is carried by an internal shuttling mechanism from the machining place to the output buffer, when the latter is empty. When the output buffer is full, the workstation sends an output request to the supervisor which commands a cart to go and take the finished part from the workstation.

When the cart is near the output buffer, it sends a signal to the workstation so that the shuttling mechanism of the output buffer can carry the part from the output buffer to the cart. Then the workstation sends an acknowledgement to the cart so that it can go and put the part into a warehouse.

The model given in Figure 4.7 shows the behavior of the workstation and emphasizes the synchronizations between its subsystems: in fact, only when the input buffer is full and when the machining place is empty is the part moved from the input buffer to the machining place and only after the part has been worked on (i.e. there is a token in place WP_Done) and when the output buffer is empty is the part moved from the machining place to the output buffer.

The interactions between the workstation and the supervisor as well as those between the workstation and the carts are shown in Figure 4.8.

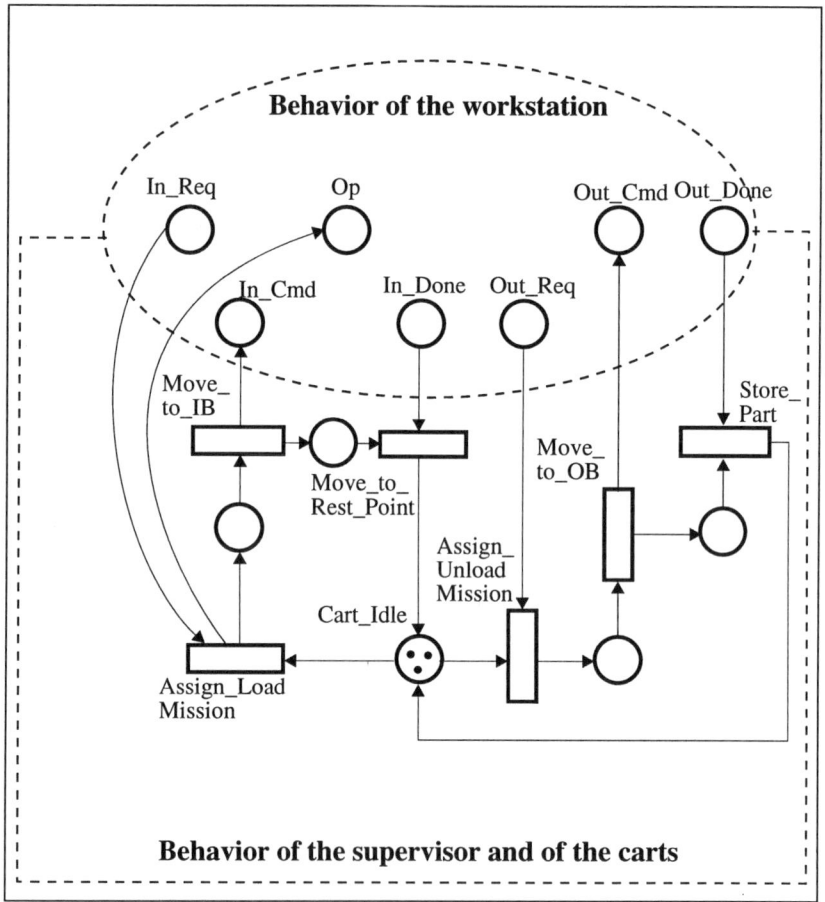

Figure 4.8 *Interactions between the workstation and its environment*

Transitions Assign_Load_Mission and Assign_Unload_Mission represent the supervisor's activity. The carts that are ready to perform new missions are modeled by the tokens contained in place Cart_Idle.

It is interesting to compare the Petri net model of the workstation with the one, shown in Figure 4.9, which is based on state-transition diagrams.

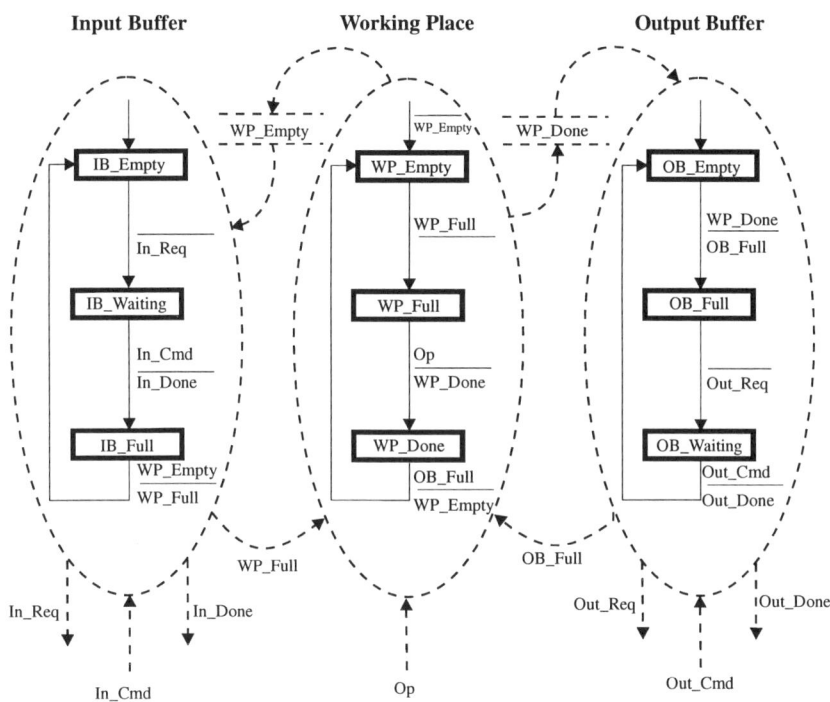

Figure 4.9 *The state-transition diagrams of the workstation*

There is one state-transition diagram for each subsystem. The synchronization between the input buffer and the machining place is achieved by means of two events, WP_Empty and WP_Full: the former notifies the input buffer that the machining place is empty, while the latter informs the machining place that the part has been carried from the input buffer to the machining place. Control store WP_Empty is needed because the input buffer could receive a WP_Empty event when it is in a state from which no transition is triggered. Similarly, the synchronization between the machining place and the output buffer is based on another pair of events, WP_Done and OB_Full.

4.3 Properties of Petri nets

The success of Petri nets depends not only on their expressive power but also on the many kinds of analysis that they encourage.

Analysing a Petri net means determining whether a given property holds or not. Properties can be studied either in relation to a particular initial marking or to the structure of the net. The former are called behavioral properties, while the latter are called structural properties.

In the remainder of this section, the most important behavioral properties will be illustrated.

4.3.1 Reachability

It is often necessary to determine whether a given marking, which has a particular meaning in the real system, can eventually be reached; for example, such a marking could correspond to a dangerous situation in the real system.

In general terms, the reachability problem can be defined as follows: given a Petri net (N, M_0) and two markings, M and M', verify whether M' is reachable from M, i.e. there is a sequence of transition firings which changes the marking of the net from M to M'.

It has been shown that the reachability problem is decidable, although, in general, it takes at least exponential space and time to be verified.

Reachability can be direct or indirect, as indicated by the following definitions.

Definition 2 *Given two markings, M and M', M' is directly reachable from M, iff there is a transition, t, enabled in M whose firing changes the state of the net from M to M'. The notation $M[t\rangle M'$ indicates the direct reachability of M' from M through t.*

Reachability is a transitive property, but not a symmetric one. The transitive closure of direct reachability yields the more general relation of (indirect) reachability from one marking to another.

Definition 3 *Given two markings, M and M', M' is reachable from M, iff there is a sequence, $\sigma = t_1 t_2 \cdots t_n$, of transition firings which changes the marking of the net from M to M'. Two equivalent notations are used in this case: $M[\sigma\rangle M'$ or $M[t_1\rangle \cdots [t_n\rangle M'$.*

Given a Petri net, $PN = (N, M_0)$, its reachability set, written as $R(N, M_0)$, is the set of all the markings reachable from M_0. For the sake of simplicity, we use a simpler notation, i.e. $R(M_0)$, to denote the reachability set of the Petri net, $PN = (N, M_0)$, being considered. Any element of this set will be referred to as a reachable marking. $R(M_0)$ is assumed to include M_0.

The reachability set of a Petri net can easily be derived from its reachability graph; this is because each node contains a reachable marking. The reachability set obtained from the reachability graph shown in Figure 4.4 contains five markings: $\{M_0, M_1, M_2, M_3, M_4\}$. $M_0[T1\rangle[T2\rangle M_2$ and $M_3[T2\rangle[T5\rangle[T1\rangle M_1$ are examples of indirect reachability.

Often we are not interested in knowing whether a specific marking M is reachable or not, since we need to know only whether a marking M' which covers M is reachable or not. Coverability is defined below.

Definition 4 *Given two markings, M and M', M' covers M iff $M'(p) \geq M(p)$ for each $p \in P$. M' is said to strictly cover M iff M' covers M and $M' \neq M$.*

A marking, M, is said to be coverable iff there is a reachable marking, M', that covers M.

4.3.2 Boundedness and safeness

Given a Petri net, $PN = (N, M_0)$, it is interesting to determine whether the number of tokens contained in each place is bounded for any reachable marking or not, and if so, what the maximum value is.

Definition 5 *A Petri net is k-bounded ($k > 0$) iff the number of tokens in each place does not exceed k for any reachable marking.*

This property is important because if the Petri net models a real system, some places often turn out to represent buffers which are capable of storing only a limited number of elements. Boundedness is needed to guarantee that the system, if it is implemented according to the model, never runs out of resources.

Safeness is a special case of k-boundedness.

Definition 6 *A Petri net is safe iff it is 1-bounded.*

The set of all the reachable markings of a k-bounded net is evidently finite and has a cardinality not greater than $(k + 1)^{|P|}$ ($|P|$ is the cardinality of the set of the places of the net); for a safe net this limit is $2^{|P|}$.

The Petri net shown in Figure 4.1 is safe.

4.3.3 Liveness

The notion of liveness is related to the one of deadlock-free operation; in fact, if a net is live it has no deadlock. A deadlock occurs when a marking is reached in which no transition is enabled.

Liveness can refer to a single transition or to the whole net.

Definition 7 *A transition, t, is:*

1. dead if t is never enabled in any reachable marking;

2. *L1-live (or potentially firable) if there is at least one reachable marking in which t is enabled;*

3. *live if for any reachable marking, M, there is a marking, M', that is reachable from M and, further, t is enabled in M'.*

Definition 8 *A Petri net is live if all its transitions are live.*

The Petri net shown in Figure 4.1 is live. However, if the initial marking of that net had had only one token in place P3, the net would not be live. In fact, after the firing of transition T3, no other transition could fire.

4.3.4 Reversibility

A Petri net is reversible if, for any reachable marking, M, M_0 is reachable from M; therefore, the state of a reversible net can always assume its initial value.

Moreover, it is often useful to know whether there is some other state which is always reachable. In general, any marking which can be reached from any reachable marking is called a home-state. The presence of a home-state denotes a periodic system.

The Petri net shown in Figure 4.1 is reversible.

As shown by Murata (1989), the properties of boundedness, liveness and reversibility are independent of each other.

4.4 Analysis of behavioral properties

In general, the behavioral properties of a given Petri net can be determined by examining the collection of its reachable markings; however, the number of reachable markings is finite only if the net is bounded. In such a case, we can, in principle, enumerate all the reachable markings and show them using two equivalent structures: the reachability tree or the reachability graph.

If the net is unbounded, only the structures that show the coverable markings, i.e. the coverability tree or the equivalent coverability graph, can be built.

The reachability tree as well as the coverability tree can be built according to the algorithm given below.

Assign the initial marking to the root of the tree and label the root *new*; *while* there is a node, N, that is labeled *new do* (the marking contained in N will be referred to as M)

1. *if* no transition is enabled in M *then* label N *dead-end*

2. *else*

(a) *for each* transition, t, enabled in M *do*

   i. compute the marking, M', which is obtained from M when t fires;

  ii. *if* there is a node, N'', which is an ancestor of N (i.e. on the path from the root to N) and which contains a marking, M'', that is strictly covered by M', *then*
set $M'(p)$ to ω for each p for which $M'(p) > M''(p)$;

 iii. add a new node, N', containing M' and draw an arc labeled with t from N to N';

 iv. *if* there is a node, N'', which is an ancestor of N' and contains the same marking as N', *then* label N' *old else* label N' *new;*

(b) label N *examined.*

The special symbol ω means infinity. It has the property that

$$\forall n \in \mathcal{N} : \omega > n, \ \omega \pm n = \omega, \ \omega \geq \omega$$

Looking at the tree, we can immediately obtain the results given below regarding behavioral properties.

1. The Petri net is bounded iff ω does not appear in any marking; if the net is bounded, the tree is a reachability tree, otherwise it is a coverability tree.

2. The Petri net is safe iff the markings associated with the nodes contain only zeroes and ones.

3. A transition, t, is dead iff t does not appear as a label of any arc.

4. If we have a reachability tree, we can say that a given marking, M, is reachable iff there is a node containing M.

5. If we have a coverability tree, we can say that a given marking, M, is coverable iff there is a node containing a marking, M', that covers M. The reachability problem cannot generally be solved by means of the coverability tree, because of the approximation we have introduced using the symbol ω: in fact, in some cases ω could represent only even numbers or only odd ones.

6. Any marking corresponding to a node labeled dead-end denotes a deadlock; in fact, no transition is enabled in that marking, thus all further evolution is blocked.

The reachability tree for the net given in Figure 4.1 is shown in Figure 4.10.

According to the above algorithm, we first introduce the root, which is node N_0. The node number is displayed on the right of the rectangle that represents the node. Only one transition, $T1$, can fire in the initial marking: its firing leads to marking M_1, which is stored in node N_1. Two transitions are enabled in M_1: $T2$, whose firing leads to marking M_2 (contained in node N_2), and $T3$, whose firing leads to marking M_3 (contained in node N_3).

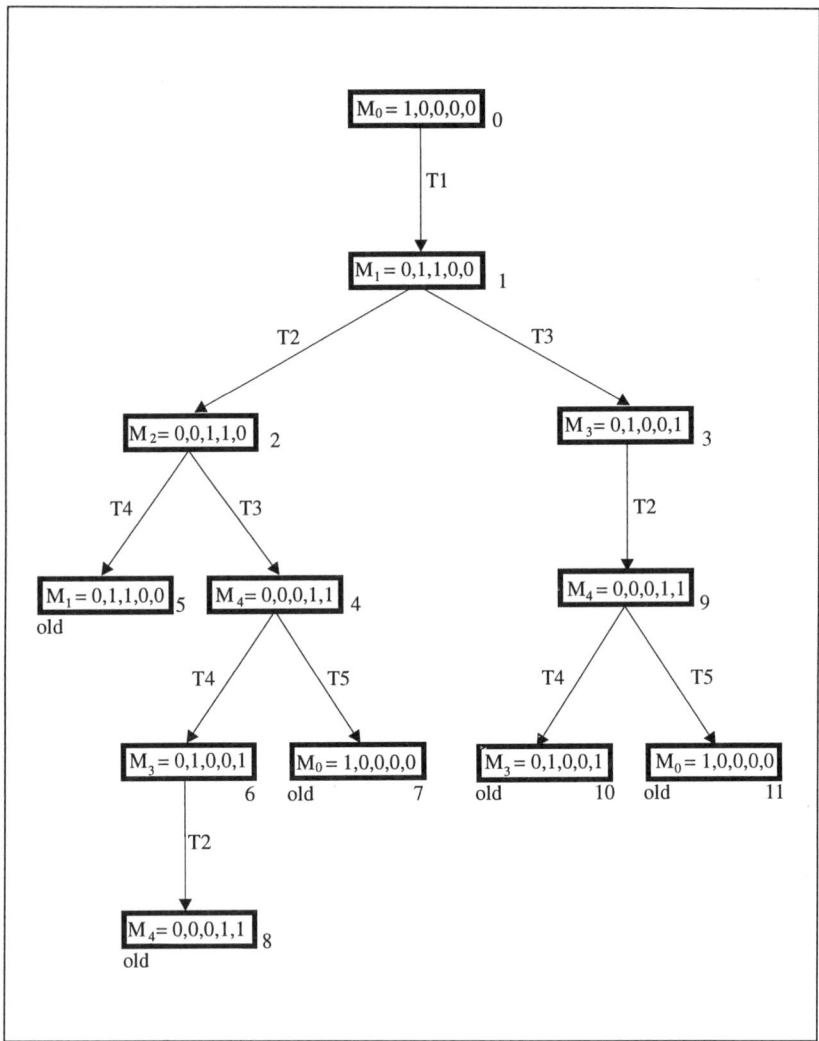

Figure 4.10 *The reachability tree for the net given in Figure 4.1*

From M_2, two markings, M_4 and M_1, are obtained: M_4, which is contained in node N_4, is generated when $T3$ fires, while M_1, which is contained in node N_5, is generated when $T4$ fires. N_5 will not be processed any more, because it has the same contents as N_1 and N_1 is an ancestor of N_5. N_4 originates two markings: M_3, when $T4$ fires, and M_0, when $T5$ fires. Two nodes are added: N_7, which contains M_0, and N_6, which contains M_3. N_7 is marked old. From N_6, only one node is obtained: it is node N_8, which has the same contents as its ancestor N_4. Similarly, we add the remaining nodes, N_9, N_{10} and N_{11}.

Given a reachability (or coverability) tree, if we merge the nodes which contain identical markings, we obtain the corresponding reachability (or coverability) graph. In fact, the above algorithm can easily be modified as follows: instead of introducing a new node, N', and connecting an existing node, P, to N' with an arc whose label is t, if a node, N, containing the same marking as N' already exists, we can simply connect P to N with an arc whose label is t.

The reachability graph shown in Figure 4.4 corresponds to the reachability tree given in Figure 4.10.

An example of a coverability graph is given in Figure 4.11. It refers to the unbounded net that is shown in Figure 4.5; of course, the unbounded place is $P2$.

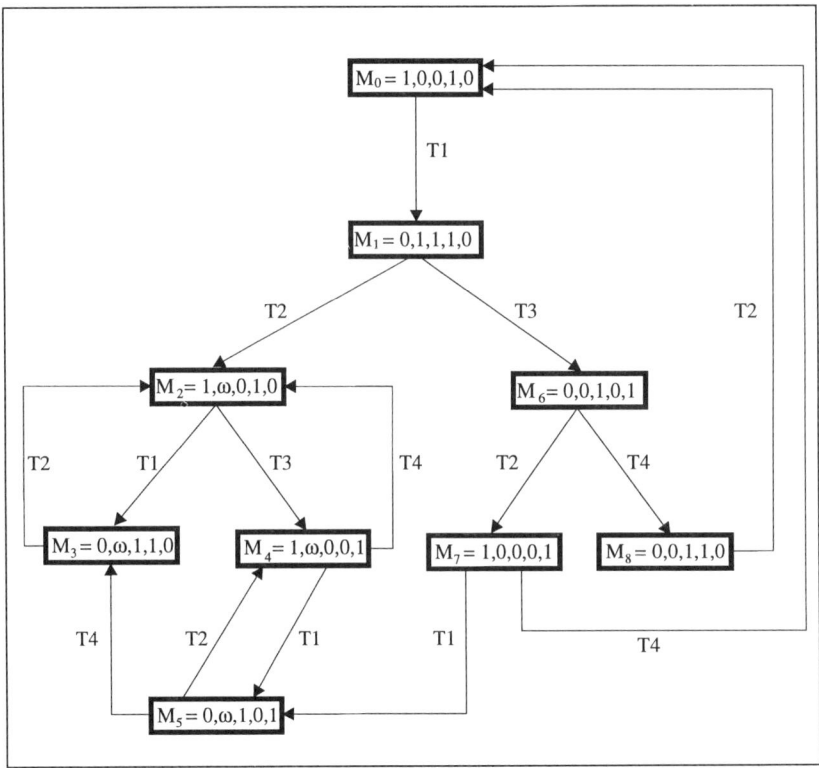

Figure 4.11 *The coverability graph for the net given in Figure 4.5*

4.5 Subclasses of Petri nets

Since the construction of the reachability tree involves the enumeration of all the reachable markings, because of the large amount of space required, it can be afforded only for small nets. However, if the structure of Petri nets is restricted, some subclasses of Petri nets are obtained for which behavioral properties, such as liveness and safeness, can be studied without the construction of the reachability tree.

For the sake of simplicity, the nets considered in this section are ordinary, according to the following definition.

Definition 9 *A Petri net is said to be ordinary iff the weight of each arc is one. In this case, the Petri net structure is a 3-tuple, $N = (P, T, F)$.*

There is no loss of generality, because ordinary nets have the same modeling power as non-ordinary ones (i.e. those introduced with the first definition).

In order to give the results in a simpler way, we also assume that the net structure (N) is strongly connected, i.e. there is a directed path from each node to any other node.

It is also convenient to introduce the following notations:

1. $\bullet t = \{p|(p,t) \in F\}$ denotes the set of all the input places of t;
2. $t\bullet = \{p|(t,p) \in F\}$ denotes the set of all the output places of t;
3. $\bullet p = \{t|(t,p) \in F\}$ denotes the set of all the input transitions of p;
4. $p\bullet = \{t|(p,t) \in F\}$ denotes the set of all the output transitions of p.

Such notations can be extended to subsets of places as well as to subsets of transitions: for instance, if $S \subseteq P$, then $\bullet S$ denotes the set of all the transitions which are input transitions for any place included in S.

Finally, we assume that the Petri net structure (N) has no isolated places and no isolated transitions, therefore we exclude the existence of some place, p, for which $\bullet p = p\bullet = \emptyset$ (where $\emptyset$ denotes the empty set) as well as the existence of some transition, t, for which $\bullet t = t\bullet = \emptyset$.

Following Murata (1989), we introduce five subclasses: state machines, marked graphs, free-choice nets, extended free-choice nets, and asymmetric-choice nets.

4.5.1 State machines

Definition 10 *In a state machine (SM), each transition, t, has exactly one input place and one output place, i.e.*

$$\forall t \in T : |\bullet t| = |t\bullet| = 1$$

It should be noted that the notation $|s|$ denotes the cardinality of set s. SMs cannot represent synchronizations, because transitions cannot have two or more input places. If the initial marking of an SM has only one token, such an SM is equivalent to a state-transition diagram (without events and actions).

It is easy to prove that a state machine, $SM = (N, M_0)$, is live iff M_0 contains at least one token. In addition, an SM is safe iff M_0 contains exactly one token.

4.5.2 Marked graphs

Definition 11 *In a marked graph (MG), each place, p, has exactly one input transition and one output transition, i.e.*

$$\forall p \in P : \; |\bullet p| = |p \bullet| = 1$$

MGs cannot represent conflicts, because two transitions cannot have a common input place. The net shown in Figure 4.6 is a marked graph, while the net given in Figure 4.1 is not, because transitions $T4$ and $T5$ are in conflict.

The properties of a marked graph, $MG = (N, M_0)$, can be studied very easily if it is transformed into a marked directed graph, whose arcs correspond to the places of N (because each place has exactly one incoming arc and one outgoing arc) and whose nodes correspond to the transitions of N; further, the tokens of M_0 (i.e. the initial tokens) are placed on the arcs of the marked directed graph that correspond to the places in which they are contained.

The marked directed graph for the net given in Figure 4.6 is shown in Figure 4.12. For the sake of simplicity, the short names of transitions are used.

A marked directed graph can be covered by directed circuits so that each arc appears in at least one circuit. A directed circuit is a sequence of nodes, $N_1 \ldots N_i N_{i+1} N_n$, satisfying the following properties: the nodes are all different, an arc connects N_n to N_1, and for any pair of consecutive nodes, N_i and N_{i+1}, an arc connects N_i to N_{i+1}.

It has been proved that an MG is live iff the corresponding marked directed graph has at least one token on each directed circuit. An MG is safe iff the corresponding marked directed graph has exactly one token on each directed circuit.

In the graph shown in Figure 4.12, there are three directed circuits: (T_1, T_2, T_3), $(T_1, T_4, T_5, T_2, T_3)$ and (T_4, T_5, T_6). Each directed circuit has one initial token, so the marked graph is live and safe.

If we transform the marked graph given in Figure 4.6 into the one shown in Figure 4.13, we immediately realize that the new net has a deadlock, as no transition is enabled even in the initial marking.

Looking at the corresponding marked directed graph shown in Figure 4.14, we see that only two of the three directed circuits (T_1, T_2, T_3), $(T_1, T_2, T_4,$

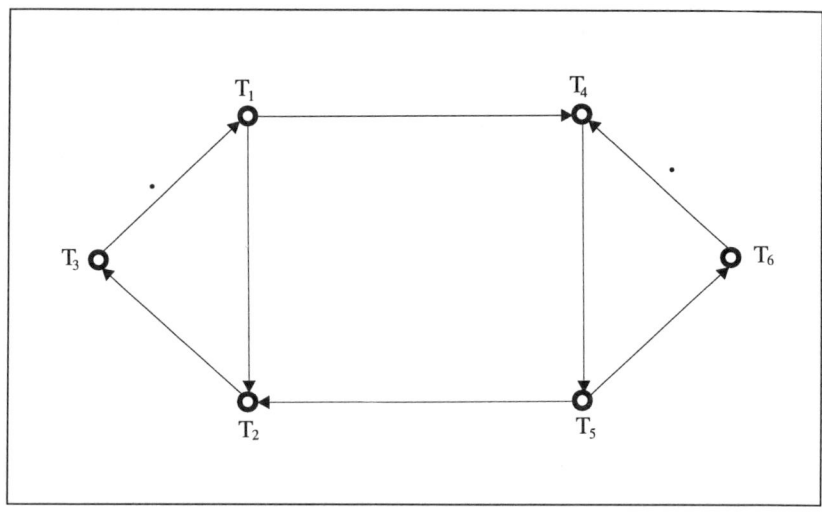

Figure 4.12 *The marked directed graph for the net given in Figure 4.6*

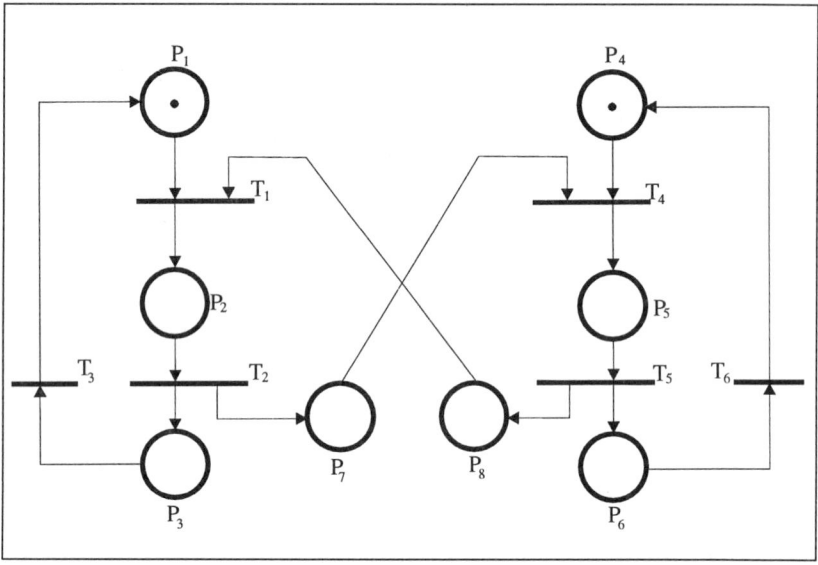

Figure 4.13 *The modified sender/receiver model exhibiting a deadlock*

T_5), (T_4, T_5, T_6), i.e. the first and the third, have initial tokens. In order to avoid a deadlock, we must give the second circuit some tokens; for example, we can place one token on arc $T_5 \rightarrow T_1$ (by putting a token into place P_8) or on arc $T_2 \rightarrow T_4$ (by putting a token into place P_7) or we can even place one token on each of those arcs.

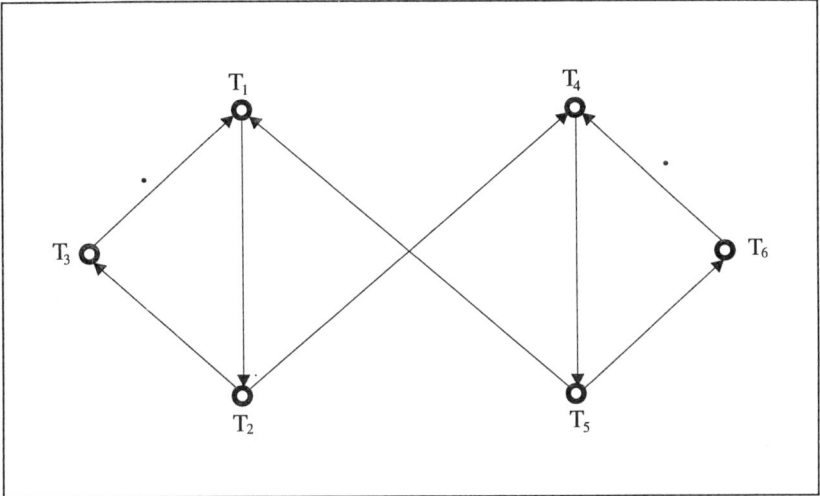

Figure 4.14 *The marked directed graph for the net given in Figure 4.13*

Another result states that the total number of tokens on each directed circuit of a live MG does not change under any firing.

4.5.3 Free-choice nets

Definition 12 *In a free-choice (FC) net, each place that has two or more output transitions is the only input place for each of its output transitions, i.e.*

$$\forall p \in P : \ |p\bullet| = 1 \ \vee \ \bullet(p\bullet) = \{p\}$$

An FC net is able to represent both synchronizations and simple conflicts which are called free choices. A free choice takes place when two or more transitions have one common input place, but this place is their only input place, so if one such transition is enabled, both or all of them are enabled and any can be selected to fire.

Before giving the properties of FC nets, we introduce the notions of siphon and trap.

Definition 13 *A non-empty subset, S, of the places of a net structure, N, is a syphon iff any transition that has an output place in S also has an input place in S, i.e.*

$$\bullet S \subseteq S\bullet$$

A syphon has the property that if it has no tokens in a given marking, it will remain without tokens in any subsequent marking.

Definition 14 *A non-empty subset, Q, of the places of a net structure, N,* *is a trap iff each transition that has an input place in Q also has an output place in Q, i.e.*

$$Q\bullet \subseteq \bullet Q$$

A trap has the property that if it has some tokens (i.e. it is marked) in a given marking, it will be marked in any subsequent marking.

Siphons and traps can be determined by solving a set of logic equations, as shown by Murata (1989). The result of the union of two syphons (or of two traps) is another syphon (or trap).

It has been proved that:

1. a free-choice net, $FC = (N, M_0)$, is live iff each syphon of N contains (including the case of equality) a marked trap (in M_0);

2. a live free-choice net, $FC = (N, M_0)$, is safe iff N is covered by strongly connected state machines, each of which has exactly one token in M_0.

The FC net shown in Figure 4.15 is live, because it has one syphon, $\{P1, P2\}$, and one marked trap, which is equal to the syphon. This net is also safe: in fact, it is covered by two state machines, as shown below the FC net in Figure 4.15, and each of them has one token in the initial marking.

The free-choice net shown in Figure 4.16 is not live, because syphon S_2 does not contain any marked trap. In fact, if transition $T2$ fires first, then no other transition is enabled.

4.5.4 Extended free-choice nets

Definition 15 *In an extended free-choice (EFC) net, any two places that have one common output transition must have all their output transitions in common, i.e.*

$$\forall p_1, p_2 \in P : \ p_1\bullet \cap p_2\bullet \neq \emptyset \ \Rightarrow \ p_1\bullet = p_2\bullet$$

EFC nets are able to represent extended free choices. An extended free choice takes place when two or more transitions have all their input places in common: therefore, if one such transition is enabled, both or all of them are enabled and any can be selected to fire.

An EFC net can be transformed into an equivalent FC net, as shown in Figure 4.17, thus the properties of an EFC net can be studied on the equivalent FC net.

4.5.5 Asymmetric-choice nets

Definition 16 *In an asymmetric-choice (AC) net, if any two places, P_1 and P_2, have one common output transition, then the set of the output*

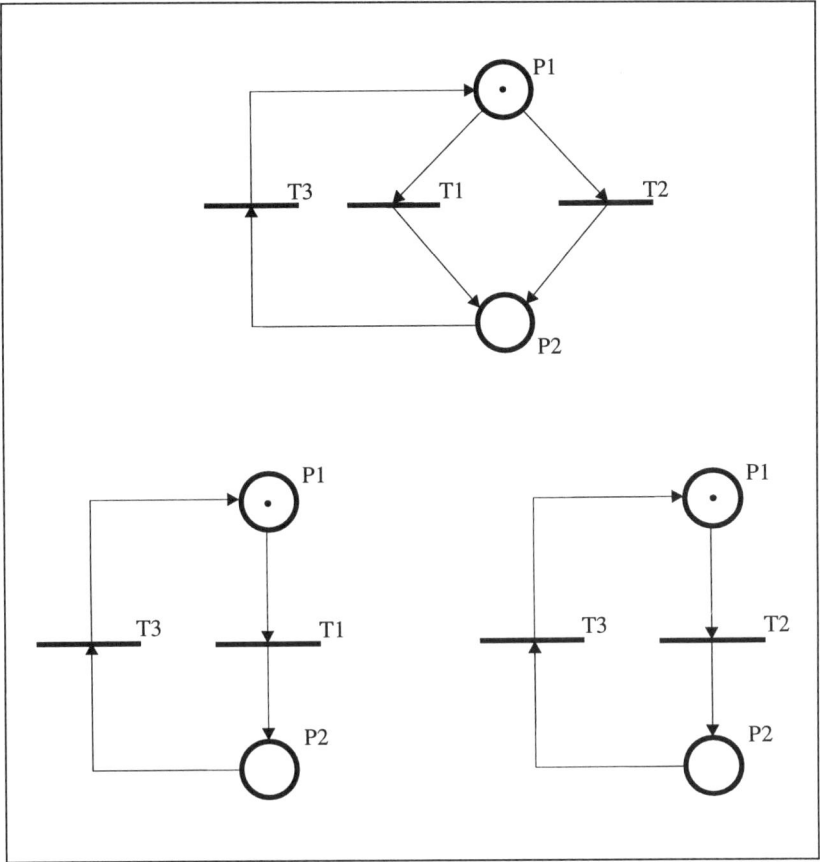

Figure 4.15 *A safe FC net*

transitions of P_1 is a subset of the set of the output transitions of P_2 or vice versa, i.e.

$$\forall p_1, p_2 \in P : \ p_1\bullet \cap p_2\bullet \neq \emptyset \ \Rightarrow \ p_1\bullet \subseteq p_2\bullet \vee p_2\bullet \subseteq p_1\bullet$$

AC nets include all the other subclasses, i.e. SMs, MGs, FC nets and EFC nets.

AC nets are able to represent asymmetric confusion but symmetric confusion cannot be modeled. Confusion denotes a situation in which concurrency and conflict are closely related, as shown in Figure 4.18.

Symmetric confusion takes place when two transitions, such as $T1$ and $T3$, are concurrent, but, at the same time, each of them is in conflict with another transition $(T2)$. We have asymmetric confusion when two transitions, such as $T1$ and $T2$, are concurrent, but if one of them $(T2)$ fires first, the other $(T1)$ will be in conflict with another transition $(T3)$. Asymmetric

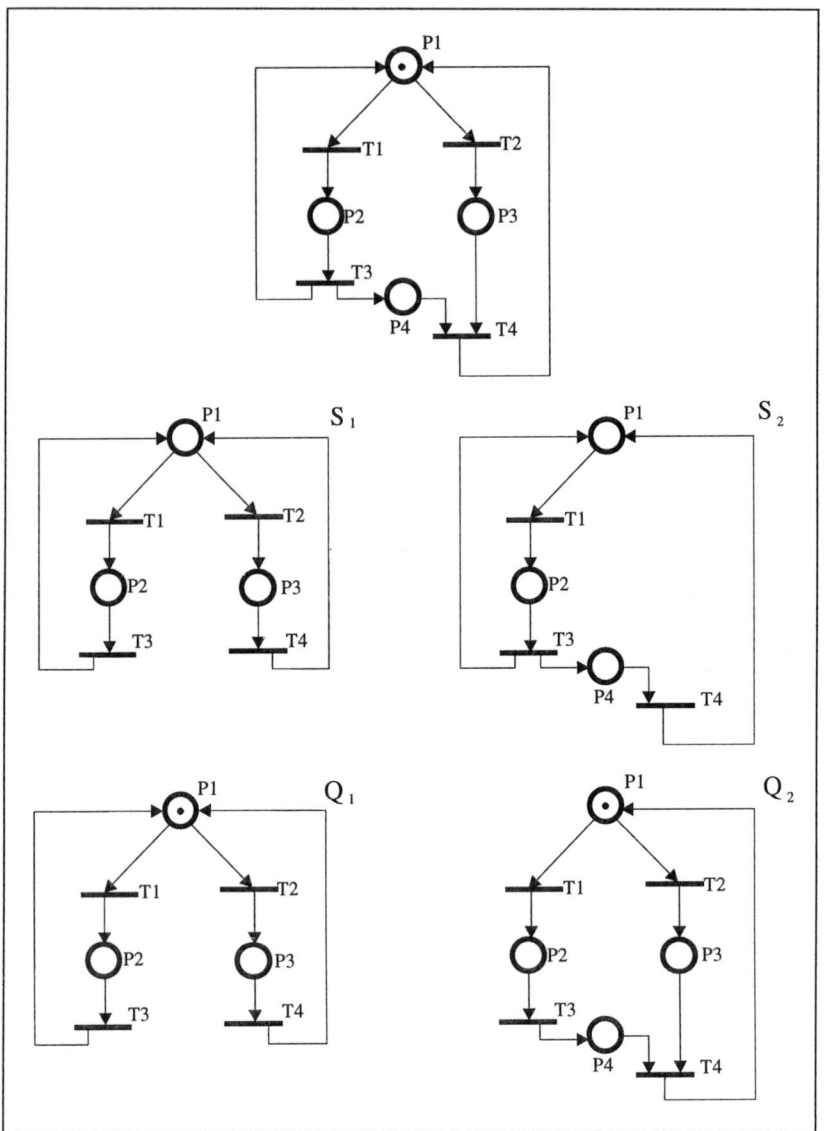

Figure 4.16 *An FC net which is not live*

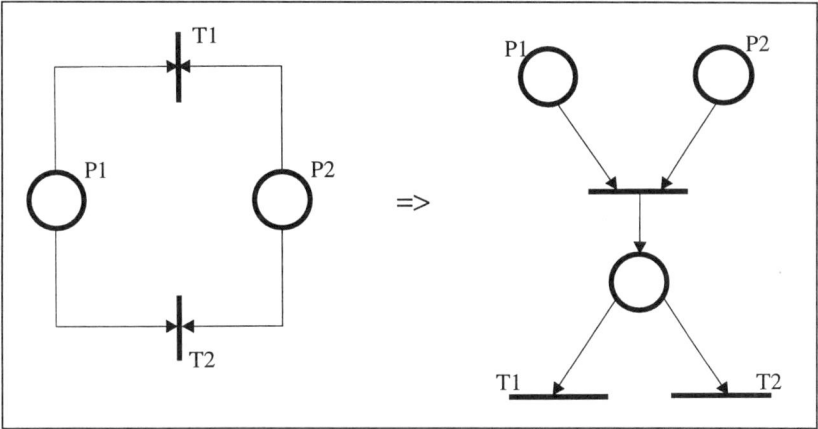

Figure 4.17 *Transformation of an EFC net into an equivalent FC net*

confusion is present in the net shown in Figure 4.1; in fact, $T4$ and $T3$ are concurrent, but, when they are both enabled, if $T3$ fires first, $T4$ will be in conflict with $T5$.

It has been proved that an asymmetric-choice net, $AC = (N, M_0)$, is live if, but not only if, every syphon of N contains a marked trap (in M_0).

4.6 Reduction rules

When the complexity of a model is too high, we can try to reduce it by applying reduction rules which preserve the properties of the original model. The reduced model, then, can be analysed with the techniques illustrated previously.

Following Murata (1989), we present some transformations, shown in Figure 4.19, which preserve the properties of liveness, safeness and boundedness. Therefore, if the reduced net enjoys some of those properties, the same holds for the original net.

1. Fusion of places in series (Figure 4.19(a)). If there is a transition, T, which has only one input place, P, and only one output place, Q, and if T is the only output transition of P, then P and Q can be merged into one place and T as well as the arcs from P to T and from T to Q can be removed. In fact, a token in P enables only T, so merging P and Q into one place does not affect the behavior of the net.

2. Fusion of transitions in series (Figure 4.19(b)). If there is a place, P, which has only one input transition, T, and only one output transition, U, and if P is the only input place of U, then T and U can be merged into one transition and P as well as the arcs from T to P and from P to

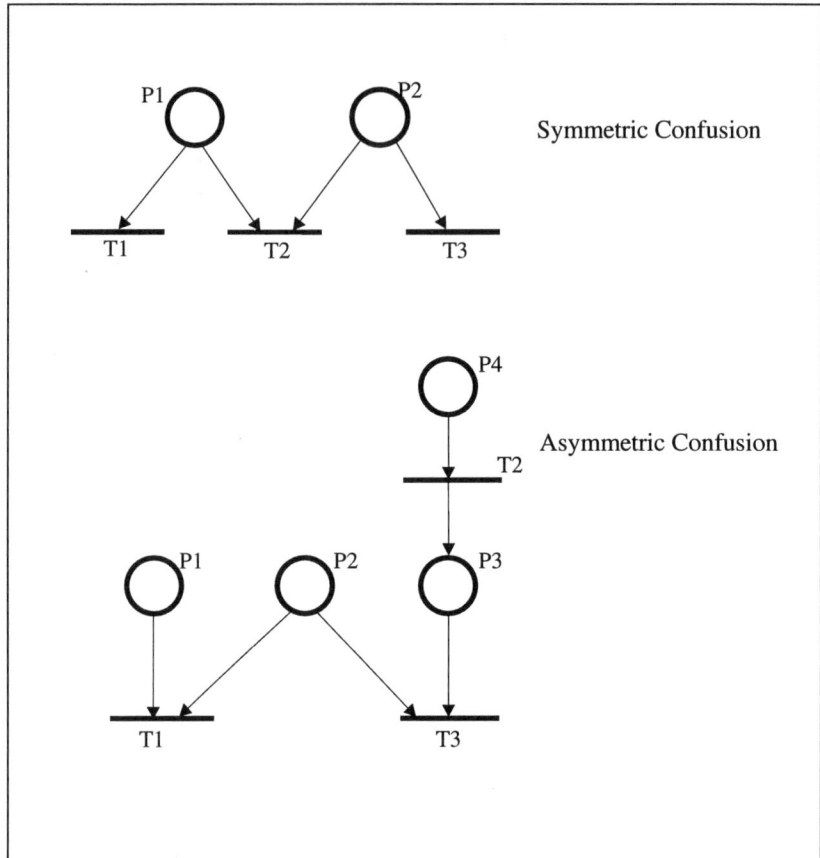

Figure 4.18 *Symmetric and asymmetric confusion*

U can be removed. In fact, the firing of T always enables U, so merging T and U into one transition does not affect the behavior of the net.

3. Fusion of places in parallel (Figure 4.19(c)). If there is a place, P, which has only one input transition, T, and only one output transition, U, and if there is another place, Q, which has the same input and output transitions as P, then P and Q can be merged into one place which has only one input transition, T, and only one output transition, U. In fact, P and Q receive tokens at the same time and it is necessary for U to be enabled that both P and Q have tokens, so just one place is needed to make U fire after T.

4. Fusion of transitions in parallel (Figure 4.19(d)). If there is a transition, T, which has only one input place, P, and only one output place, Q, and if there is another transition, U, which has the same input and output

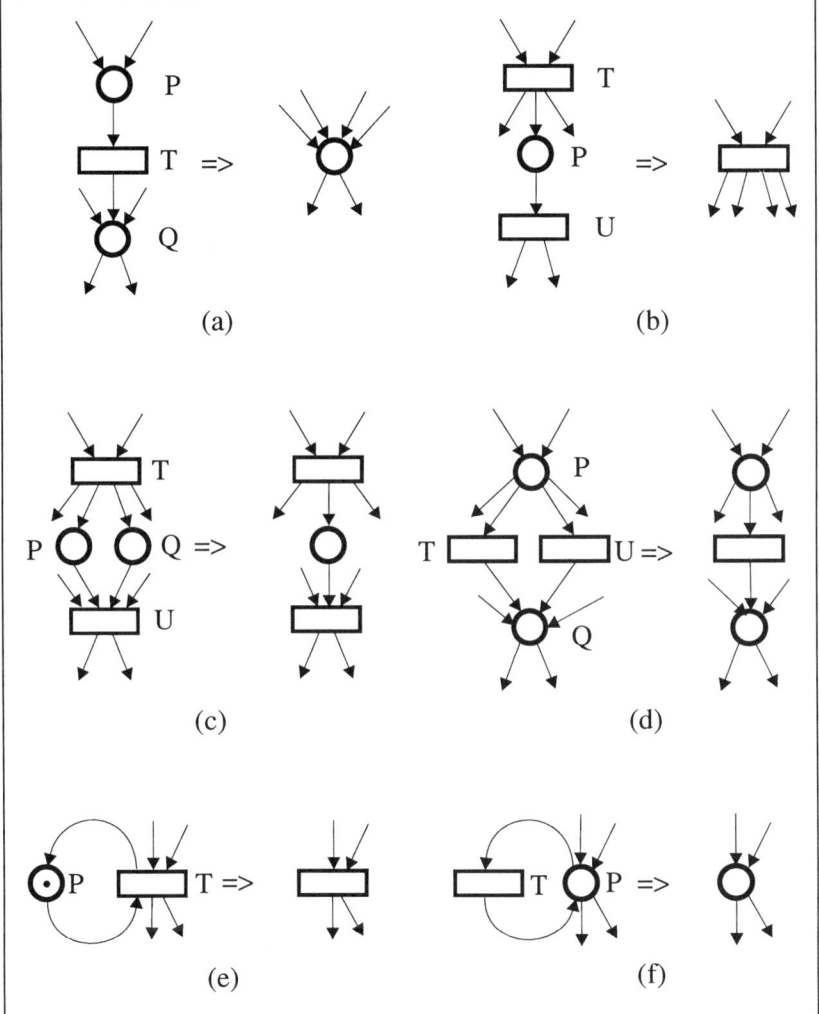

Figure 4.19 *Reduction rules*

places as T, then T and U can be merged into one transition which has only one input place, P, and only one output place, Q. In fact, it does not matter which path a token has to follow from P to Q, so just one transition is needed to make tokens move from P to Q.

5. Removal of self-loop places (Figure 4.19(e)). If there is a place, P, which is marked (i.e. it has a token in the initial marking) and has the same transition, T, as its only input transition and its only output transition, then P as well as its incoming and outgoing arcs can be removed. In

fact, the firing of T depends on the tokens contained in the other input places of T.

6. Removal of self-loop transitions (Figure 4.19(f)). If there is a transition, T, which has the same place, P, as its only input place and its only output place, then T as well as its incoming and outgoing arcs can be removed. In fact, the firing of T does not change the marking of the net.

The reduction of the AC net shown in Figure 4.1 is illustrated in Figure 4.20. In the first step (Figure 4.20(b)), we merge two pairs of places in series, $P2 - P4$ and $P3 - P5$. Then, we remove $T4$, which is a self-loop transition (Figure 4.20(c)). Subsequently, we merge two places in parallel (Figure 4.20(d)) and two transitions in series (Figure 4.20(e)), thus a trivial net, which is live and safe, is obtained.

It is easy to verify that the net shown in Figure 4.16 cannot be reduced using any of the above-mentioned transformations.

Instead of trying to reduce a complex model, we can do the opposite: we can start from a simple model (the original model) and then refine it progressively using suitable synthesis rules (that preserve the properties of the original model) until it reaches the required level of detail. Rules for marked graphs are discussed by Murata (1989).

4.7 Timing constraints

The lack of an explicit notion of time in ordinary Petri nets is an obstacle to their use as a performance evaluation tool. In fact, the standard firing rule of Petri nets states that an enabled transition will fire, but it does not specify when this will occur. Moreover, the firing of a transition is an action that changes the current marking instantaneously.

Many extensions to Petri nets have been proposed which enable the analyst to associate timing constraints with transitions or places.

In the remainder of this section, attention will be focused on a widely used extension, called timed Petri nets (TdPN), first proposed by Ramchandani (1974).

A TdPN is a pair (PN, τ), where PN is a standard Petri net, $PN = (P, T, F, W, M_0)$, and τ is a mapping from T to $\mathcal{R}_0^+$, which assigns a nonnegative fixed firing duration, called release delay, to each transition. A transition with a release delay equal to 0 is said to be immediate.

The firing of a transition, T, changes the marking of a TdPN in two distinct steps:

1. when T fires, say, at instant t_1, the input tokens are removed from the input places of T;

2. at instant $t_2 = t_1 + \tau(T)$, the output tokens are added to the output places of T.

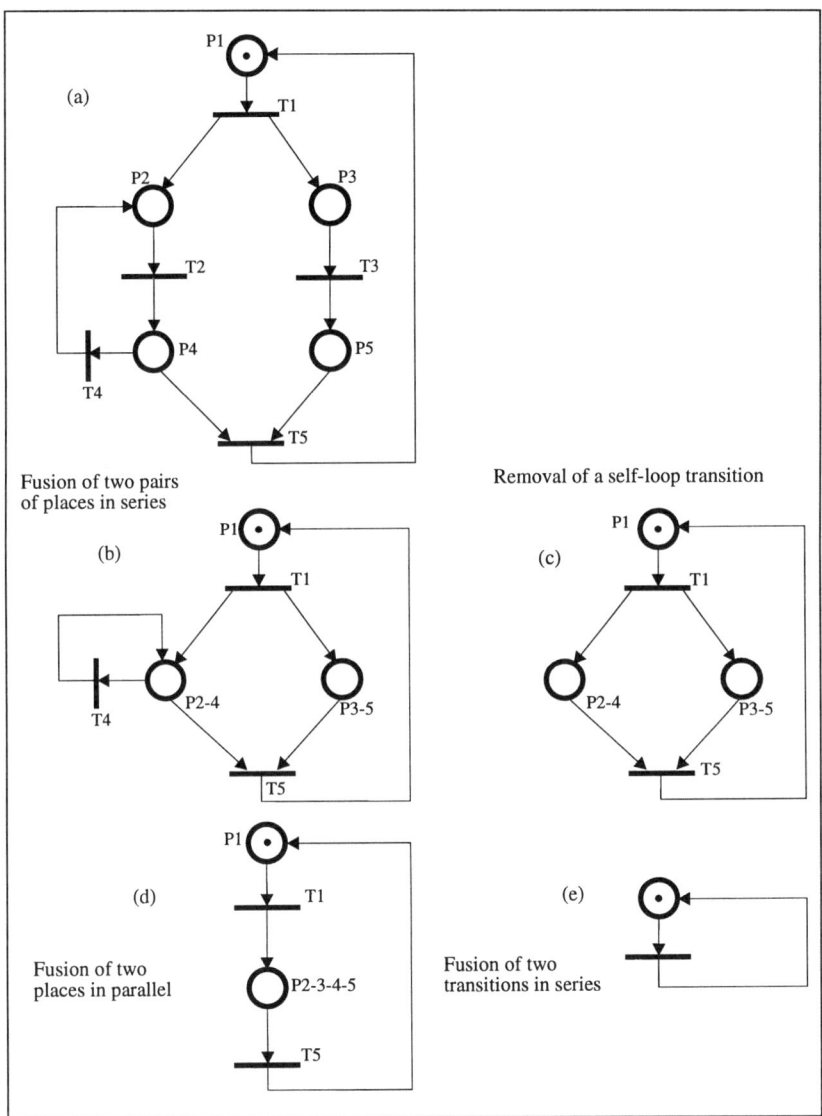

(a)

Fusion of two pairs
of places in series

Removal of a self-loop transition

(b)

(c)

(d)

Fusion of two
places in parallel

(e)

Fusion of two
transitions in series

Figure 4.20 *The reduction of the net shown in Figure 4.1*

Such an extension to the firing rule allows a specific duration to be associated with each transition, but it does not yet determine when an enabled transition will fire. However, most properties of TdPNs are only studied under the assumption that each transition fires as soon as it is enabled, thus this assumption will hold henceforth in this section. For the sake of simplicity, conflicts are ignored in this section, so only marked graphs are considered. Conflicts will be dealt with in the next chapter when priorities will be associated with transitions.

According to the extended firing rule, several firings of the same transition can take place at the same time. In fact, if it is assumed that a transition, T, which features a release delay of 10 time units and has only one input place, P, and only one output place, Q, is enabled at instant t_1 because there is one token in P, then T immediately starts the first firing by removing this token from P. If P receives another token at an instant in between t_1 and $t_3 = t_1 + 10$, say at instant $t_2 = t_1 + 5$, at the same instant T starts the second firing by removing that token from P. Therefore, if no other token arrives, two concurrent firings of T are taking place during the interval $[t_2, t_3]$. The first firing ends at instant t_3, the second one at instant $t_4 = t_1 + 15$. If we wish to make sure that the firings of a given transition are serialized, we must add a self-loop place (with one token in the initial marking) to that transition.

An example of a TdPN is shown in Figure 4.21.

It models a simple production system consisting of one workstation and one cart. The workstation behaves as follows.

1. Its initial state is Idle.

2. When it is idle (i.e. a token is in place Idle), it asks the cart for a part and waits for the part. In fact, transition Issue_In_Req fires and puts a token into place In_Req and a token into place W.

3. When the cart is ready to deliver a part to the workstation (i.e. a token is present in place Part_Ready), the workstation takes the part. Transition Input_Part represents the action of transferring the part from the cart to the workstation. When the action is done, a token is put into place Unloaded and another is put into place W_Enabled: the former indicates that the cart is allowed to come back to its rest point, while the latter enables the workstation to start working on the part.

4. After the workstation has taken the part, transition Work fires; when the firing is over, the workstation becomes idle again.

Initially, the cart is ready at a rest point located between the workstation and a warehouse containing raw parts. When the cart receives a request, transition Load_and_Move fires so as to represent the actions of taking a raw part from the warehouse and carrying it to the workstation. A token in place W_U indicates that the cart waits until the workstation has taken the

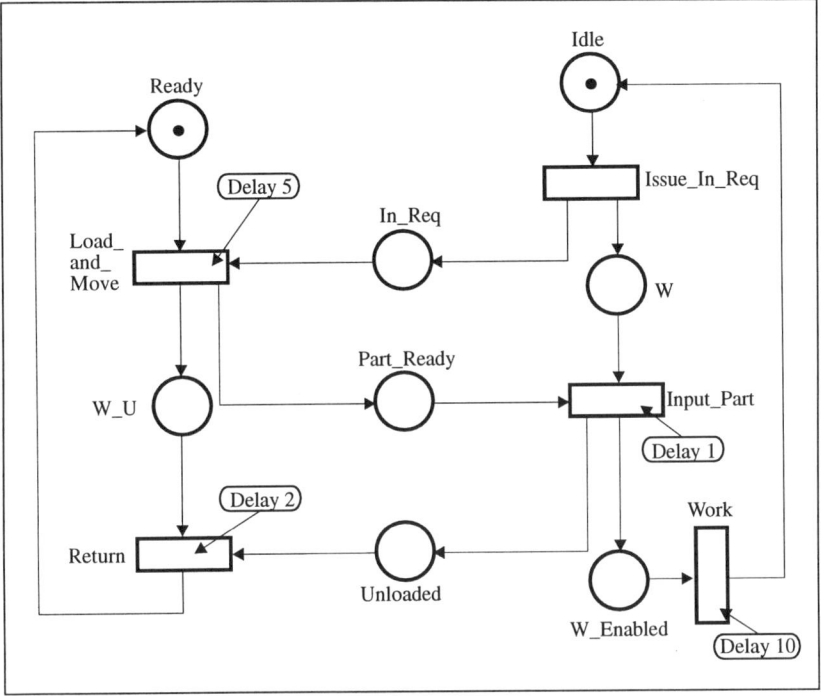

Figure 4.21 *A net with timing constraints*

part from it. When a token is put into place Unloaded, transition Return fires and the cart comes back to its rest point.

All transitions but Issue_In_Req have a release delay, as illustrated in Figure 4.21. These delays are associated with mechanical actions; since transition Issue_In_Req represents a communication from the workstation controller to the cart controller, its duration (compared with the durations of the other transitions) is negligible, so this transition is considered to be immediate.

The diagram given in Figure 4.22 enables us to observe the evolution of the model through time. It shows the number of tokens in some selected places: a bar indicates that a token is put into the place being considered at a certain instant and that, at the same time, it is removed because a transition which has that place as an input place fires.

The main result we obtain from such a diagram is the low utilization of the cart: in fact, it is ready, i.e. a token is in place Ready, for 50% of time.

If we consider a production system including two identical workstations which are served by one cart, we obtain the diagram shown in Figure 4.23.

In this case, the cart is always busy: in fact, as soon as a token is put into place Ready, it is immediately removed because a request is pending. In the

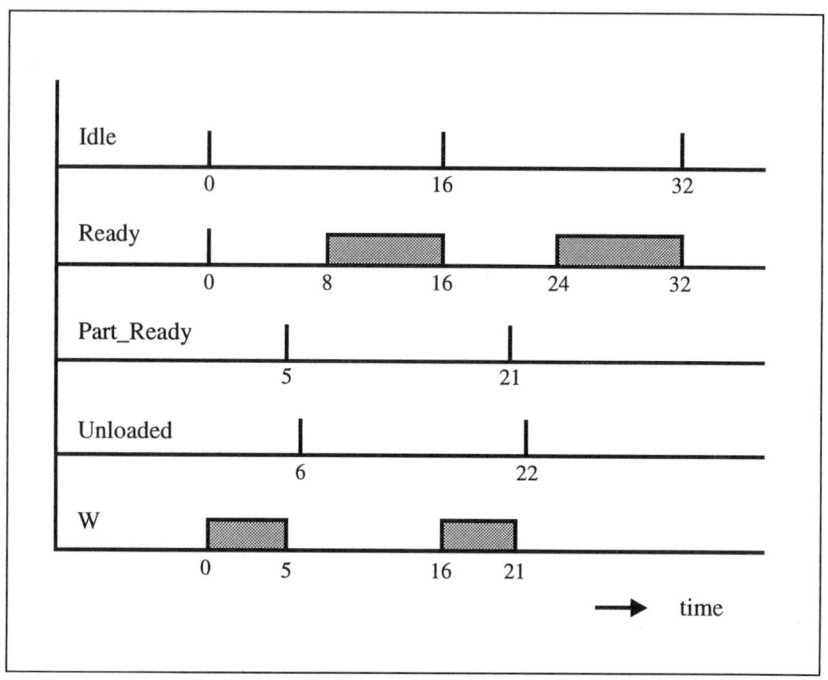

Figure 4.22 *Temporal diagram for the net given in Figure 4.21*

interval $[0..5[$ there are two tokens in place W denoting both workstations waiting for parts. Subsequently, one workstation at a time will be waiting for a part.

Other well-known kinds of time-dependent nets include time Petri nets (Merlin and Farber, 1976), stochastic Petri nets (Molloy, 1982) and generalized stochastic Petri nets (Ajmone Marsan, Conte and Balbo, 1984).

4.7.1 Timed marked graphs

In this subsection we present an important result concerning marked graphs with deterministic release delays. This subclass of TdPNs is called timed marked graphs.

For the sake of simplicity, only strongly connected marked graphs (SCMGs) will be considered. An SCMG is an MG in which any two places can be the ends of a directed path. A directed path from a place, p_1, to another place, p_n, is a sequence of places and transitions, $p_1 t_1 p_2 t_2 \ldots t_{n-1} p_n$, in which t_i is both an output transition of p_i and an input transition of p_{i+1}. The same transition cannot appear more than once in a directed path. A directed path in which p_1 and p_n denote the same place is called cycle.

In a timed SCMG, after an initial transient, the time, called cycle time

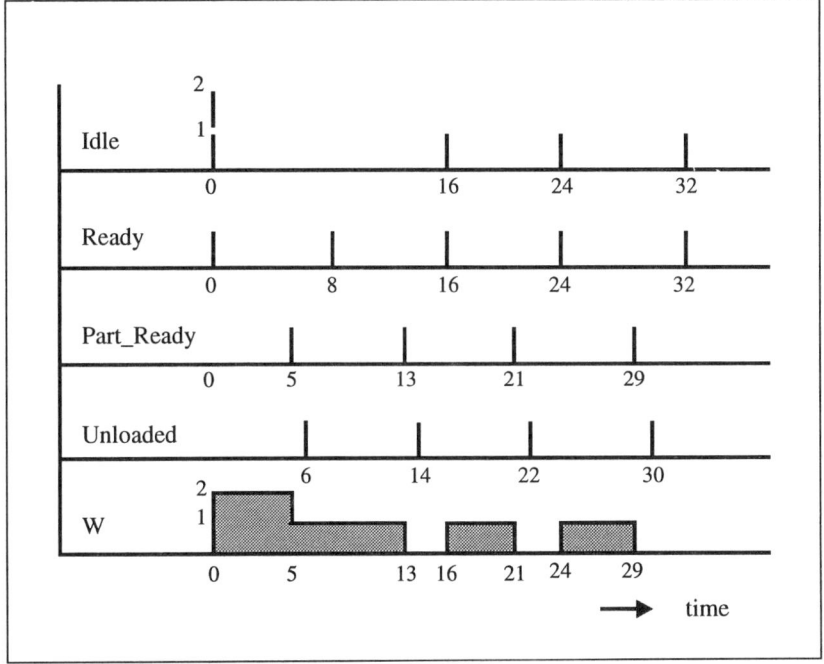

Figure 4.23 *Temporal diagram for the net given in Figure 4.21 with two tokens in place Idle*

(C), which elapses between two subsequent firings of the same transition is constant and equal for all transitions. Ramamoorthy (1980) has proved that the cycle time of a timed SCMG can be computed using the following formula:

$$C = \max_k \left(\frac{T_k}{N_k} \right), \quad k = 1, 2, \ldots, q$$

where:

$$T_k = \sum_{t_i \in L_k} \tau(t_i)$$

$$N_k = \sum_{p_i \in L_k} M(p_i)$$

and

1. q is the number of cycles of the SCMG;

2. L_k is the k-th cycle;

3. T_k is the sum of the release delays of all the transitions belonging to the k-th cycle;

4. N_k is the number of tokens that circulate in the k-th cycle.

Cycle	Transitions in cycle		T	N
α	Load_and_Move	Return	7	1
β	Load_and_Move Return	Input_Part	8	1
γ	Issue_In_Req Input_Part	Load_and_Move Work	16	1
δ	Issue_In_Req Work	Input_Part	11	1

Table 4.1 *T and N values for the cycles of the net given in Figure 4.21*

The performance of a system represented by a timed SCMG is thus completely determined by its cycle time.

Using the above formula, we can compute the cycle time of the net given in Figure 4.21: it has four cycles whose T and N values are reported in Table 4.1.

Therefore, we have

$$C = \max\{7, 8, 16, 11\} = 16$$

so each transition starts firing every 16 time units, as shown in Figure 4.22.

If there were two workstations instead of just one, the value of N would change for some cycles. In particular, N would double for γ and δ and would remain unchanged for α and β, so the cycle time would become

$$C = \max\{7, 8, \frac{16}{2}, \frac{11}{2}\} = 8$$

It should be noted that, on the basis of the results concerning marked graphs, the net shown in Figure 4.21 is live and safe, because each of its four circuits has exactly one initial token.

Bruno, Castella, Pavesio and Pescarmona (1993) extended Ramamoorthy's result to the marked graphs in which the firing of each transition can have a duration that falls within a predefined interval.

4.8 High-level nets

The first kinds of Petri nets that appeared in the literature are known as Condition/Event nets (CE-nets) and Place/Transition nets (PT-nets).

In CE-nets, any place contains at most one token, because places are interpreted as boolean conditions, while transitions represent events: in fact, an event occurs only when its preconditions are true (i.e. each of its input places contains one token), and after it occurs its postconditions are true (i.e. each of its output places contains one token).

In PT-nets, places can contain several tokens: in fact, places are interpreted as data buffers and transitions as data-driven computations.

Such kinds of nets turned out to be inadequate when complex real-world systems had to be modeled, because models based on such nets rapidly became too large.

Substantial progress was made when tokens were allowed to possess individual features and, during firing, transitions were allowed to read the features of input tokens and to write the features of output tokens.

Two major kinds of extended nets were proposed: Predicate/Transition nets (PrT-nets) (Genrich and Lautenbach, 1981) and Colored Petri nets (CP-nets) (Jensen, 1981).

A recent reformulation of CP-nets (Jensen, 1991) incorporates and integrates the original contributions of the above-mentioned extensions.

Instead of giving a formal definition of CP-nets, which would be difficult to read for non-specialists, we present a simple example.

The example, given in Figure 4.24, concerns the machining of raw parts by a pool of workstations. A raw part can be machined only by a workstation that is able to do it. After a workstation has machined a part, the part becomes finished and the workstation either is ready to work on another part or must perform a set-up. A workstation must perform a set-up every time it has machined two parts.

Places have a name and a color, which is similar to a type in programming languages; the color is shown boxed. Colors are described in a data dictionary associated with the net. The colors of the example are listed below.

Part is the union of two components (technically, it is a Cartesian product of the values of those components), namely the part code and the code of the workstation which is able to process the part.

Part_Code is the set of the part codes. We have four part codes (literal values): p_1, p_2, p_3 and p_4.

Wst_Code is the set of the workstation codes; it contains the values: w_1, w_2 and w_3.

I is the set of the integer values belonging to a specified interval.

Wst is the union of two components, namely the workstation code and the number of machinings performed since the last set-up. This number will be referred to as the operation counter of the workstation.

The initial marking includes four raw parts, (p_1, w_1), (p_2, w_1), (p_3, w_1) and (p_4, w_4), and three workstations, $(w_1, 0)$, $(w_2, 0)$ and $(w_3, 0)$.

Arcs and transitions can have inscriptions. If the arc being considered leaves a place, P, its inscription specifies which token has to be taken from

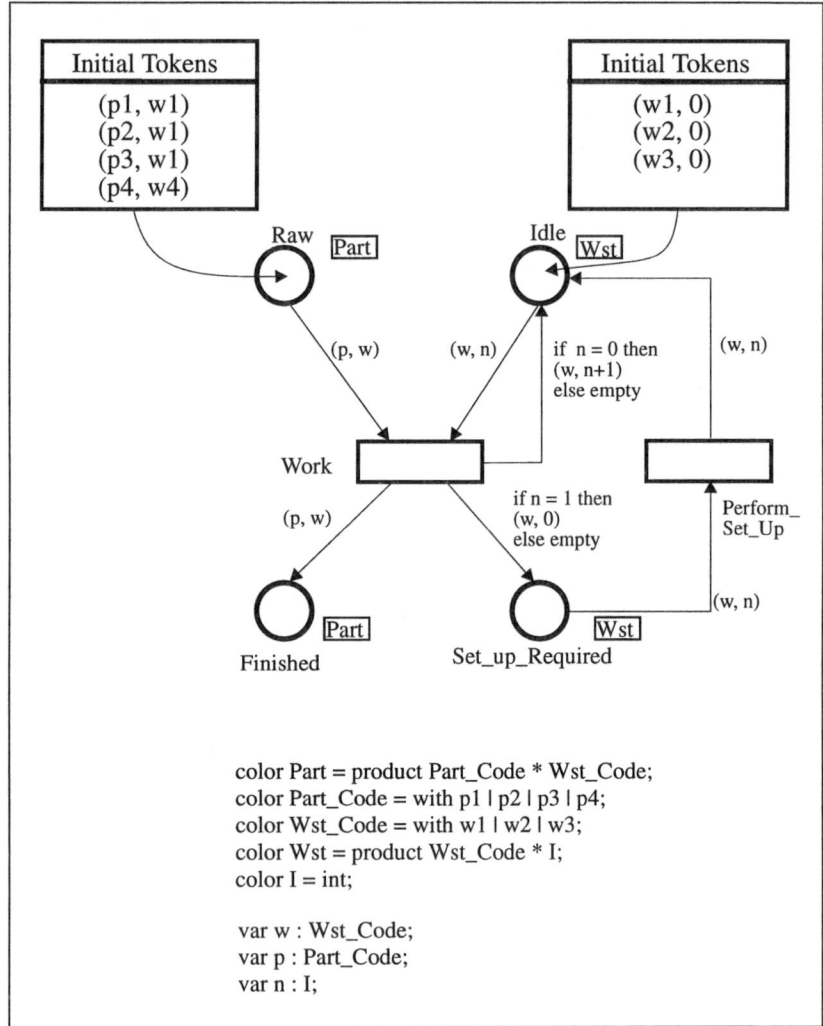

Figure 4.24 *A Colored Petri net*

P; if the arc enters a place, Q, its inscription specifies which token has to be put into Q.

The inscription of an arc must be consistent with the color of the place to which the arc is connected. For example, the inscription of arc *Raw* → *Work*, i.e. (p, w), is consistent with the color, Part, of place Raw; p and w are variables and they are declared in the data dictionary.

Transition Work has two input places, Raw and Idle; since the inscriptions of the arcs, *Raw* → *Work* and *Idle* → *Work*, which enter Work contain the same variable, w, w must be bound to the same value when tokens are taken from the corresponding places. If no such binding is possible, transition Work will not be allowed to fire.

There are three pairs of tokens which, initially, enable transition Work: $(p_1, w_1) - (w_1, 0)$, $(p_2, w_1) - (w_1, 0)$, and $(p_3, w_1) - (w_1, 0)$. One of those pairs will be selected randomly when the transition fires.

The inscriptions of the outgoing arcs of a transition determine the contents of the tokens that will be put into its output places; variables appearing in such inscriptions are bound to the values of the tokens extracted from the input places.

The inscription of arc $Work \rightarrow Idle$ specifies that a token has to be delivered to place Idle only if the value contained in the operation counter of the token which has been taken from place Idle is zero: in fact, a workstation returns into state Idle after processing the first part since the last set-up. When a token is delivered to place Idle, the value of its operation counter is 1. The action, empty, which is performed when the boolean condition of the inscription of arc $Work \rightarrow Idle$ is false, means that no token will be delivered to the output place.

The inscription of arc $Work \rightarrow Set\_up\_Required$ specifies that a token has to be delivered to place Set_up_Required only if the value contained in the operation counter of the token which has been taken from place Idle is 1: in fact, a workstation, after processing the second part since the last set-up, must perform a new set-up. When a token is delivered to place Set_up_Required, the value of its operation counter is 0.

Transition Perform_Set_up only moves tokens from place Set_up_Required to place Idle.

A transition can also have an inscription, called guard, which is a boolean expression: in such a case, the transition is allowed to fire if and only if the inscriptions of both its incoming arcs and its guard are satisfied.

The firing rule in CP-nets is more general than in Petri nets: in fact, a transition, when it fires, can take one token, several tokens or even none from an input place, depending on the inscriptions of its incoming arcs; further, it can deliver one token, several tokens or even none to an output place, depending on the inscriptions of its outcoming arcs.

The last example, shown in Figure 4.25, models the well-known problem of the five dining philosophers.

Philosophers alternately think and eat; when they want to eat, they sit down at a round table where there are five forks. Each philosopher needs two forks to eat, hence he must pick up one fork on the left and another on the right. The problem is that, if all philosophers pick up one fork on the same side and wait for the fork on the other side, they will all wait for ever (the system enters a deadlock).

The solution is that each philosopher before eating picks up both forks simultaneously. This is shown in Figure 4.25: places T, H and E contain

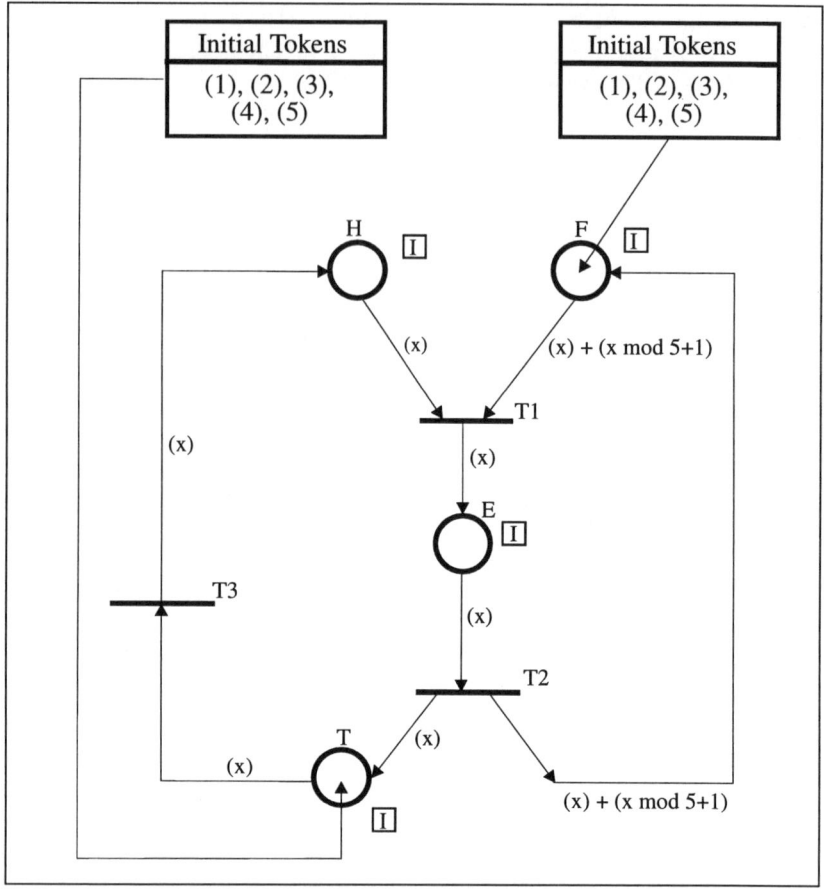

Figure 4.25 *The CP-net for the five dining philosophers problem*

thinking philosophers, hungry ones and eating ones, respectively; place F contains available forks. Philosophers and forks are numbered from 1 to 5.

Each philosopher, i, is allowed to eat only when both his left fork, i, and his right fork, $i \bmod 5 + 1$, are available in place F. Transition T1, when it fires, moves one token (the philosopher who can eat) from place H to place I and removes two tokens (the forks corresponding to such a philosopher) from place F. It should be noted that m tokens are involved when an arc inscription is made up of a sum of m parentheses, thus two tokens are removed from place F when T1 fires and two tokens are delivered to place F when T2 fires.

4.9 Summary

This chapter has outlined the basic notions of Petri nets and has illustrated some subclasses which enable the analyst to study important properties, such as liveness, without enumerating all the reachable markings. It has also described timed Petri nets, i.e. nets with deterministic timing constraints, and has given a short introduction to Colored Petri nets.

The literature on Petri nets is very rich and is growing very quickly in both the fields of theoretical studies and practical applications, a recent survey being the book edited by Jensen and Rozenberg (1991).

5

Protob

Protob is both a modeling and a development language for event-driven systems. It combines the most important features of high-level timed Petri nets with those of extended dataflows and organizes them within an object-oriented framework.

Protob is the result of research started at the end of 1984. Looking back at the activities carried out so far, we can identify three major milestones:

1. the definition of Prot nets (Bruno and Marchetto, 1986), i.e. high-level nets translatable into Ada-based concurrent programs;

2. the definition of Protob as both a graphical language and a technique for organizing models into cooperating objects (Baldassari and Bruno, 1991);

3. the development of an environment, Artifex (Artis, 1992), which simulates Protob models and automatically generates executable distributed programs from such models.

This chapter reviews the major features of Protob and also illustrates the simulation of models, the construction of client-server models and the integration of services.

5.1 Protob nets

This section illustrates the basic components of Protob nets, namely places, transitions and tokens. In addition to the graphical representation, textual information complementary to the net is provided in a data dictionary which will be referred to as the script.

The script contains sections of code written in a standard programming language, such as C or Ada. However, for the sake of simplicity, the examples in this chapter will adopt an informal but intuitive syntax.

5.1.1 Places and tokens

A place can contain several tokens at a time; all the tokens contained in a given place are of the same type. Each place has three attributes: the place name, the place type and the number of tokens in the initial marking (such tokens are called initial tokens). The first two attributes are strings, while the third is an integer number which can be omitted if the place has no initial tokens.

The place type denotes the type of the tokens that are contained in the place. For example, place P in Figure 5.1(a) is of type Part and contains tokens that represent mechanical parts waiting to be processed.

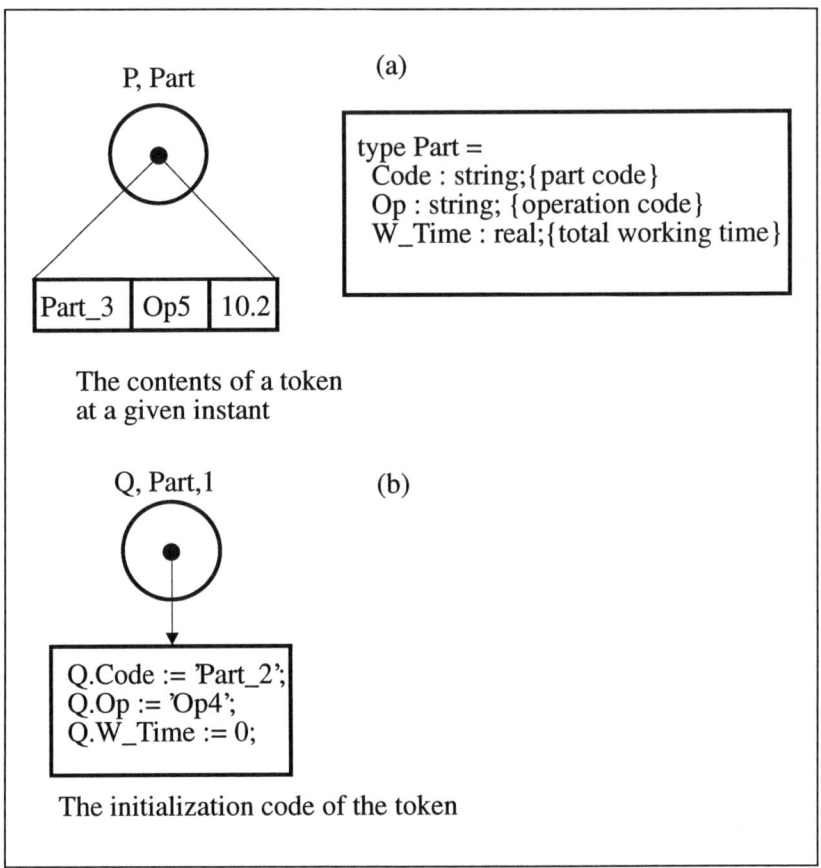

Figure 5.1 *Places, place types and initial tokens*

Type Part consists of three attributes (or fields): a string, Code, which contains the part code, a string, Op, which contains the code of the operation to be performed on the part, and a real number, W_Time, which stores the overall duration of all the operations performed on the part.

Type definitions are collected in the script.

The contents of the token which is in place P at a given instant are shown in Figure 5.1(a). Tokens are usually depicted as dots.

If the tokens in a place contain no information, a special type, nul, is used. For the sake of simplicity, if the place type is nul, it can be omitted.

Places are queues (not sets) of tokens, thus when a token is put into a place, it is added to the end of the queue. Tokens are ordered in places on the basis of their arrival times.

As shown in Figure 5.1(b), a piece of code, called token-initialization code, can be associated with each initial token, so that its contents are initialized. In a token-initialization code, the place name is used as a reference (or handle) to the token and the dot notation *place_name.field_name* enables the programmer to refer to the token's field that must be initialized.

5.1.2 Transitions

Transitions are the processing units of the model. They carry out token-driven computations.

If predicates, priorities and delays are ignored for the moment, a transition fires as soon as it is enabled (i.e. none of its input places is empty) and firing consists in removing one token from each of its input places and adding one token to each of its output places. The tokens taken from the input places are called input tokens, while those delivered to the output places are called output tokens.

In Protob, there is no weight function associated with arcs, so, during firing, just one token is taken from an input place and just one token is delivered to an output place.

Since tokens usually contain information, applying the standard firing rule strictly, i.e. removing and destroying input tokens and generating and delivering output tokens, would be awkward. In fact, if an input token carries information which must not be lost, the transition, before destroying it, has to perform an action to copy its contents into an output token; this action has to be written by the programmer. In such a case, it would be more convenient to turn that input token into an output token. When an input token becomes an output token, we say that it is propagated by the transition.

In most cases, the propagation of tokens is done automatically in Protob, so no action at all has to be written.

The rules presented below illustrate the details of the propagation of tokens.

Token propagation rules and the actions of transitions

An input token can be either moved into an output place (in this case it is a propagated token) or destroyed and an output token that is not a propagated token is generated by the transition itself.

When a transition fires, it can execute an action. The action is a piece of code which has visibility on the tokens (propagated, destroyed and generated) acted on by the transition. The action can modify the contents of propagated tokens and initialize the contents of generated tokens, as well as invoke external subprograms.

If the transition has to generate tokens, they will be generated before the action is executed, so that their fields can be initialized during the action. If the transition has to destroy tokens, they will be destroyed after the action is executed, so that the values they carry can be copied into other tokens.

The propagation of input tokens depends on the types of the input and output places of the transition, as shown below.

1. If there is only one input place, P, of a given type, T, and if there is only one output place, Q, of the same type, then the token taken from P is propagated to Q.

2. If there is an input place, P, and if there is no output place of the same type, the token taken from P is destroyed.

3. If there is an output place, Q, of a given type, T, and if there is no input place of the same type, the transition first generates a new token of type T and then delivers it to Q.

4. If there are two or more input places of the same type, the tokens taken from such places are destroyed, because they cannot be propagated unambiguously. For the same reason, if there is only one input place, P, of a given type, T, and if there are two or more output places of type T, the token taken from P is destroyed. When the propagation of an input token cannot be performed automatically, it is always possible to write some statements into the action which copy the values to be propagated from that input token into an output token.

5. An exception to the above case occurs when the same place, P, is both an input place and an output place of a transition. In this case, the token taken from P is always delivered to P.

A transition which illustrates how tokens are propagated is shown in Figure 5.2.

Transition Produce_Part has two input places, Raw of type Part and Ready of type Wst (Wst is an abbreviation of workstation), and two output places, Finished of type Part and Set_up of type Wst. Type Part is the same as the one shown in Figure 5.1(a). Type Wst is made up of four fields: a string, Code, which keeps the workstation code, a string, Op, which contains the code of the operation that the workstation is able to perform,

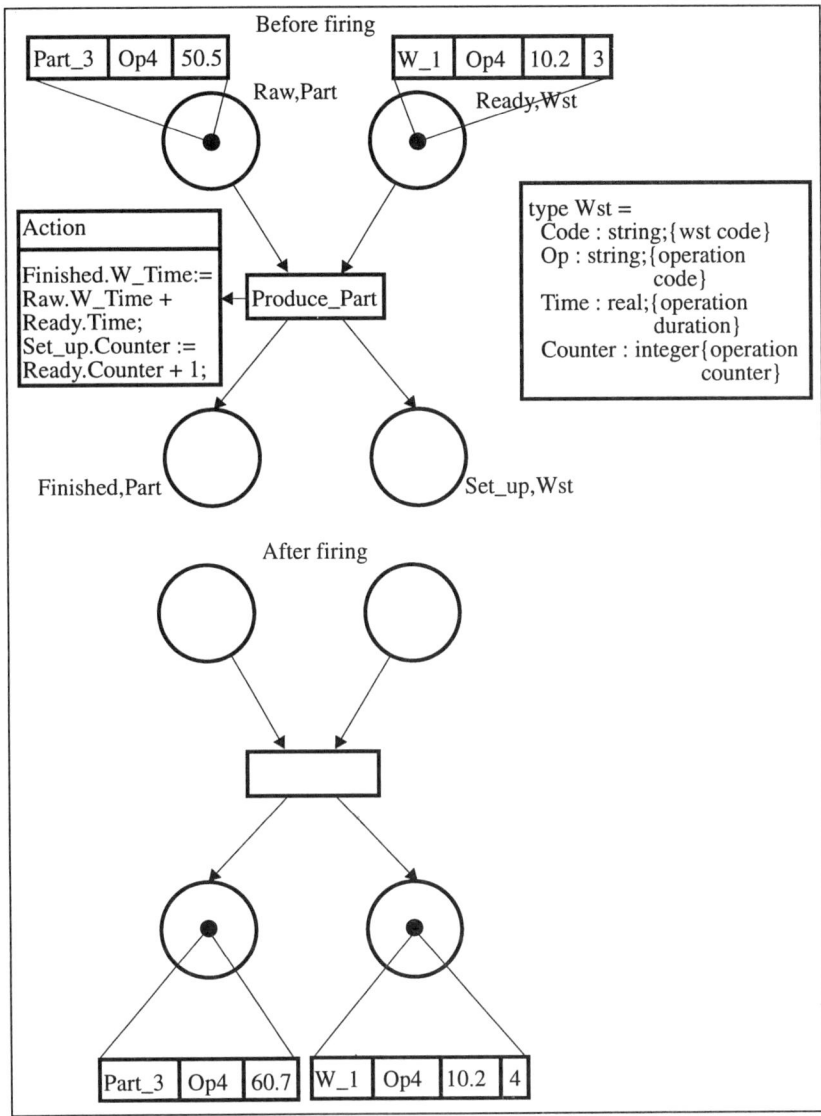

Figure 5.2 *A transition that propagates tokens and modifies their contents*

a real number, Time, which indicates the duration of this operation, and an integer number, Counter, which is used to count the total number of the operations performed by the workstation so far.

Transition Produce_Part shows that when both a raw part and a ready workstation are available, the workstation works on the part, and then the part will be considered to be finished and the workstation will have to perform a set-up. Produce_Part is responsible for updating the W_Time attribute of the finished part and the Counter attribute of the workstation.

According to the token propagation rule, the token taken from place Raw is moved into place Finished, while the token taken from place Ready is moved into place Set_up.

In an action, tokens are referred to by place names. A propagated token can be referred to using both the name of the input place from which it is taken and the name of the output place to which it is delivered. In the example given in Figure 5.2, place names Raw and Finished are both bound to the token taken from place Raw, while place names Ready and Set_up are both bound to the token taken from place Ready.

The action performed by Produce_Part modifies the contents of both tokens as follows: the W_Time field of the token taken from place Raw is incremented by the duration of the current operation (provided by the Time field of the token taken from place Ready); the Counter field of the token taken from place Ready is incremented by 1. The contents of such tokens after the firing of Produce_Part are also shown in Figure 5.2.

If a field of a propagated token has to be modified in the action, it is customary to use the input place name when the old value of the field (i.e. the one before the action) is involved, and the output place name when a new value produced by the action is indicated. The assignment Set_up.Counter := Ready.Counter+1; is an example of this convention.

Tokens are usually taken from places in an FIFO order (i.e. the oldest token first) unless the transition has a predicate.

Predicates

It is often necessary to take not the oldest tokens from the input places of a transition when it fires, but those tokens which satisfy a particular condition, called predicate. The predicate is a boolean expression which can be associated with a transition.

If there is a tuple of tokens (i.e. a collection of tokens, one for each input place of the transition) that satisfy the predicate, such tokens are selected and removed from the input places even if they are not the oldest ones. If it is possible that two or more tuples satisfy the predicate at the same time, a clause must be added to the predicate: this clause defines the order in which the input places of the transition have to be examined, thus such tuples can be given different priorities and the one with the highest priority will be selected. If an input place does not appear in the predicate, the oldest token of its queue is taken.

If a transition has a predicate, the condition that has to be satisfied for it to be enabled is more restricted: in fact, such a transition is enabled iff none of its input places is empty and iff there is a tuple of input tokens which satisfy the predicate.

A predicate is shown in Figure 5.3. Place types are the same as the ones shown in Figures 5.1 and 5.2.

The predicate states that tokens taken from places Raw and Ready must have identical values in their Op_Code and Op fields, respectively. In this way, a part is allowed to be processed only by a workstation that is able to perform the operation needed by the part. The only pair of tokens satisfying the predicate is the one which is made up of the first token in place Raw and the second one in place Ready. Tokens in places Raw and Ready are numbered on the basis of their arrival times.

Priorities

When two or more transitions are enabled at the same time, the order in which they fire can be determined by using priorities. The priority is a non-negative integer number, which is written, separated by a comma, after the transition name. The default priority (lowest priority) is zero and can be omitted.

Priorities can be used to decide the order in which transitions in conflict (i.e. transitions having a common input place) have to be selected to fire.

In general, priorities are used to define the relative importance of some transitions that happen to be enabled simultaneously. When two or more transitions with the same priority are enabled at the same time, t, and no other transition with a higher priority is enabled at time t, one of them is selected to fire in a non-deterministic way.

In the example shown in Figure 5.4, place Server is a common input place for transitions Serve_In and Serve_Out. Serve_Out has a higher priority, thus, when both are enabled, Serve_Out will be selected to fire.

5.2 Temporal behavior

The introduction of timing constraints into the model enhances its descriptive power and facilitates a careful analysis of the performance of the system being considered.

In Protob, timing constraints can be associated with transitions and determine two different behaviors, which are referred to as delayed release and delayed firing.

Delayed release (of tokens). When a transition is selected to fire, first it takes the input tokens from its input places and, if it is necessary, it

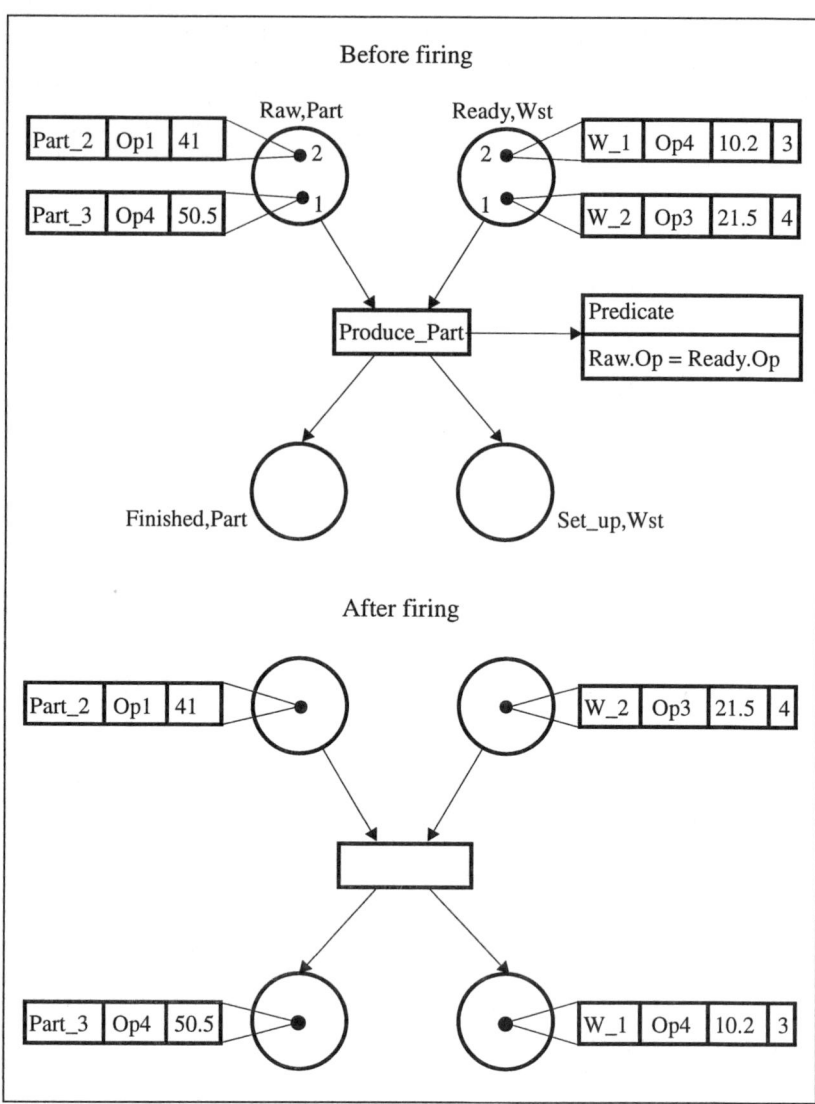

Figure 5.3 *A transition with a predicate*

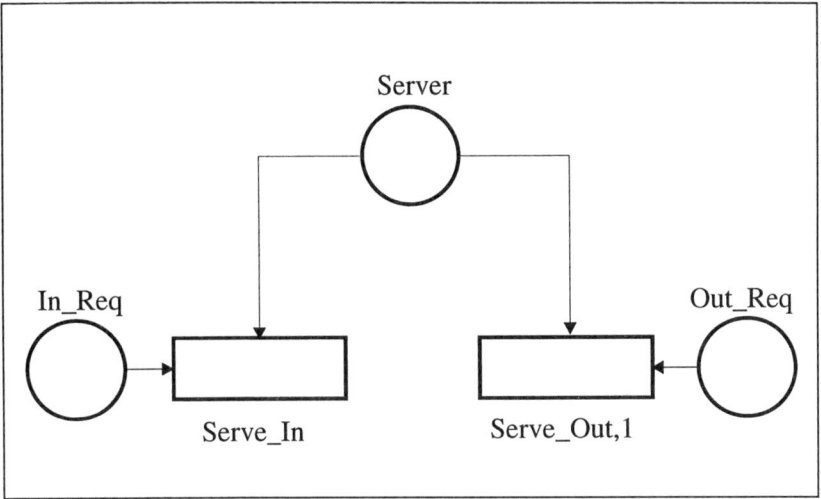

Figure 5.4 *Transitions with different priorities*

generates new empty tokens, then it performs the action and, finally, it holds the tokens in a private storage area for a specified interval of time, called release delay. The release delay of a transition can be set by calling a primitive (`delay`) in its action. Primitive `delay` has two parameters: the name of the transition and the value (a real number) of the delay. When the delay expires, the transition destroys the input tokens that do not have to be propagated and delivers the others to the output places. The release delay of a transition can be set in any action of the model.

Delayed firing. When a transition is enabled, it does not fire immediately, but it waits for a specified interval of time, called firing delay, to elapse. Then, if all the input tokens that enabled the transition are still in their places, having been in these places all that time, the transition fires as above. The firing delay of a transition can be set by calling a primitive (`time-out`). Primitive `time-out` has two parameters: the name of the transition and the value (a real number) of the delay. This primitive is usually invoked in the action of another transition: in fact, since the action of a transition, t, is executed after its firing delay has elapsed, if the firing delay of t is changed in its action, this change will affect the next firing and subsequent ones, but not the current firing.

Transitions characterized by delayed firing are called delayed-firing transitions and their name is followed by T (this letter stands for time-out). Such transitions are also called time-out transitions, because they model time-out situations very easily. A delayed-firing transition can also have a release delay.

Transitions that exhibit delayed release only are called delayed-release transitions or simply delayed transitions. Transitions with no delay are called immediate transitions.

The value of a delay can be given by a real constant or a real variable; it can also be the result of a function call or the result of the evaluation of an expression. Therefore, the delay can be deterministic or stochastic and, further, it can depend on the contents of the transition's input tokens.

Two examples of delayed transitions are given in Figure 5.5.

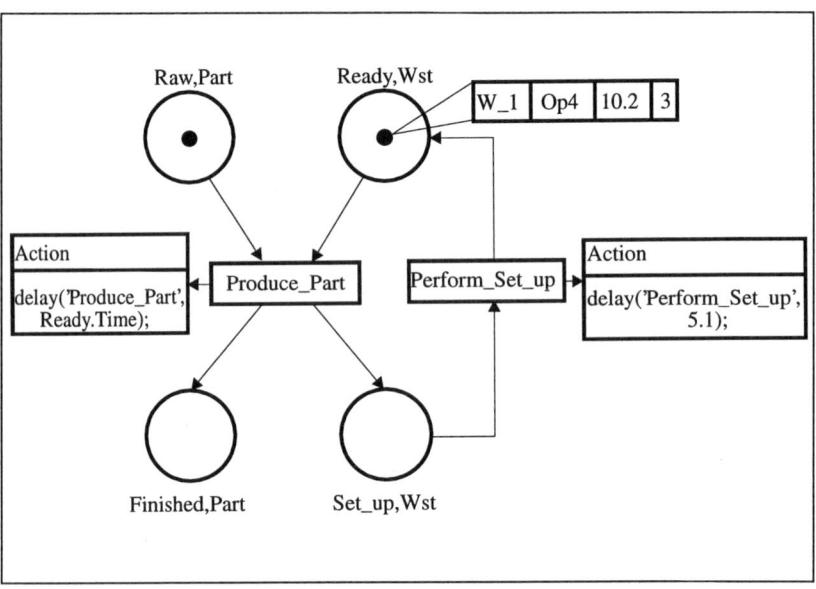

Figure 5.5 *Delayed-release transitions*

Transition Produce_Part has a delay that depends on the contents of the input token taken from place Ready, so it delivers its output tokens after an interval of time corresponding to the duration of the operation performed on the part. Since set-up activities are assumed to have constant duration, the delay of transition Perform_Set_up is given by a numerical constant (5.1).

The behavior through time of the net shown in Figure 5.5 is illustrated in Figure 5.6.

1. At instant $t1$, transition Produce_Part begins firing.

2. In the interval $]t1..t2[$, tokens are held by Produce_Part. When a transition is holding tokens, a dot is shown inside the rectangle.

3. At instant $t2$, tokens are delivered to the output places of Produce_Part. Then, transition Perform_Set_up begins firing.

4. In the interval $]t2..t3[$, Perform_Set_up holds its input token.

5. At instant $t3$, that token is delivered to place Ready.

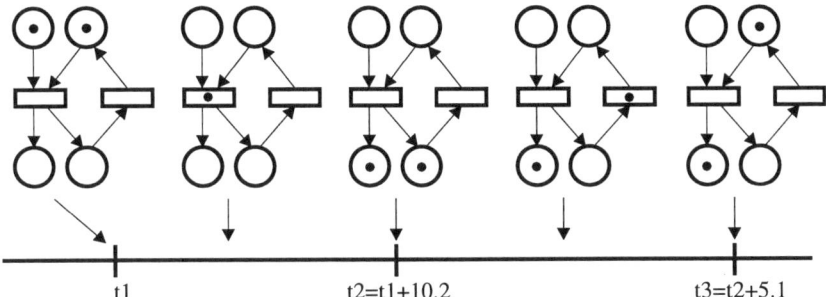

Figure 5.6 *The evolution over time of the model shown in Figure 5.5*

A delayed-firing transition, Manage_Time_Out, appears in Figure 5.7, which presents a fragment of a sender. The sender sets the value of a time-out, issues a message, starts the time-out, and then waits for the acknowledgement. If the time-out expires before the acknowledgement is received, a retransmission has to be performed, so the sender issues the message again, starts the time-out, and then waits for the acknowledgement. The sender stops operating when the acknowledgement is received or after two retransmissions. In the latter case, an error is signaled.

Manage_Time_Out is a delayed-firing transition, so its firing delay must be set by another transition: in fact, it is set by Set_Time_Out, which is the first transition to fire.

After a message has been sent by transition Send_Message, the state of the sender is Waiting_for_Ack. Then, transition Manage_Time_Out is enabled, but it does not fire immediately. It waits for the firing delay (of 10 time units) to expire. If, in the meantime, a token is put into place Ack, transition Receive_Ack fires, thus disabling Manage_Time_Out. However, if the time-out expires, Manage_Time_Out fires and delivers a token into place Retransmissions_to_be_Checked.

The token that circulates in places Ready_to_Send, Waiting_for_Ack and Retransmissions_to_be_Checked keeps a counter of retransmissions. Whenever the time-out expires, this counter is incremented. If no acknowledgement is received after two retransmissions, a failure is signaled.

Transitions Signal_Failure and Enable_Retransmission are in conflict, but the former is of higher priority and it also has a predicate that restricts the cases in which it can fire. Such transitions represent a frequent situation of conflict which can be managed in two ways.

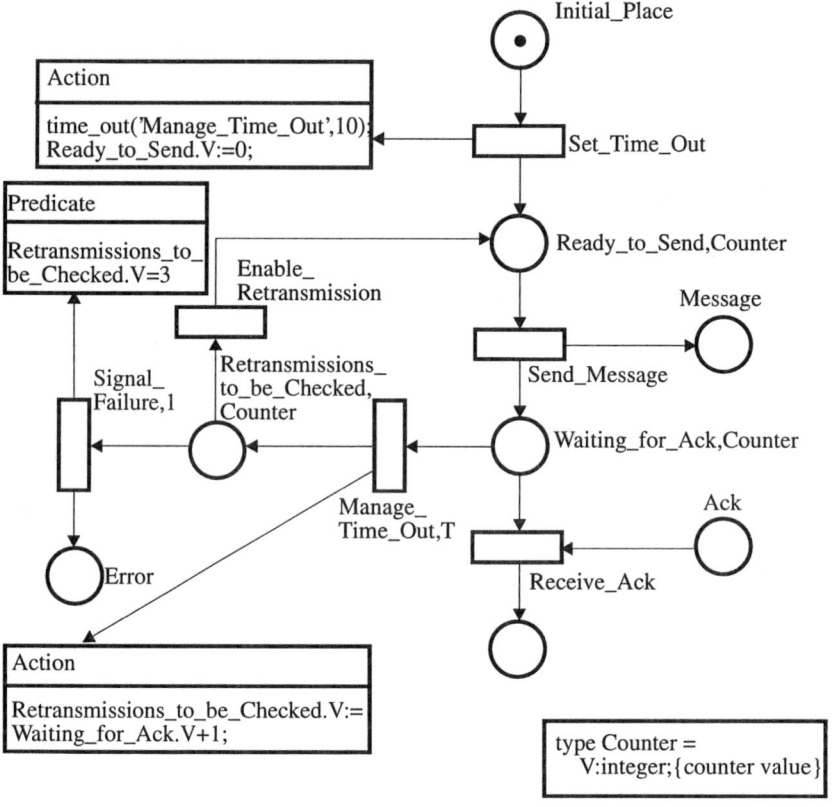

Figure 5.7 *A net including a delayed-firing transition*

1. The transitions can be given equal priorities and opposite predicates, so that when the predicate of one transition is satisfied, the predicate of the other is not and vice versa.

2. Alternatively, one transition can be given a predicate and a priority that is higher than the priority of the other transition, which is given no predicate. The former transition is tried first, thus such a pair of transitions has the same semantics as an if-then-else construct.

As a final comment on the temporal behavior of transitions, it has to be mentioned that a transition can give rise to several concurrent firings and that each firing can have a different delay. For example, if x tokens were contained in place Raw and x in place Ready at a given instant in the model shown in Figure 5.5, then transition Produce_Part would perform x simultaneous firings and each firing would involve a pair of input tokens (one taken from place Raw and the other from place Ready) and would exhibit a specific release delay (depending on the Time attribute of the token taken from place Ready).

Thus, a transition acts as an infinite capacity processing unit, which is able to perform an activity as soon as it is enabled. If we want to restrict this capability so as to limit (say, to n) the number of concurrent firings of a given transition, we can connect a self-loop place (with n initial tokens of type nul) to that transition.

5.2.1 Simulation of the model

We are now in a position to study how the model evolves over time. The evolution of the model is of a discrete nature, so attention is focused only on the instants at which something occurs and all the others are ignored. Any instant of interest concerns an event, i.e. a fact that affects the behavior of the model. Events are related to transitions and can be of two types, called *end of release delay* and *end of firing delay*.

The algorithm we use to make the model evolve over time is typical of discrete event simulation and is sketched below. The current instant is kept in variable Current_Time, while future events (with respect to Current_-Time) are ordered on the basis of their occurrence instants and are stored in list Event_List. When an event whose occurrence instant is τ is inserted into Event_List, it is put as the last of the events whose occurrence instant is τ, or it is put before the first event whose occurrence instant is higher than τ.

1. Set Current_Time to 0.

2. Select the highest-priority transition, t, that is enabled at Current_Time:

    (a) If t is immediate, execute its action and deliver its output tokens.

    (b) If t is a delayed transition, execute its action and insert an *end of release delay* event whose occurrence instant is equal to Current_Time + the value of the release delay into Event_List.

    (c) If t is a delayed-firing transition, insert an *end of firing delay* event whose occurrence instant is equal to Current_Time + the value of the firing delay into Event_List.

    If the firing of t causes a delayed-firing transition whose firing delay has already begun to be disabled, then cancel the *end of firing delay* event associated with that transition from Event_List.

3. If there are other transitions enabled at Current_Time, return to the previous step.

4. Set Current_Time to the occurrence instant of the first event in Event_-List.

5. Extract all the events whose occurrence instants are equal to Current_-
   Time from Event_List and process them as follows.

   (a) If the event refers to the end of a release delay, then deliver the tokens
       held by the corresponding transition to the output places.

   (b) If the event refers to the end of a firing delay, execute the action of
       the corresponding transition; then, if the transition has no release
       delay, deliver its output tokens, otherwise insert an *end of release
       delay* event whose occurrence instant is equal to Current_Time + the
       value of the release delay into Event_List.

6. If Current_Time is greater than (or equal to) the simulation interval,
   then stop, otherwise go back to step 2.

The current simulation time can be obtained by calling a primitive
(`get_time`) in any action. Primitive `get_time`, which is a function returning
a real value, is needed to perform time-based computations.

5.3 Views

If a model is large, it can be decomposed into portions (or submodels),
called views. Each view of a model has a different name.

Places with identical names can appear in several views, as they are
graphical representations of the same logical place. However, two places
with identical names cannot appear in the same view.

A transition appears in just one view, because we want the context of a
transition (i.e. its input and output places) to be defined in only one site.

A view has a graphical representation given by a square with rounded
corners. To be more precise, the term view denotes a portion of the model,
while the term view symbol refers to the icon that represents a view. A
view symbol has an identifier that is identical to the name of the view to
which it refers.

A view can contain a view symbol: this means that such views are interrelated and also facilitates the navigation from one view to another. View
symbols with identical names can appear in different views in the same way
as places can.

A decomposition into views of the model shown in Figure 5.5 is presented
in Figure 5.8. There are two views and each includes a view symbol that
refers to the other.

A view symbol can be connected to places using arcs, called view arcs, so
that the places of the current view which also appear in the view represented
by the view symbol can be indicated. The direction of a view arc, which is
drawn between a place of the current view and a view symbol, must show
how the place is used by the transitions that are contained in the view
referred to by the view symbol; therefore

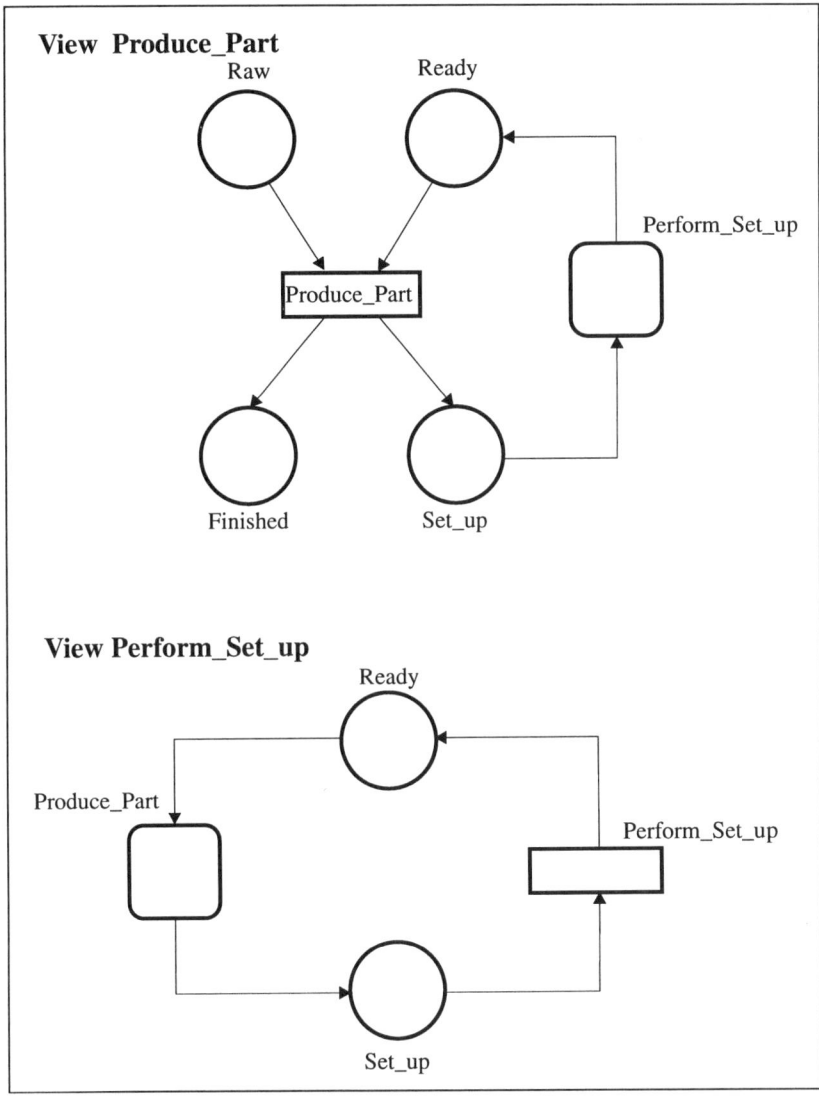

Figure 5.8 *The decomposition into views of the model shown in Figure 5.5*

1. if such a place is used in the view only as an output (input) place of some transitions, then the view arc is directed from the view symbol (place) to the place (view symbol);

2. if such a place is an input place for some transitions and is also an output place for other transitions, then the view arc is bidirectional.

Since view symbols are intended for browsing purposes, view arcs are not mandatory.

Another example regarding views is presented in Figure 5.9: Get_Raw_-Part and Deliver_Finished_Part model the input buffer and the output buffer of the workstation shown in Figure 4.7.

5.4 Object orientation

Models in Protob can be structured according to the principles of object orientation.

An object models a system's component and its behavior is given by a Protob net. Since objects are based on nets, it is natural that they interact by sending and receiving tokens. Special places, called input places (or input ports) and output places (or output ports), are introduced so that an object is enabled to communicate with other objects.

Input places receive tokens from other objects. An input place is drawn as a double circle; it has a name and a type and contains a queue of tokens.

When an object has to send a token to other objects, it puts the token into an output place. An output place is drawn as a circle with a triangle inscribed. Output places do not hold tokens, because when a token is put into an output place, it is immediately delivered to the destination object(s).

The collection of all the input and output places of an object forms its interface. Such places are also called interface places. The other places are called internal places or simply places.

In Figure 5.10(a), an informal model showing the interaction between a Client object and a Server object is presented.

The Client object asks the Server to perform a service by sending a token through an output port (Request). An oriented arc, called link, connects Request to an input port (Req) of the Server object.

A link stands for an immediate communication, so when the Client object puts a token into output port Request, this token is immediately delivered to input port Req of the Server object.

After sending the request, the Client object waits for the reply. The Server object performs the service and sends the reply from an output port (Rep), which is linked to an input port (Reply) of the Client object.

The ports connected by a link must be of the same type.

The structure of objects in Protob is a tree and the object corresponding

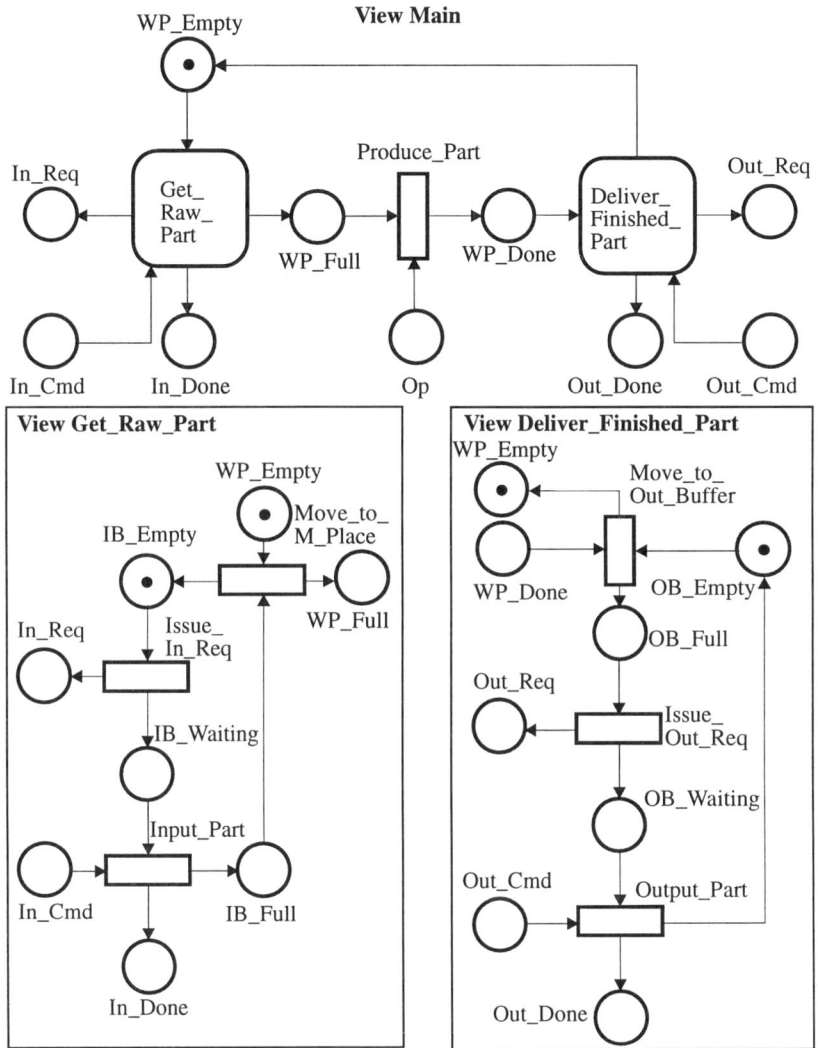

Figure 5.9 *The model of the workstation decomposed into views*

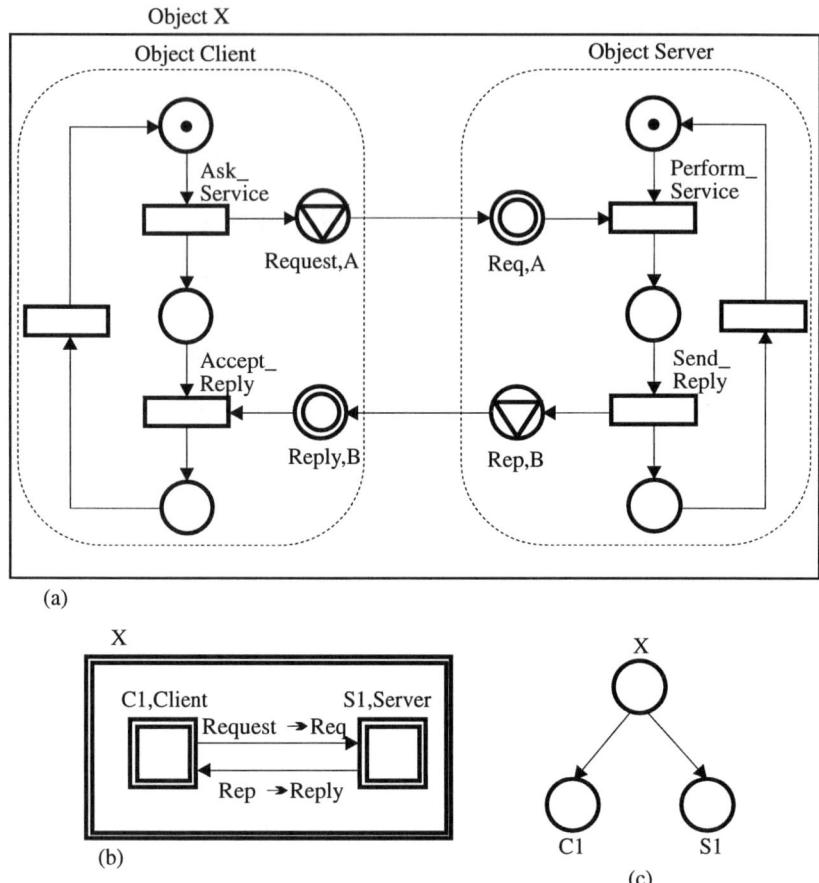

(a)

(b)

(c)

Figure 5.10 *Objects based on nets*

to the root, which is also referred to as the top-level object, represents and contains the overall model. If an object, A, contains another object, B, then there is an oriented arc directed from node A to node B in the object tree. If an object contains other objects, it is called a compound object and the objects it contains are called its component objects. A compound object is the only owner of its component objects.

Objects are graphically represented by a double square. Composition is graphically represented, too, because the model associated with an object can contain icons which represent other objects, as shown in Figure 5.10(b). Object X contains two objects, C1 and S1, and the corresponding object tree is given in Figure 5.10(c).

For the time being, only fixed composition is considered, therefore a compound object has a number of components which cannot be changed.

Every object belongs to a class and every class has a model associated with it. For this reason, the icon representing an object has two identifiers: the first is the object name, the second is the name of the class to which the object belongs.

As shown in Figure 5.11, we can build an application (or a new class) by selecting suitable classes from a library of existing classes, instantiating objects belonging to these classes and then connecting objects with appropriate links. In fact, class C, which represents an application, contains one object, C1, of class Client and one object, S1, of class Server. Class C is a compound class, because it contains objects (belonging to other classes).

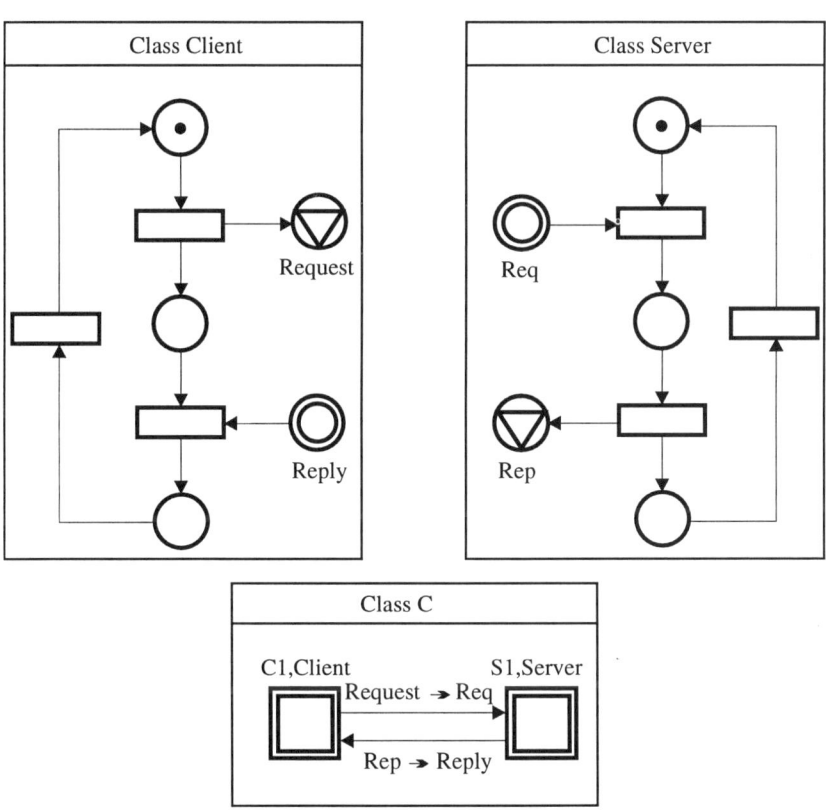

Figure 5.11 *Classes and objects*

A compound class has visibility on the interfaces of its component objects, so that it can logically link an output port of an object to an input port of another object, provided that the ports to be connected are of the same type. Actually, a link connects one object to another object but its label specifies which output port of the source object and which input port of the destination object are involved in the connection. Therefore, the label of a link is written as `output port` → `input port`.

Protob objects are easy to put together, in accordance with the metaphore of *software chips* (Cox, 1986); in fact, an object does not know the other objects it will interact with and the interaction is only based on the tokens that it sends and receives through its interface, so it is the task of the compound class to set suitable links between its component objects.

A compound class can also contain places and transitions, in addition to its component objects, as shown in Figure 5.12. In such a case, connections can be drawn between the places of the compound class and its component objects.

Class C contains three objects: one, C1, of class Client and two, S1 and S2, of class Server. It routes the requests coming from C1 to either S1 or S2. The request issued by C1 is put into place X, then it is routed either to place Y or to place Z. When a token is put into place Y (Z), it is immediately delivered to an input port, called Req, of object S1 (S2). S1 and S2 directly reply to C1.

A connection, such as the one from C1 to X, which is drawn from a component object to a place of the compound class, is called a bottom-up link, while a connection, such as the one from Y to S1, which is drawn from a place of the compound class to a component object, is called a top-down link. On the other hand, the term link denotes a connection between peer objects, i.e. objects that are components of the same compound class.

The label of a bottom-up (top-down) link specifies which output (input) port of the component object is involved in the connection.

Bottom-up links and top-down links connect only places of the same type.

A place that has an outgoing top-down link does not hold tokens, so, when it receives one, it immediately forwards this token to the object(s) to which it is connected. A place that has an incoming bottom-up link contains a queue of tokens, and thus it can be connected only to transitions.

Top-down links and bottom-up links can involve either internal places or interface places of the compound class that contains them, as illustrated in Figure 5.13. In fact, a top-down link can connect an input port of a compound class, A, to an input port of a component object, B, and a bottom-up link can connect an output port of a component object, C, to an output port of A. In the first case, the token that A receives from outside is immediately routed to B, while, in the second case, the token that A receives from C is sent immediately outside.

The output ports that have several outgoing links and the internal places that have several outgoing top-down links are also called derouting places. As will be illustrated in the next section, a mechanism, called token routing

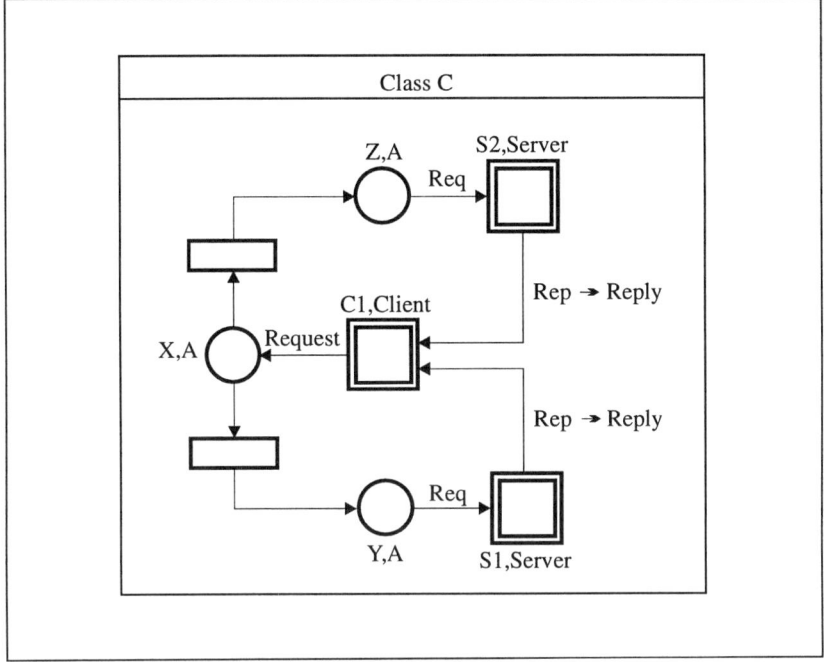

Figure 5.12 *A compound class*

protocol, will be used to determine whether the token sent through a derouting place has to be broadcast to all the objects the place is connected to or whether it has to be sent to a specific object only.

If a model contains objects exhibiting large interfaces (with many ports), then it will be crowded with too many connections. In order to avoid such a drawback, we can use compound links.

A compound link stands for a set of links, which can have different directions. It can be drawn with one arrow, with arrows at both ends or even without any arrow, because the user is free to indicate the most important information flows.

A compound link, which is drawn from one object to another, connects a compound port of the first object to a compound port of the second. A compound port is a named sequence of ports; a class can have several compound ports. If the compound link has one arrow, its label consists of the name of the source compound port, the arrow symbol and the name of the destination compound port. If the compound link has no arrow or has two arrows, the dot notation `object_name.compound_port_name` is used to identify each port precisely.

Two compound ports, A and B, can be connected by a compound link, provided that the following conditions are satisfied:

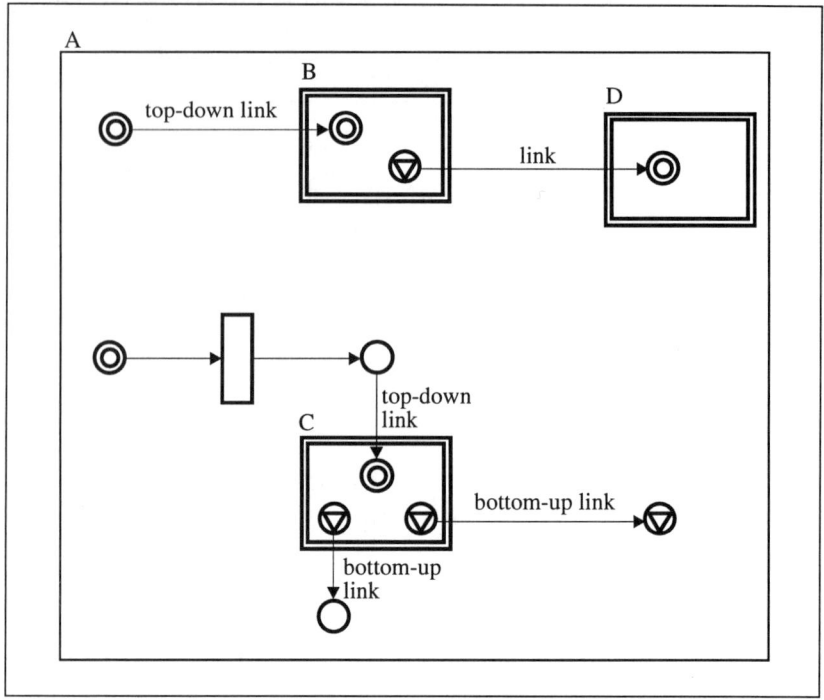

Figure 5.13 *Types of links*

1. A and B must have n ports each; these ports are referred to as $A_1 \ldots A_n$ and $B_1 \ldots B_n$;

2. for each i $(1 \le i \le n)$, places A_i and B_i must be of the same type, and if A_i is an input port, B_i must be an output port, and vice versa.

Compound links and compound ports are illustrated in Figure 5.14. Classes Client and Server have one compound port each. Further, when a compound link is drawn between an object of class Client and an object of class Server, it represents a pair of links and its direction means that the client object takes the initiative in the dialogue with the server object.

5.4.1 Local variables and parameters

An object can have local variables to store information that pertains to its overall behavior. For example, a local variable can be used to count the number of firings of a given transition.

Local variables can be acted on in the actions of transitions. They can also appear in predicates; however, they cannot be used to synchronize the firing of a transition: in fact, the predicate is evaluated only if each input

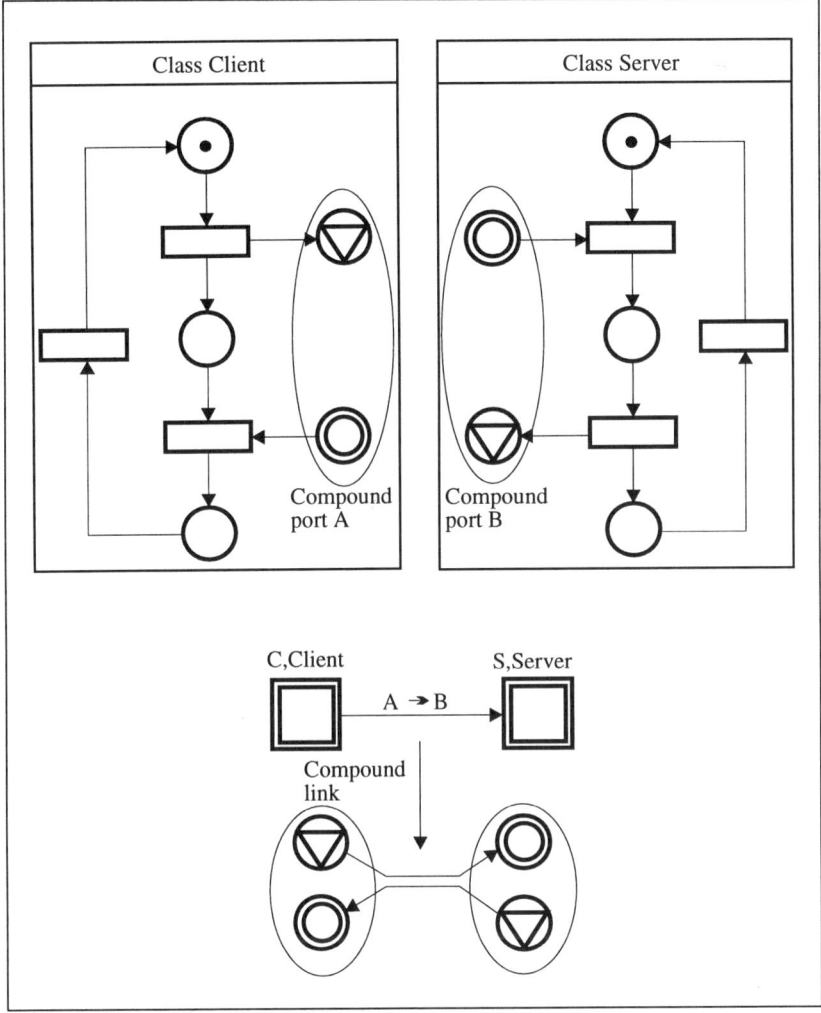

Figure 5.14 *Compound links and compound ports*

place of the transition contains at least one token and only when a new
token has been put into an input place of the transition.

Local variables are initialized in a piece of code, called initial action,
which is executed before any transition fires.

An object, X, can also have parameters: they are like local variables,
but they must be given initial values by the compound object, Y, which
contains X. A compound object will use a primitive (set_parameter) to
set the initial values of the parameters of its component objects. The first
argument of primitive set_parameter is the name of the component object

and it is followed by a sequence of items separated by commas, each item having the form `parameter_name` → `value`.

The example given in Figure 5.15 shows a variant of the sender described in Figure 5.7. An object of this class models the lowest layer of a communication protocol. It waits for a message to be received from a higher layer and then sends the message to the corresponding layer of the receiver. Since the message can be lost, the Sender object waits for an acknowledgement. If it does not receive the acknowledgement within a given interval after the transmission, it retransmits the message. Retransmission can be repeated several times until the maximum number of permitted trials is reached, then a failure is signaled.

Class Sender has two parameters, Time_Out and Max, so that both the duration of the time-out and the number of retransmissions can be specified when an object of this class is generated.

In Figure 5.15, class X, which includes an object S of class Sender, sets the parameters of S by invoking primitive `set_parameter` in its initial action.

The objects of class Sender also have two local variables, namely Failure_-Counter and Success_Counter. The former counts retransmissions, whilst the latter counts the number of successful transmissions.

The initial action of class Sender initializes those local variables and also sets the firing delay of transition Manage_Time_Out, because this delay is provided by a parameter and never changes thereafter.

Parameters are transmitted top-down along the object tree, because the initial action of a compound object is executed before the initial actions of its component objects. The top-level object has no parameters. There is an option that makes the component objects of the top-level object automatically read their parameters from a parameter file. This option is useful when the top-level object is a mere collection of other objects: in such a case, the user can avoid writing the (often long) initial action of the top-level object which would only serve to set the parameters of its component objects. Further, the user can change the parameter file without changing the model.

5.4.2 Using local variables

A simple case study consisting of a timer and a client is presented below.

The client can send the timer the length of the interval after which it has to receive a signal (or interrupt). The interval is expressed as an integer number of periods of the system clock. After receiving the interrupt, the client can send another interval length.

The client can ask for the remaining part of the current interval from the timer and the timer must reply immediately.

The first model of the timer, given by class Timer1, is shown in Figure 5.16.

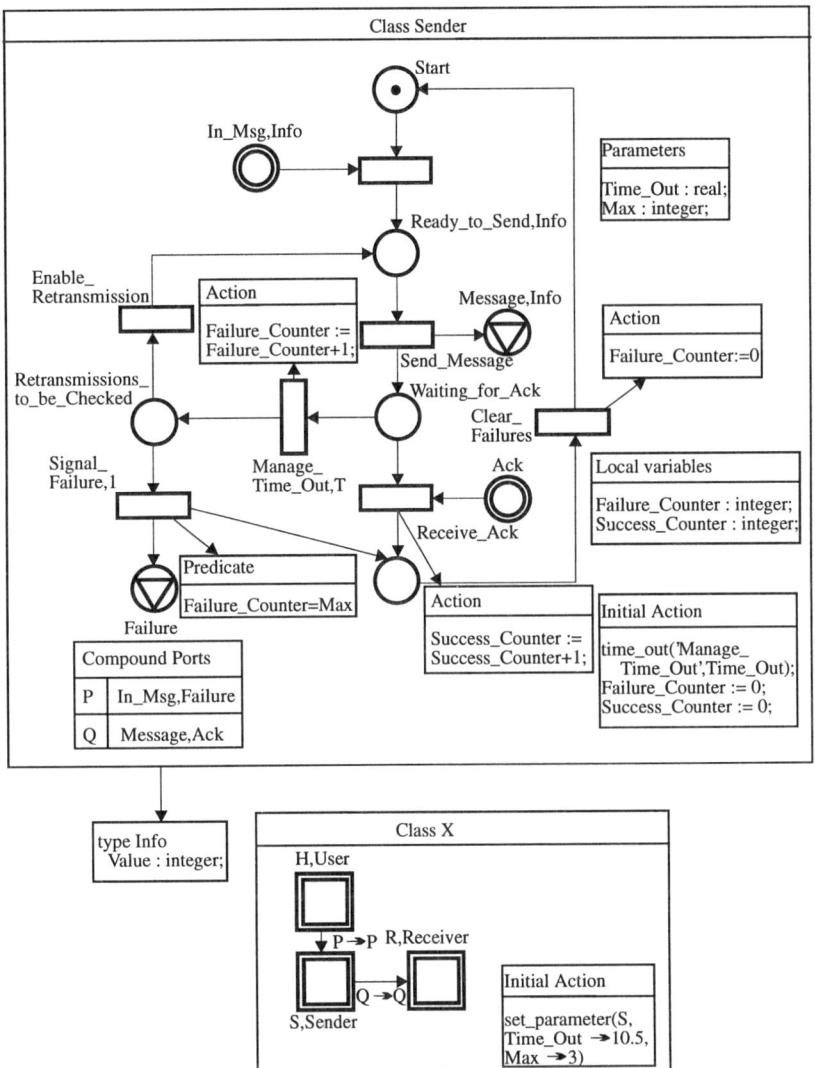

Figure 5.15 *Parameters and local variables*

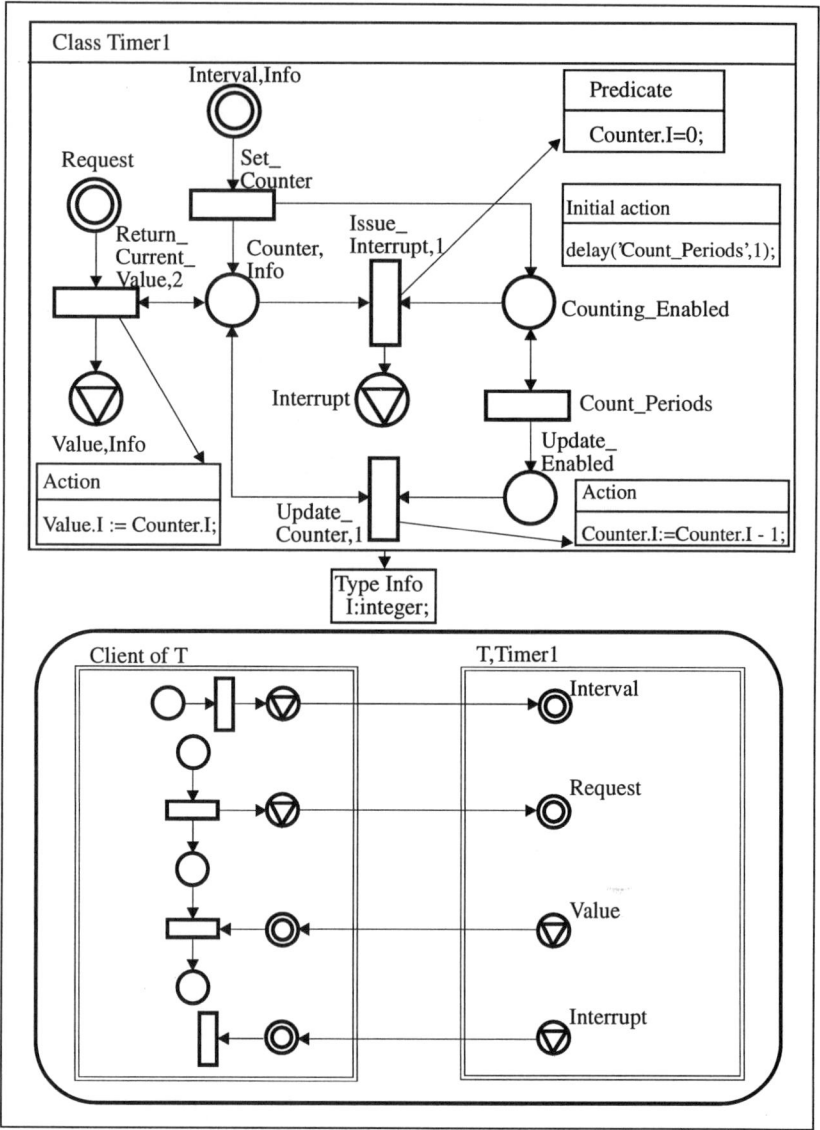

Figure 5.16 *The first model of the timer*

The units of simulation time are assumed to correspond to the periods of the system clock.

When the interval length is received by an object of class Timer1 at its input place Interval, transition Set_Counter copies the token into place Counter, which keeps the current value of the timer counter. That token is automatically copied because of the token propagation rule, thus no action is associated with Set_Counter. Set_Counter also puts a token into place Counting_Enabled, thus transition Count_Periods will be enabled.

Count_Periods is a delayed transition: its release delay is constant, so it is set in the initial action of the class. Count_Periods puts a token into place Update_Enabled to cause transition Update_Counter to fire.

Update_Counter decrements the counter in the token contained in place Counter. Since Update_Counter has a greater priority than Count_Periods, it fires before the next firing of Count_Periods, so the decrement of the counter is guaranteed to take place at the end of every period of the system clock. Such a decrement is an immediate action (because Update_Counter has no delay), thus the token in place Counter is practically always available (as decrements take place in zero time). Therefore, when a request for the current value of the counter is received, it is immediately satisfied. However, if Count_Periods and Update_Counter were merged into one transition, the token in place Counter would be available only at the ends of every period of the system clock; therefore, the reply to a request for the current value of the counter would be delayed until the end of the current period of the system clock. However, only if the period of the system clock is greater than one unit of simulation time is such a delay appreciable.

When the counter is 0, transition Issue_Interrupt fires. It has a greater priority than Count_Periods, so, when the counter is 0, no additional period will be counted.

When a request for the current value of the counter is received, transition Return_Current_Value provides it. It has the greatest priority, because the request must be satisfied immediately.

A possible interaction between the client and the timer is also sketched in Figure 5.16.

The model of the timer is simple, but inefficient; this is because transition Count_Periods fires a number of times equal to the interval length.

A more efficient and more compact model is shown in Figure 5.17. It contains only two transitions and uses two local variables, namely Start and Interval_Length. Transition Issue_Interrupt is delayed and its release delay is equal to the length of the interval. Its action copies the current time, i.e. the instant at which the interval begins, into local variable Start and copies the length of the interval into local variable Interval_Length. Primitive get_time returns the current simulation time.

Transition Return_Current_Value returns the current value of the timer, which is computed by subtracting the time elapsed since the beginning of

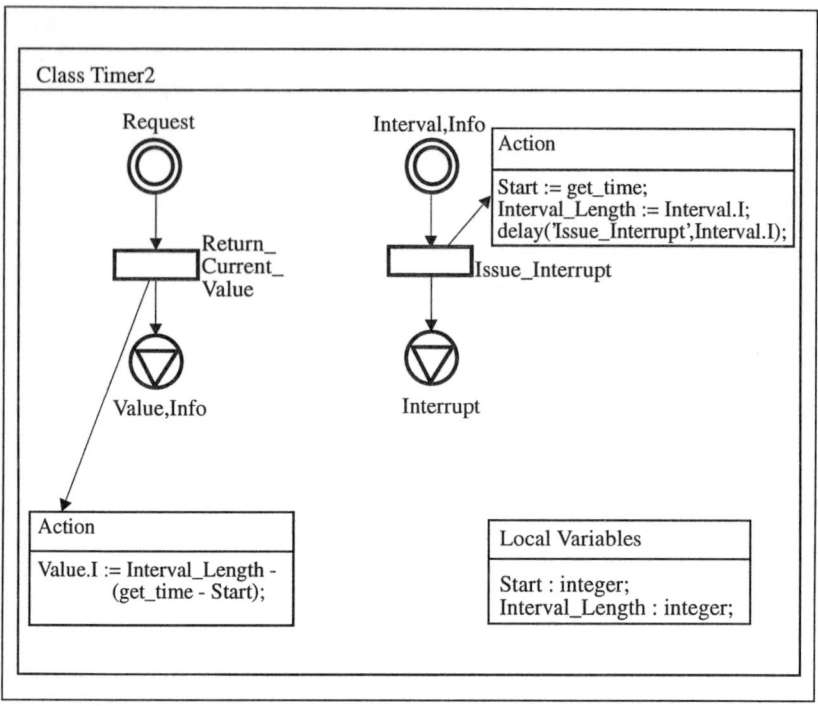

Figure 5.17 *The second model of the timer*

the interval from the interval length. This time is obtained by subtracting the value contained in local variable Start from the current simulation time.

5.5 Building client server models

When there is a derouting place, i.e. a place connected to several objects, the question arises as to which path a token, sent through that place, has to take. For example, the interaction between one server, S1, and two clients, C1 and C2, is illustrated in Figure 5.18.

When a client needs a service, a token is sent from output place Request of the client to input place Req of S1. When the service has been performed, a token is sent from output place Rep of S1 to input place Reply of the client that made the request for the service. Therefore, there is a link from S1 to each client and such a link connects output place Rep of S1 to input place Reply of the client. The right client to which S1 has to reply is selected on the basis of the token routing protocol which is illustrated below.

Each object in the model has a unique address (also called identity) which depends on its position in the object tree. Addresses are values belonging

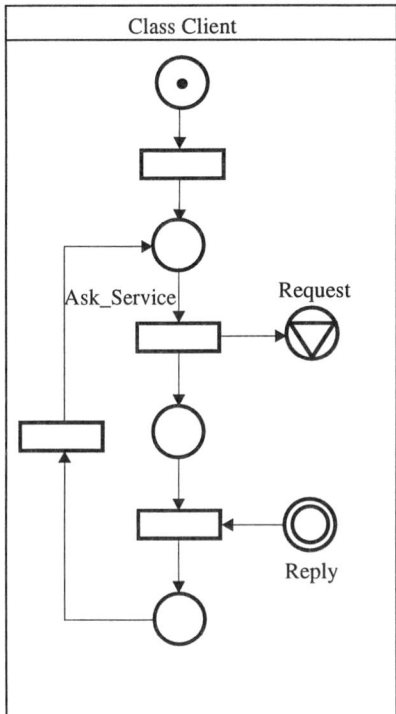
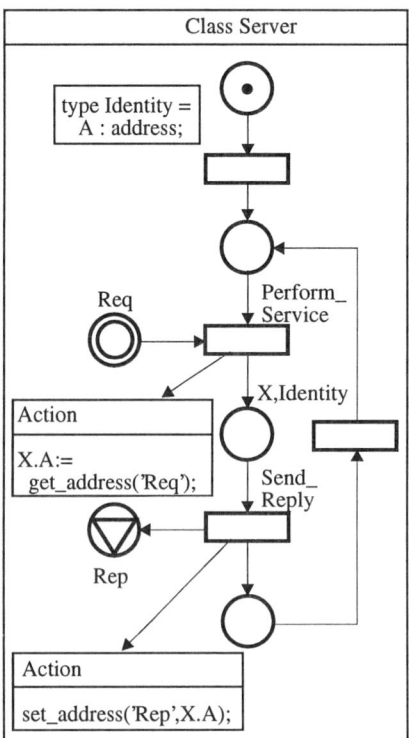

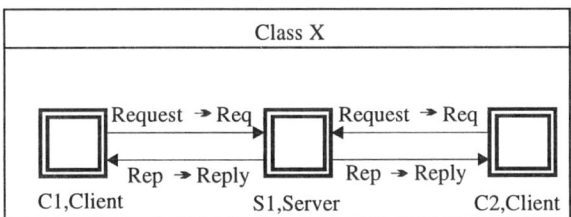

Figure 5.18 *How a server replies to the right client when there are many clients and one server*

to a predefined type (Address); they can be kept in local variables as well as in tokens. Addresses are managed by two primitives:

1. `get_address`. It takes as a parameter the name of an input place and returns the address of the sender object. Every token sent by an object is automatically stamped with the address of the sender object (the address is stored in a hidden attribute of the token). When the token is received by the destination object, the transition that gets the token can call (in its action) `get_address` (passing it the token that is referred to by the input place name) so as to obtain the address of the sender object. The address can be copied into a local variable or into an attribute of a token which is being acted on by the transition.

2. `set_address`. It takes as parameters the name of an output place and the address of the destination object. When a transition sends a token through a derouting place, it can select the destination object from among the several objects that are linked to the derouting place by calling `set_address`. This primitive copies the address of the destination object into a hidden attribute of the token, so that the token will be sent only to the object whose identity matches that address. Otherwise, if a token leaves an object through a derouting place and its destination address has not been set, it is copied and sent to each object that is connected to the derouting place. In one case, we have selective routing, while in the other we have broadcasting. Broadcasting is the only protocol that can be used when the addresses of the destination objects are unknown.

The server shown in Figure 5.18, on receiving a request, extracts the address of the client from the input token by calling `get_address`, then copies this address into the token delivered to place X. When the reply has to be sent to the client, transition Send_Reply, by calling `set_address`, stamps the output token with the client's address which is read from the token taken from place X. The server could use a local variable, instead of a token, to keep the client's address; however, the model shown in Figure 5.18 is more general and can easily be extended to cope with many services being performed concurrently by the server.

Let us now suppose that several servers are available, as shown in Figure 5.19: there are two servers, S1 and S2, and two clients, C1 and C2, and each client sends service requests alternately to each server.

Before issuing the first request, each client must receive the addresses of all the servers so as to be able to route requests properly. Therefore, each server must send a token to all the clients to which it is connected in order to let them know of its existence. Since the address of the destination object is not set by the server, the token is broadcast.

According to the *software chip* metaphor, an object (and the corresponding class) must not depend on the number and the identities of the

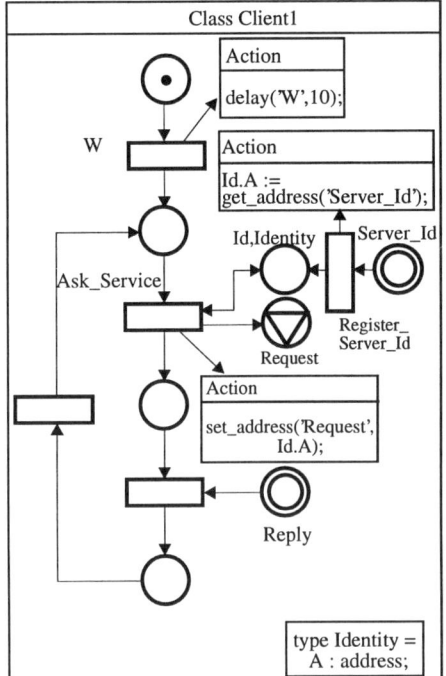

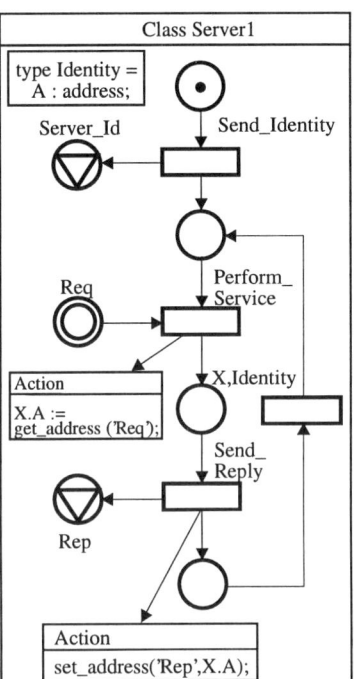

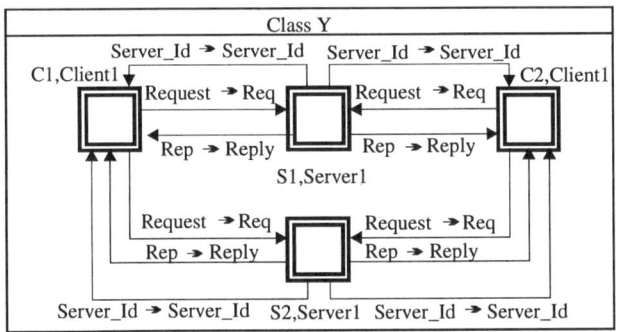

Figure 5.19 *How to make several clients interact with several servers*

objects to which it will be connected. Thus an object cannot 'a priori' select the object to which an output token has to be actually sent. An object must first receive the identities of the objects it has to communicate with, then it will be able to send tokens selectively.

In fact, a client receives the identity of each server at its input place Server_Id, then it extracts the server address and puts it into the token delivered to place Id. Place Id is used as a datastore of the identities of servers.

The first action of a client, which is carried out by transition W, is to wait for a given period of time during which all the identities of the servers are assumed to be received. Then, the client sends a service request to the server whose address is the first in the queue of place Id. When transition Ask_Service ends firing, it adds the token that has been previously taken from place Id to the bottom of the queue of this place. In this way, clients follow a round-robin technique when sending service requests to servers.

The server shown in Figure 5.19, after the firing of transition Send_Identity, exhibits the same behavior as the server given in Figure 5.18.

5.6 Inheritance

The notion of inheritance is well-defined for textual languages, but here it has to be adapted to a graphical language, such as Protob. For the sake of simplicity, only some hints are given in this section and attention is focused on single inheritance.

When a class, B, inherits from another class, A, the rules listed below must be observed.

1. Class B maintains all the input and output places of class A. This corresponds to the standard rule that the inheriting class provides the same services as the inherited class.

2. Class B can redefine and extend the behavior of class A (additional input and output places can be introduced as well). With textual languages, this rule means that B can redefine some services of A and can provide additional services. In Protob there is no corresponding notion of service, even if a reasonable interpretation could associate a service with a path in the net which starts from an input place and ends at an output place. For the sake of simplicity, we relate inheritance to views, as they are the portions into which a Protob net is decomposed; therefore, class B can selectively inherit the views of class A, further it can modify inherited views as well as include new views (which provide additional features).

A simple example is given in Figure 5.20, where classes Client1 and Server1 inherit and extend the classes shown in Figure 5.18.

The portion of the net that has been inherited is shown dashed. It can be noted that in class Client1:

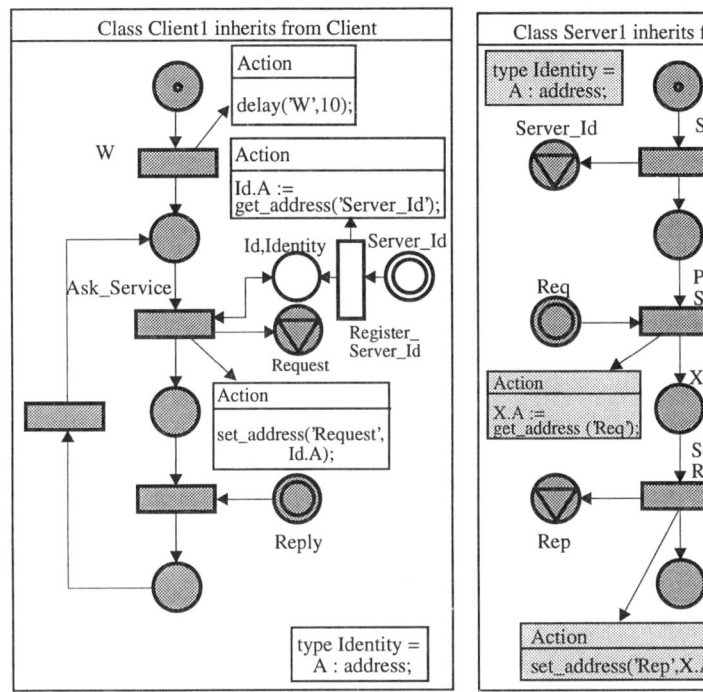

Figure 5.20 *Inheritance of nets*

1. transition Ask_Service has an additional input/output place, Id, and its action has been extended;

2. a new transition, Register_Server_Id, as well as a new input place, Server_-Id, have been introduced;

3. transition W has been given an action while it had none in class Client.

   Class Server1 has an additional output place, Server_Id.

5.7 Adding services to net-based objects

So far, an object has been considered as a token-driven machine, which receives tokens and sends tokens according to a net-based behavior. However, the common notion of object presents it as a supplier of services where a service involves some manipulation of the object's internal data structure and can be based on services provided by other objects as well.

The two points of view from which we can look at an object, i.e. the net-based point of view and the service-based point of view, are not antithetic, but, as shown in Figure 5.21, they can be profitably integrated so that a more expressive representation is obtained.

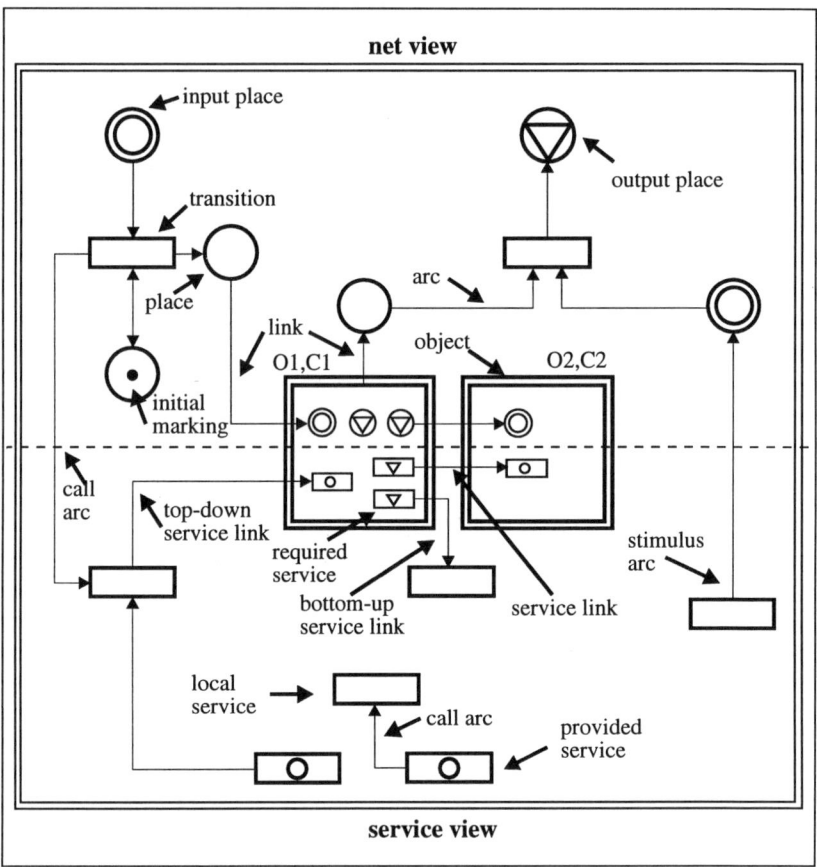

Figure 5.21 *Symbols and connections used in the net model and in the service model*

The net-based point of view is attractive, because it describes the object's behavior graphically, moreover it encompasses the other one, as discussed below.

1. Each transition can be thought of as a sort of service which will be performed when the state of the object, i.e. the marking of the net, enables its execution.

2. The execution of a service can be described by an equivalent net model. In fact, the execution of a service, S, can be represented by an input place, P, an output place, Q, and a transition, T, which connects P to Q, because calling S is equivalent to first sending a token containing

the input parameters to P and then waiting for the reply token which contains the output parameters and is issued through Q.

On the other hand, if the object is naturally thought of as a supplier of services or it has no complex dynamics, the service-based point of view is more compact than the equivalent net model, because, after all, a service can be represented by one icon, while the equivalent net model requires three icons. Anyhow, the two points of view can coexist as explained below.

In addition or as an alternative to the net model, a Protob object (or class) can have a service model consisting of three groups of services:

1. provided services, which the object makes available to the other objects;

2. local services, which can be called only by the owner object;

3. required services, which are called by the object but have to be provided by other objects.

The service interface is made up of a provided interface, which groups all the provided services, and a required interface, which groups all the required services.

Pictorially, services are represented by rectangles (just as transitions); in addition, provided services have a circle inside the rectangle and required ones have a triangle inside the rectangle. The icons of services are shown in Figure 5.21.

Service invocation between peer objects, i.e. objects that are components of the same compound object, is represented by an oriented arc, called a service link, which connects a required service of the caller object to a provided service of the called object. The services which are connected by a service link can have different names, but their formal parameters must be congruent.

Service invocation between a compound object and a component object is represented by a link that connects a service of the compound object to a provided service of the component object (such a link is called a top-down service link) or by a link that connects a required service of the component object to a service of the compound object (such a link is called a bottom-up service link).

Sometimes, the net model and the service model must interact and this can take place in two ways.

1. A transition (in its action or predicate) calls a service. In order to show such an interaction, we can draw an arc, called a call arc, from the transition to the service. A call arc is optional.

2. A service stimulates the net. Such a stimulus is given by a token that the service puts into a place of the net and it is indicated by an oriented arc, called a stimulus arc, connecting the service to the place.

Call arcs and stimulus arcs are shown in Figure 5.21.

5.7.1 Using services and nets

Combining nets and services often leads to more compact models, as exemplified below.

We can transform the timer model given in Figure 5.17 into the one shown in Figure 5.22 by replacing transition Return_Current_Value as well as its input and output places with a provided service, Time_Request.

The contents of Time_Request are similar to the action of transition Return_Current_Value. The client, too, is simpler (as compared with the one shown in Figure 5.16), because it no longer needs to send a request token and to wait for a reply token, but it calls service Get_Timer_Value directly in the action of a transition. Get_Timer_Value is a required service and, as such, it is a placeholder for the actual service, Time_Request, to which it is connected by a service link.

Yet another version of the timer model is given in Figure 5.23 which shows the usage of the stimulus arc.

In this case, a new provided service, Set_Timer, has been introduced: its contents are similar to the action of transition Issue_Interrupt in Figure 5.17. Since a stimulus arc connects Set_Timer to place Counter_Enabled, the last (implicit) action of Set_Timer consists in putting a token into this place. Transition Issue_Interrupt is, then, enabled and fires with a delayed-release behavior.

The client, too, is slightly changed with respect to Figure 5.22, because the interval length has to be given to the timer by means of service invocation.

5.8 Comparison with structured analysis

Protob can be regarded as a rigorous and executable language which integrates the functional and control models used in structured analysis.

This section presents some guidelines on how models based on dataflows, either simple or extended with control features, can be transformed into Protob models.

The conversion of simple dataflow diagrams into Protob models is illustrated in Figure 5.24 and is based on the rules listed below.

1. Each dataflow is viewed as a flow of tokens and is represented by a place in the Protob net; the place name is given by the dataflow label and the place type is obtained from the definitions of the data dictionary which specify the information flowing in the dataflow. A place corresponding to a dataflow is called dataflow place. Places A, B, C and E in Figure 5.24(a) are dataflow places; place types have been omitted.

2. Datastores, too, are mapped onto places, which are called datastore places. In general, a datastore place has one initial token, which represents the overall information contained in the datastore, and is always

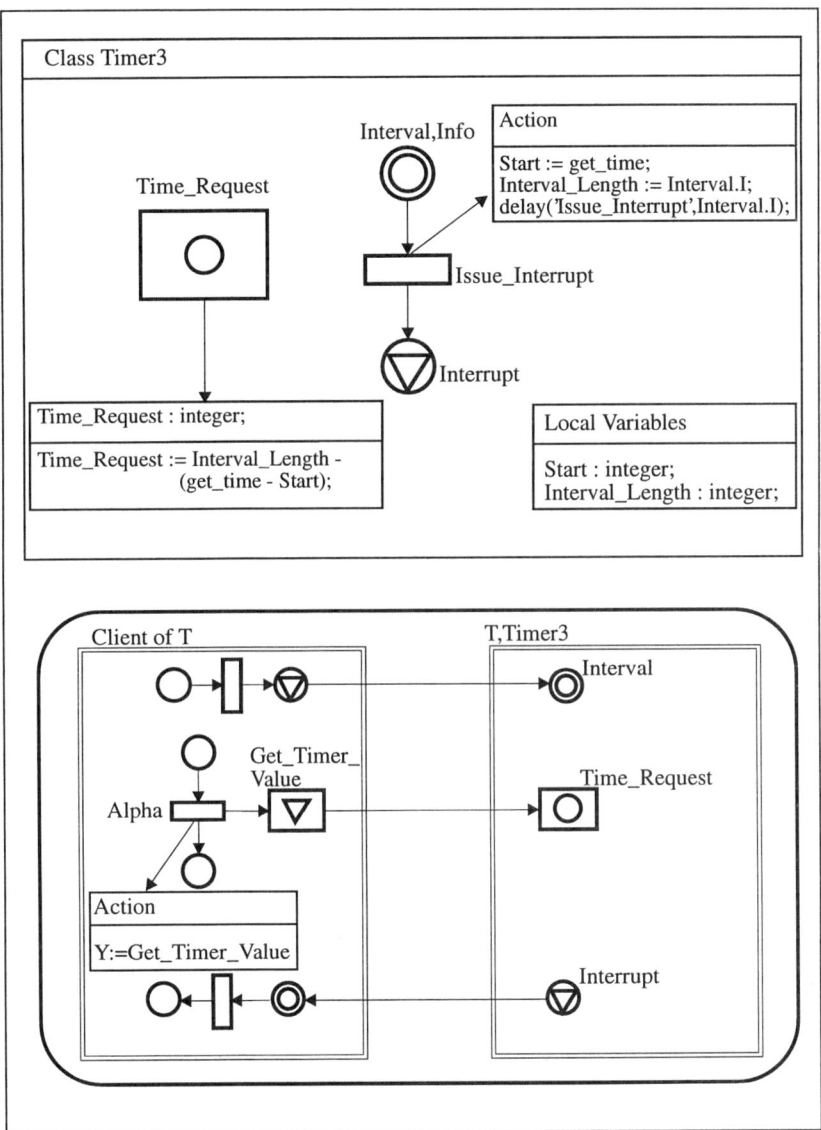

Figure 5.22 *The third model of the timer*

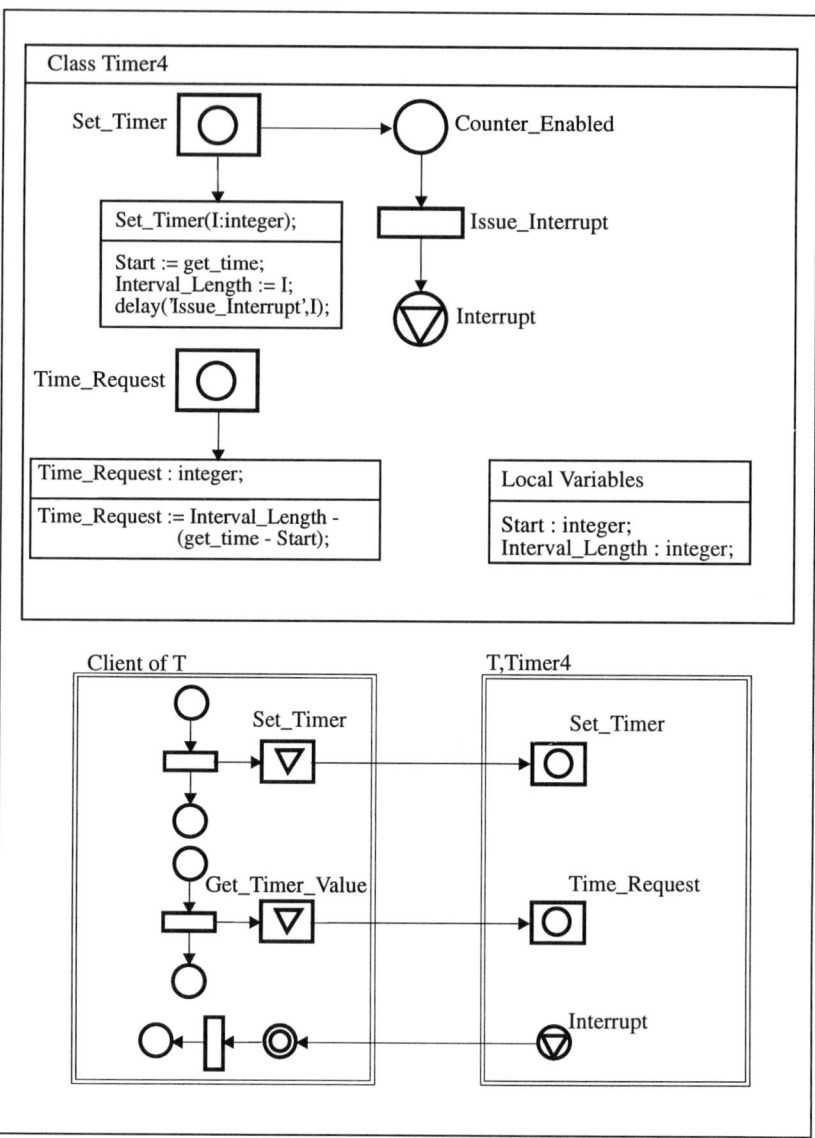

Figure 5.23 *The fourth model of the timer*

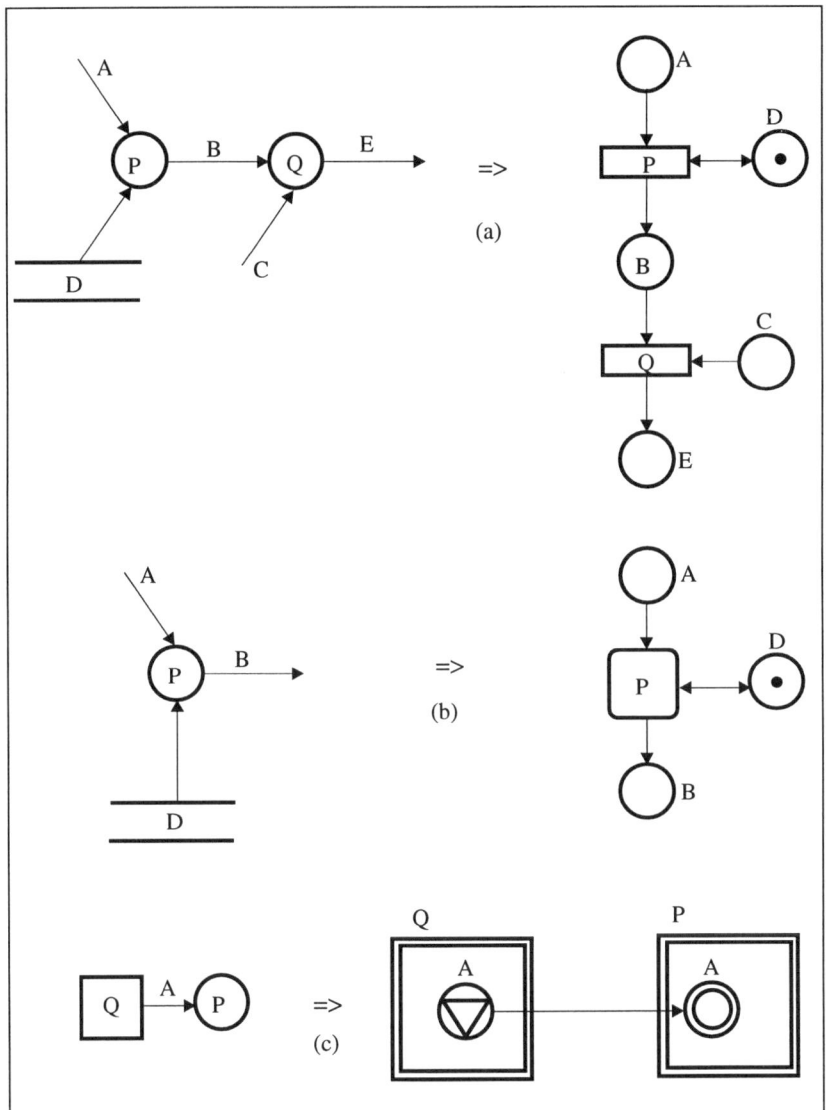

Figure 5.24 *Transformation rules from DFDs into Protob nets*

connected to transitions by means of bidirectional arcs. Place D in Figure 5.24(a) is a datastore place.

3. A simple process is mapped onto a transition if, when it is executed, it removes one token from each input dataflow and datastore and delivers one token to each output dataflow and datastore. Otherwise, the process has to be transformed into a Protob view in which its behavior will be detailed. A transition corresponding to a process is called a functional transition and a view corresponding to a process is called a functional view. A simple process is called a transition process if it can be mapped onto a Protob transition. Processes P and Q in Figure 5.24(a) are transition processes, so they are converted into (functional) transitions. Process P in Figure 5.24(b) cannot be mapped onto a transition, so it is transformed into a functional view.

4. A compound process is transformed into a Protob view or into a Protob object, depending on the complexity of its behavior.

5. Agents are represented by Protob objects, so their behavior can be modeled. A context diagram containing an agent, Q, and the system being considered, P, is shown in Figure 5.24(c): agent Q gives rise to object Q and compound process P is represented by object P, which contains the overall model.

The transformation of extended dataflows into Protob nets is illustrated in Figure 5.25. Additional rules concerning state-transition diagrams and the interaction between control processes and functional processes are presented below.

When a state-transition diagram is transformed into a Protob view (called a control view)

1. States are mapped onto places (called state places).

2. A new place (called an event place) is introduced for each event.

3. A new place (called a command place) is introduced for each process that is enabled or disabled by the state-transition diagram; the name of such a place is *Process*_Enabled where *Process* stands for the name of the process involved. Likewise, a new place (called a command place, too) is introduced for each process that is triggered by the state-transition diagram; the name of such a place is *Process*_Triggered.

4. State-transitions are mapped onto Protob transitions.

The control process (C) in Figure 5.25(a), triggers a transition process (P). Then, in the equivalent net, transition T, which corresponds to the state-transition from state X to state Y, puts a token into command place P_Triggered so as to enable one execution of functional transition P. Likewise, as shown in Figure 5.25(b), when a control process enables or disables a functional process, P, a command place whose name is *P*_Enabled is introduced into the corresponding Protob net. When P has to be enabled, a

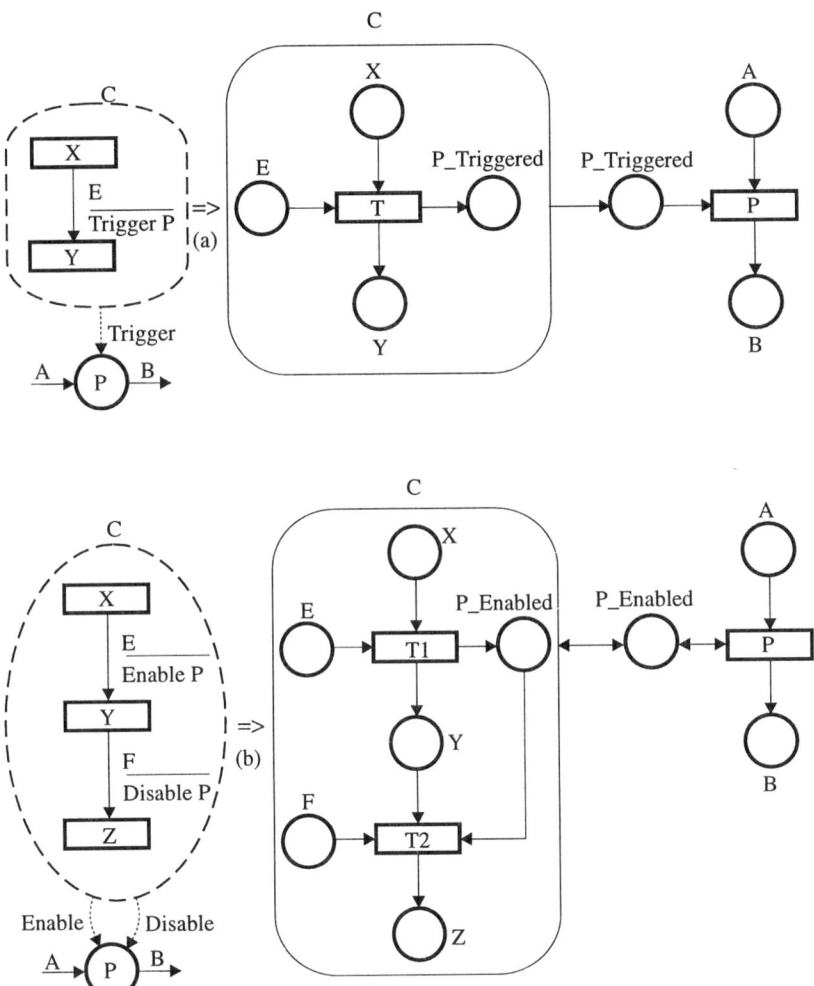

Figure 5.25 *Transformation rules from DFDs into Protob nets (continued)*

token is put into place *P_Enabled*; when P has to be disabled, that token is removed from place *P_Enabled*.

The previous rules handle the major steps in the transformation of dataflow diagrams into Protob nets. For the sake of simplicity, additional details, such as the removal of the input data of a controlled functional process when it is disabled, or the removal of an event when the control process to which the event is directed is unable to accept it, are not considered here.

Converting models based on dataflows into Protob nets offers many advantages, which are summarized below.

1. The net is more rigorous and more expressive than the functional model, because the conditions that determine the execution of a process are shown precisely and graphically.

2. Functional models and control models end up having the same semantics, so there is no reason why they should be kept separate. They can be merged into a single kind of representation consisting of elements of two types: transitions, which represent state-transitions and transition (functional) processes, and places, which represent dataflows, datastores, states, events, control flows and control stores.

3. The data dictionary is given a formal content because token types as well as the predicates and the actions of transitions are written in a standard programming language rather than in a pseudo-code.

4. When extended dataflows are used, multiple threads of control must be represented by separate state-transition diagrams which interact with control flows, thus synchronization between state-transition diagrams entails a pair of control flows. If, instead, a net is used, synchronization can easily be represented by transitions, so the resulting model is simpler.

5. If a compound process is transformed into a Protob object, the submodel associated with that object will be less tightly coupled with the overall model (as compared with the dataflow model) and, therefore, it will be easier to reuse it in other applications.

5.9 Summary

This chapter has presented Protob, an operational modeling and development language based on object-oriented nets. Protob objects are parameterized building blocks, so they can easily be put together to form more powerful objects or even final applications. This capability enables the developer to effectively reuse ideas, and not only pieces of code.

As will be discussed in Chapter 8, Protob models can be translated into concurrent programs automatically. Many event-driven applications have been developed so far, e.g. supervisors of production systems and logistic systems, supervisors of communications systems and measuring systems, and embedded systems for telephone traffic monitoring and for toll collection on highways. The complexity of such models ranges from few classes and few objects to dozens of classes and thousands of objects, while some classes have up to two hundred transitions.

6

Quid

We have seen in Chapter 3 that the Class-Relationship (CR) formalism and the Entity-Relationship (ER) formalism are strongly related and that CR can be considered as an extension to ER. In fact, a class supplements the data structure represented by an entity with all the services that operate on this data structure. Therefore, in this chapter it is assumed that CR models include ER models.

CR is not generally provided with operational semantics, so there is no linguistic support that enables the analyst to work with objects and with associations between objects at a conceptual level. Consequently, CR models have to be translated into models based on lower-level languages, but this transformation causes a reduction in expressiveness, as discussed below.

ER models are usually translated into relational tables (Elmasri and Navathe, 1989), thus the distinction between entities, which represent real objects in the application domain, and relationships, which represent associations between objects, is lost. Relational tables are acted on by means of relational languages, which operate at a lower level: in fact, an association between objects has to be managed through the explicit join of tables and, consequently, objects have to be provided with explicit (and often artificial) identification keys. Further, many applications that feature really complex data structures cannot be implemented using a relational language (and the underlying database), because of performance and memory constraints. In such a case, ER is still used to specify the data structure, but, then, this data structure has to be managed at a lower level using a conventional programming language.

Similar comments can be made on CR models. As Rumbaugh (1987) points out, when a CR model is translated into an object-oriented program, programmers will probably implement a relationship between classes by introducing, into each class, an object variable bound to the other class, even though the relationship represents information which, conceptually, does not belong to either class. For this reason, the notion of relationship is more abstract and richer (semantically) than the notion of object variable provided by object-oriented programming languages.

In order to overcome the above-mentioned limitations, we have developed a language, called Quid (Bruno, Grammatica and Macario, 1992 and Artis, 1993), which is an operational extension to CR, and this chapter illustrates how it can be applied to information models, object models and actor models.

6.1 Operational information models

We start by presenting Quid in the context of information structures, i.e. when CR models correspond to ER models.

Models developed with Quid are made up of classes, relationships and roots.

A class represents several individuals, also called instances or objects, which have the same properties; the term property denotes either an attribute or a kind of association with other objects. Every attribute has a name and a type and the notion of type is the same as in conventional programming languages.

The model presented in Figure 6.1 refers to users that can be assigned to tasks. Specifically, a user can be assigned to a task for a given percentage of its duration. Class User has two attributes: Name, which is a string, and Role, which can assume one of two values, i.e. developer or manager. Likewise, class Task has two attributes, Name and Duration, the second indicating the length of the task in weeks.

As discussed in Chapter 2, relationships are drawn as oriented arcs, for the arrow indicates the direction in which the name of the relationship must be read. For example, relationship Works_on indicates that users work on tasks; class User is the source of relationship Works_on, while class Task is its destination. For the sake of simplicity, only binary relationships are considered in this chapter.

A relationship between classes represents the associations that can exist between the objects of the source class and the objects of the destination class. Relationships can have cardinality constraints: one-to-one (1,1), one-to-many (1,n), many-to-one (n,1) or many-to-many (m,n). Further, a relationship can impose a participation constraint as follows: if every object of the source (destination) class must be involved in at least one association, a left (right) square bracket precedes (follows) the cardinality constraint.

Relationships, too, can have attributes; relationship Works_on, shown in Figure 6.1, has one attribute, Percentage.

A relationship is called recursive if the source class and the destination class coincide.

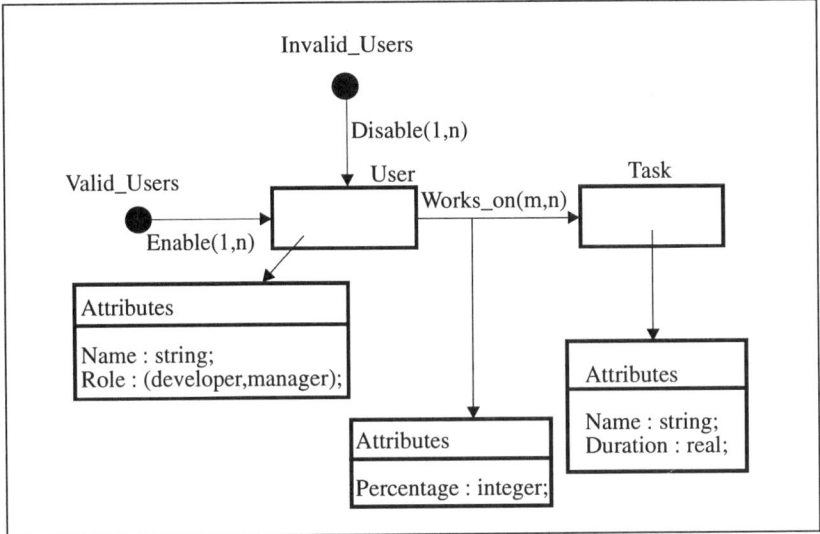

Figure 6.1 *A Quid model*

Ordering policies can be associated with relationships, as was explained in Chapter 2.

It is often necessary to mark some of the objects belonging to a given class as they exhibit a special feature. Then, we do not add a specific boolean attribute to the class so as to distinguish the objects exhibiting the special feature; instead, we introduce a root and connect it to all such objects.

A root is drawn as a small circle. It has a name and can only have outgoing relationships with cardinalities one-to-one or one-to-many. A root has no attributes.

For example, if class User in Figure 6.1 represents all the users that have been given access to a certain system in its lifetime, root Valid_Users indicates which users are currently authorized.

When a CR model is complex, it can be decomposed into views, with the constraint that the same class or root can appear in several views, but a relationship must appear in only one view.

The actual information structure represented by a CR model is a connected graph, called an object graph, whose nodes contain objects. Associations between objects are depicted as directed arcs between nodes. An object graph has several roots, i.e. those corresponding to the roots defined in the model plus one (internal) root for each class. Whenever a new object is added to the graph, an internal connection, too, is introduced to link the internal root (corresponding to the class of the object) to the node containing the object. All the roots are reachable through internal connections from a special internal root, called the primary-root, thus connectivity is guaranteed for the whole structure.

An object graph corresponding to the model given in Figure 6.1 is shown in Figure 6.2. For the sake of simplicity, internal roots have been omitted.

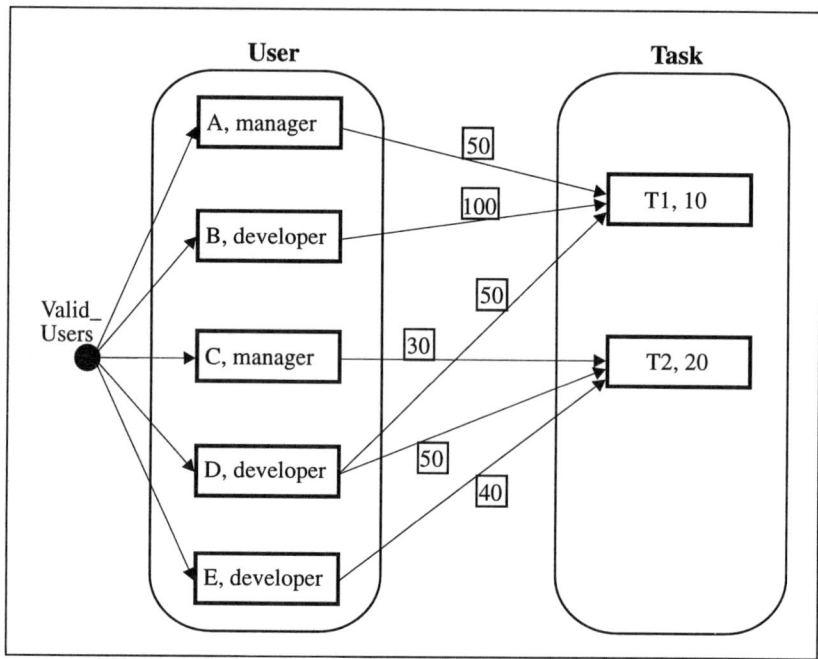

Figure 6.2 *An object graph related to the model shown in Figure 6.1*

Objects and associations are unique and can be referred to by pointers, called handles.

Quid provides statements to generate or delete objects or associations as well as to navigate the object graph.

The statements written below generate a portion of the object graph shown in Figure 6.2.

```
var U: handle(User); T: handle(Task);

Qd_new User U (name := 'A', role := manager);
Qd_new Task T (name := 'T1', duration := 10);
Qd_new Works_on U -> T (Percentage := 50);
Qd_new Enable Valid_Users -> U;
```

A keyword (Qd_new) begins the statement that generates a new object or a new association. The name of the class or of the relationship, an instance of which has to be generated, is written after that keyword. If a handle follows the class or relationship name, this handle can be used, after the execution of the statement, to refer to the newly generated element. When an association has to be introduced, the objects involved are represented by their handles: in fact, in the above code, user A and task T1, which have to be connected by a Works_on association, are represented by their handles, U and T.

Handles are variables and are declared by means of a keyword (`handle`) followed by the name, enclosed between round brackets, of a class or relationship. When an element (object or association) is generated, the values of its attributes can be set using the notation *attribute_name* := *expression*, as shown in the above code.

6.1.1 Navigation

The most important feature of Quid is navigation. Navigation is the act of traversing the object graph following the paths that are specified with a construct, called a path expression. The objects that are reached during navigation can be acted on.

A path expression denotes a set of paths in the object graph, as shown in Figure 6.3. It consists of a path source (i.e. a root name or a class name) and of a sequence of path elements, each path element being a relationship class pair, written as /R/C, where R stands for a relationship name and C for a class name. The path expression must be consistent, thus, if a path element is /R/C, then C is the destination class of R and, further, R is an outgoing relationship of the class or root that precedes R in the path expression.

Given a model that includes two classes, A and B, and a relationship, R, from A to B, if navigation must be performed from an object of B to the objects of A which are associated with it, the path element is B/rev(R)/A (where `rev` stands for reverse) instead of A/R/B.

For the sake of simplicity, the relationship name can be omitted if there is no ambiguity (i.e. R is the only relationship between A and B) and if the attributes of the relationship are not used. Therefore, instead of writing A/R/B or B/rev(R)/A, we can simply write A//B or B//A. The short form cannot be used when the relationship is recursive.

The path expression shown in Figure 6.3, i.e. R/rel_1/A/rel_2/B, denotes the ten paths listed below.

1. (R). The first path consists of the root that begins the path expression.

2. (R, A1). A1 is assumed to be the destination of the first rel_1 association leaving R.

3. (R, A1, B1). Navigation is performed depth-first, so, after an object, y_i, has been reached from a given object, x, every further path starting from y_i is explored before any other object, y_j, is reached from x. B1 is assumed to be the destination of the first rel_2 association leaving A1.

4. (R, A1, B2).

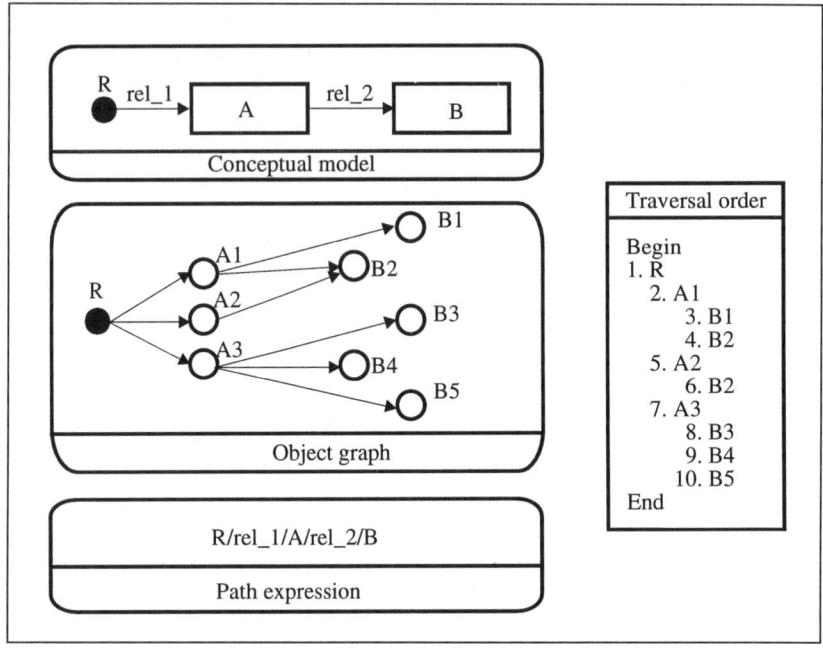

Figure 6.3 *The order in which an object graph is traversed*

5. (R, A2).

6. (R, A2, B2).

7. (R, A3).

8. (R, A3, B3). B3 is assumed to be the destination of the first rel_2 association leaving A3.

9. (R, A3, B4).

10. (R, A3, B5).

The maximum number of objects that a path can encompass is given by the length of the path expression, i.e. the number of classes (including the root) that appear in the path expression. In the above example, the length of the path expression is 3.

Given a path, its length is the number of objects it contains. A maximum path is a path whose length is equal to the length of the path expression. A subpath is a path whose length is shorter than the length of the path expression. Given a subpath, s, all the paths that include s, i.e. the paths that include all the objects of s and have additional objects, form the including set of s. In the above example, (R, A3) is a subpath, while {(R, A3, B3), (R, A3, B4), (R, A3, B5)} is its including set.

The path expression is the core of the navigational statement provided by Quid. This statement is written within two keywords, `Qd_apply` and `Qd_end`.

During the execution of a navigational statement, the objects in the current path can be referred to by means of handles. A handle, h, can be bound to an object of a certain class, C, by writing h just after C in the path expression. Likewise, a handle, k, can be bound to an association which is an instance of a relationship, R, by writing k just after R in the path expression.

A path source can be either a root or a class; if it is a class, each of its objects will be the starting point of a different navigation. However, if the path source is written as `class:handle`, there is only one starting point of navigation, i.e. the object referred to by the handle.

The major features of navigation are exemplified below; the examples refer to the model given in Figure 6.1 and to the object graph shown in Figure 6.2.

The handles used in the examples are declared as follows:

```
var U: handle(User); T: handle(Task);
    P: handle(Works_on);
```

1. Determine the involvement of each user in each task which has been assigned to him or her.

```
Qd_apply Valid_users//User U/Works_on P/Task T do
   {writeln('User ',U.Name,' works on task ',T.Name,
    ' for ',P.Percentage*T.Duration/100,' weeks');}
Qd_end;
```

In the above statement, the short form `Valid_Users//User` has been used instead of `Valid_Users/Enable/User`. An attribute of the object or association denoted by a handle can be referred to using the dot notation `handle.attribute`.

Actions, which consist of sequences of statements, can be performed during navigation. An action is introduced by a keyword (`do`) and is enclosed between curly brackets. It can be written only after the path source or after a path element and can act on all the objects (to which handles have been bound) that have been reached in the current path.

The class that precedes an action, a, is the triggering class of a, because a is performed as soon as an object of the triggering class is reached in the current path; further, any path that includes an object belonging to the triggering class of a is called a triggering path of a.

The result of the execution of the above navigational statement is:

```
User A works on task T1 for  5 weeks
User B works on task T1 for 10 weeks
User C works on task T2 for  6 weeks
```

```
User D works on task T1 for  5 weeks
User D works on task T2 for 10 weeks
User E works on task T2 for  8 weeks
```

In fact, the path expression denotes 12 paths, but the action has only 6 triggering paths. Handle U is sequentially bound to the objects corresponding to users A, B, C, D and E. When U is bound to D, T is sequentially bound to the objects corresponding to tasks T1 and T2.

2. Determine the involvement of each user, who is also a manager, in each task to which he/she has been assigned.

```
Qd_apply Valid_users//User U where {U.Role=Manager}
/Works_on P/Task T do
   {writeln('Manager ',U.Name,' works on task ',T.Name,
    ' for ',P.Percentage*T.Duration/100,' weeks');}
Qd_end;
```

The path source and the path elements can be followed by conditions, which are boolean expressions preceded by **where** and enclosed between curly brackets; if a path element (or the path source) has to be followed by both a condition and an action, the condition is written before the action. A condition restricts further navigation (and the execution of the action that follows it, if there is one) to the objects that satisfy the condition. The result of the execution of the above navigational statement is:

```
Manager A works on task T1 for  5 weeks
Manager C works on task T2 for  6 weeks
```

3. Determine for each user his/her total involvement, which results from all the tasks to which he/she has been assigned.

```
var Total: integer;
```

```
Qd_apply Valid_users//User U do
   {Total:=0;}
then do
   {writeln('User ',U.Name,' works for ',Total,' weeks');}
/Works_on P/Task T do
   {Total:=Total+P.Percentage*T.Duration/100;}
Qd_end;
```

Variables, such as Total, can be used within a navigational statement to store results depending on multiple paths. In fact, for a given user, Total accumulates the number of weeks resulting from the tasks to which he/she has been assigned. As soon as a user has been reached, an action, i.e. `Total:=0;`, clears the accumulator before the tasks associated with him or her are examined.

In some cases, it is necessary to perform an action, called a final action, after all the paths of the including set of a given subpath have been examined. A final action is preceded by **then do**, it follows a path element (or the path source) and is written after the action, if there is one. In the above example, instruction **writeln** is executed for each user after all his or her tasks have been examined.

The result of the execution of the above navigational statement is:

```
User A works for  5 weeks
User B works for 10 weeks
User C works for  6 weeks
User D works for 15 weeks
User E works for  8 weeks
```

4. The example presented above can be rewritten as follows to show how navigational statements can be nested.

```
var Total: integer;

Qd_apply Valid_Users//User U do
  {Total:=0;}
  Qd_apply User:U/Works_on P/Task T do
    {Total:=Total+P.Percentage*T.Duration/100;}
  Qd_end;
  {writeln('User ',U.Name,' works for ',Total,' weeks');}
Qd_end;
```

Variables and handles follow the same visibility rules as in conventional programming languages, so handle U, which is bound to an object by the external navigational statement, can be used in the internal one as the starting point of navigation.

6.1.2 Navigating inheritance relationships

The model given in Figure 6.4 presents a case of inheritance as classes Produced_Part and Supplied_Part are subclasses of class Part.

The model describes orders that refer to parts. Parts have one attribute, Name, and can be either produced internally or supplied by one supplier. Orders have two attributes, Name and State, and State contains one of the following values: ready, on-going, finished. Each produced part is related to one workstation, i.e. the workstation that is able to produce the part, and each supplied part is related to one supplier. Workstations and suppliers have one attribute, Name.

For each part that is referred to by an order whose state is on-going, the

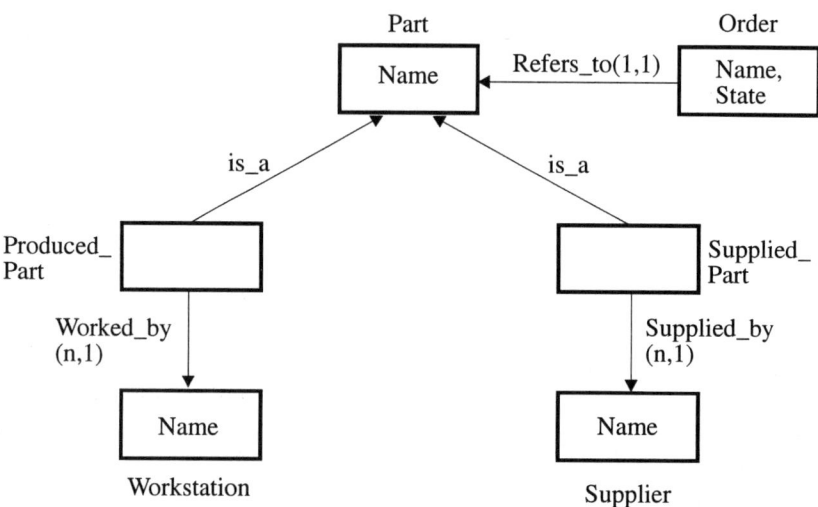

Figure 6.4 *A model featuring inheritance*

navigational statement presented below shows the name of the workstation
that machines the part (if the part is a produced one), or the name of the
supplier (if the part is a supplied one).

```
var O: handle(Order); P: handle(Part);
    W: handle(Workstation); S: handle(Supplier);

Qd_apply Order O where {O.State=on-going}
//Part P do
  {write('Part ',P.Name,' ordered by order ',O.Name);}
case of
  when Produced_Part//Workstation W do
    {writeln(' is produced by workstation ',W.Name);}
  when Supplied_Part//Supplier S do
    {writeln(' is supplied by supplier ',S.Name);}
end case;
Qd_end;
```

The path source is a class name, therefore each object of class Order
starts a navigation.

During navigation, a relationship that denotes inheritance, i.e. is_a, can be followed either from the superclass to one of its subclasses or vice versa.

In fact, we assume that there is a one-to-one mapping (called specialization mapping) from the set of the objects (called generic objects) belonging to a superclass, C, to the set which is made up of all the objects (called specific objects) belonging to the subclasses of C. The inverse mapping is called generalization mapping.

Given a superclass, C, the specialization mapping of C returns the specific object (i.e. an object belonging to a subclass of C) corresponding to a given generic object (which belongs to C), whereas the generalization mapping of C returns the generic object corresponding to a given specific object.

Therefore, a navigation, after reaching a generic object, g, that belongs to a superclass, C (e.g. an object of class Part in the above navigational statement), can continue from the specific object, s, related to g; s is obtained by applying the specialization mapping of C to g. Since the class of s is not known a priori, a case construct is used to indicate which route has to be followed for each subclass of C. The case construct in the above navigational statement contains two branches because class Part has two subclasses.

In the example presented below, navigation proceeds from a subclass to its superclass. In fact, after a specific object, s, has been reached, navigation can continue from the corresponding generic object, g, which is obtained by applying the generalization mapping related to the superclass to g.

All the on-going orders in which each supplier is involved can be listed as follows.

```
var O: handle(Order); P: handle(Part);
    S: handle(Supplier);

Qd_apply Supplier S//Supplied_Part Part P
//Order O where {O.State=on-going} do
    {writeln('Supplier ',S.Name,' supplies part ',
     P.Name,' as required by order ',O.Name);}
Qd_end;
```

In order to express that navigation must continue from the generic object corresponding to the specific object that has been reached, the superclass name is written after the subclass name, thus Part follows Supplied_Part.

6.1.3 Object-oriented navigation

When a CR model (in the true sense of the word) is used, the objects that are reached during navigation can be acted on only by invoking the services of the corresponding classes. The actions that can be performed during navigation are, then, more limited: in fact, it is possible to read the visible attributes of an object directly, but they can be modified only by calling the services of the class to which the object belongs. This new kind of navigation which must be performed on true CR models will be referred to as object-oriented navigation.

The example of object-oriented navigation that will be presented later in this subsection concerns the model given in Figure 6.5, which shows a portion of the information structure of an editor of Petri nets.

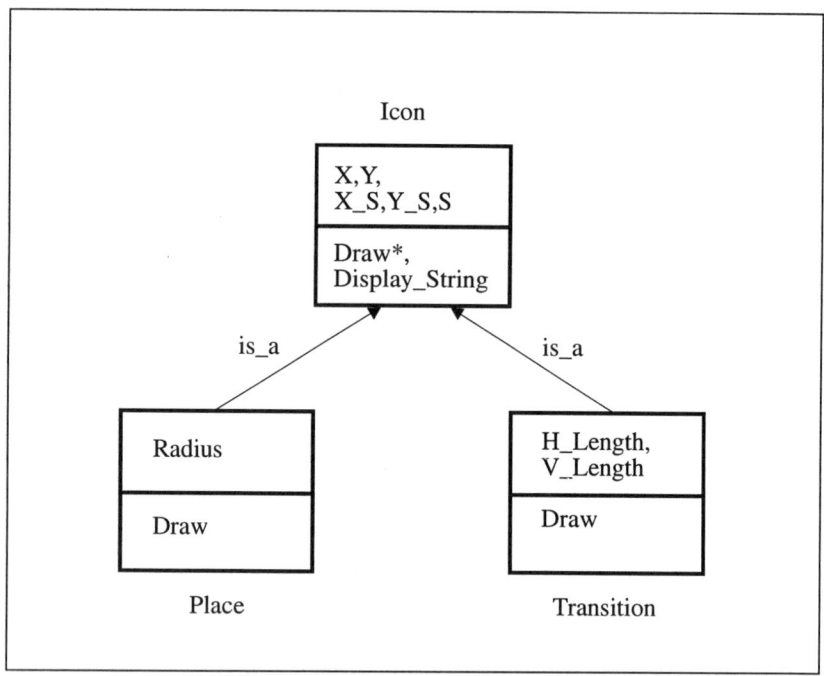

Figure 6.5 *A fragment of the information model related to a Petri net editor*

Each class is depicted as a rectangle which contains two sections: the visible attributes are listed in the upper section, while the visible services are listed in the lower section.

Class Icon represents icons, an icon being an abstraction of the actual elements, i.e. places and transitions, to be displayed. Places and transitions are drawn as circles and rectangles, respectively, so they have several common features, i.e. the coordinates, X and Y, of the center of the icon (circle or rectangle), the string, S, associated with the element, and the coordinates, X_S and Y_S, of the lower left corner of the rectangle in which S is displayed.

Class Icon has two services, Draw and Display_String: the former is an abstract service because it depends on the actual shape of the icon and thus cannot be performed by this class, the latter is implemented by this class. An abstract service is marked with an asterisk (*).

The subclasses of Icon exhibit additional features and implement service Draw. Specifically, class Place has one attribute, Radius, whilst class Transition has two attributes, H_Length and V_Length (it is assumed that the sides of the rectangle are parallel to the coordinate axes).

The navigational statement written below displays all the elements, places and transitions, of a net.

```
var I: handle(Icon);

Qd_apply Icon I do {I.Draw; I.Display_String;}
Qd_end;
```

A service call is indicated with the dot notation and the object handle precedes the service name.

6.1.4 Navigating recursive relationships

Recursive relationships can be handled by means of recursive navigational statements.

The model given in Figure 6.6 shows the structure of a bill of materials. Parts have two attributes, Name and Is_Compound: Name is a string and Is_Compound is a boolean value indicating whether the part is made up of other parts or is a single piece.

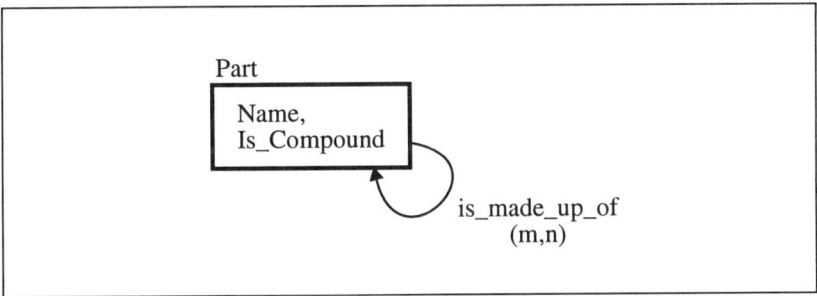

Figure 6.6 *A recursive relationship*

For a given part, the navigational statement written below lists all its direct components, the components of its components and so on.

```
var P,Q: handle(Part);

Qd_apply Part:P then do
  {if not P.Is_Compound then
     writeln('Part ',P.Name,' is simple');}
```

```
/is_made_of/Part Q do
  {writeln('Part ',P.Name,' is made up of part ',
  Q.Name);}
  reapply with Q;
Qd_end;
```

Handle P is assumed to be set outside the navigational statement as it indicates which part has to be decomposed.

The final action (the one that follows **then do**) is a conditional statement, thus will be executed only if the part is a single piece.

When the part denoted by P is compound, each of its components is referred to by handle Q; for each component of P a message is printed, then the same navigational statement is repeated (and navigation starts from the component of P being considered).

The statement **reapply with Q** causes the immediate execution of the enclosing navigational statement with a different starting point (given by handle Q). Alternatively, the recursive execution of a navigational statement can be obtained by writing it inside a recursive procedure.

6.2 Actor models

The CR framework can be used, with a different interpretation, when classes have a behavior expressed in terms of high-level nets. In this context, classes are Protob classes and relationships are interpreted as compound links which connect pairs of compound ports. When CR models are given such a meaning, they are called actor models. Further, the objects represented by an actor model will be called actors to emphasize that they represent components which play an active role, as they can take decisions and react to external events autonomously.

The example given in Figure 6.7 models routers that route clients' requests for service to free servers.

Each router is connected to several clients and to several servers. Clients and servers can be connected to only one router.

Relationship Asks_Service from class Client to class Router stands for a compound link from compound port P of class Client to compound port P of class Server. Likewise, relationship Provides_Service from class Server to class Router stands for a compound link from compound port Q of class Server to compound port Q of class Router.

The mapping from relationships to compound links is given in a separate table, as shown in Figure 6.7.

Classes Client, Server and Router are described in Figures 6.8, 6.9 and 6.10 respectively.

Class Client has one compound port, P, which is made up of output place Request and input place Reply. A client actor repeatedly issues a request, waits for the reply and prepares a new request. The time spent in preparing

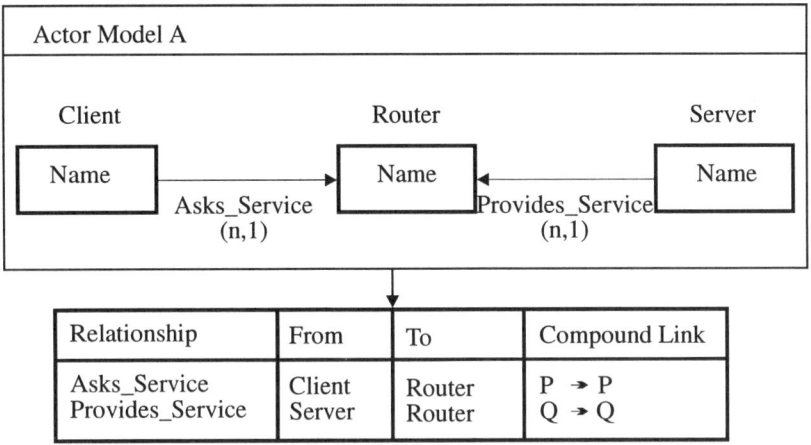

Figure 6.7 *An actor model*

a new request is not negligible, so transition Prepare_Request has a release delay, which is given by a parameter, D.

A server actor initially sends the router a token (from output place Server_Id) to let it know of its existence as well as to communicate its address.

After firing transition Send_Id, a server actor repeatedly waits for a service request, performs the service and sends the reply. Performing a service takes some time, so transition Perform_Service has a release delay, which is given by a parameter, D. There is also a local variable, N, which counts the services performed by the server actor.

A server actor can also execute a service (Performed_Services) which returns the number of services performed up to the time of the call.

Class Server has one compound port, Q, which is made up of output place Server_Id, input place Request and output place Reply.

The model of the router is a bit more complex, because it is both a server for client actors and a client for server actors.

The router dispatches service requests to free servers on a FCFS (first come first served) basis. Place Free_Server contains tokens representing free servers, each token storing the address of a free server. Place Busy_Server contains tokens representing busy servers, each token storing the address of a busy server (in field S) and the address of the client (in field C) whose service request is being dealt with by that server.

Initially, each server communicates its address to the router. The address is received at input place Server_Id, then transition Register_Server fires and copies it into the token to be put into place Free_Server. The action of

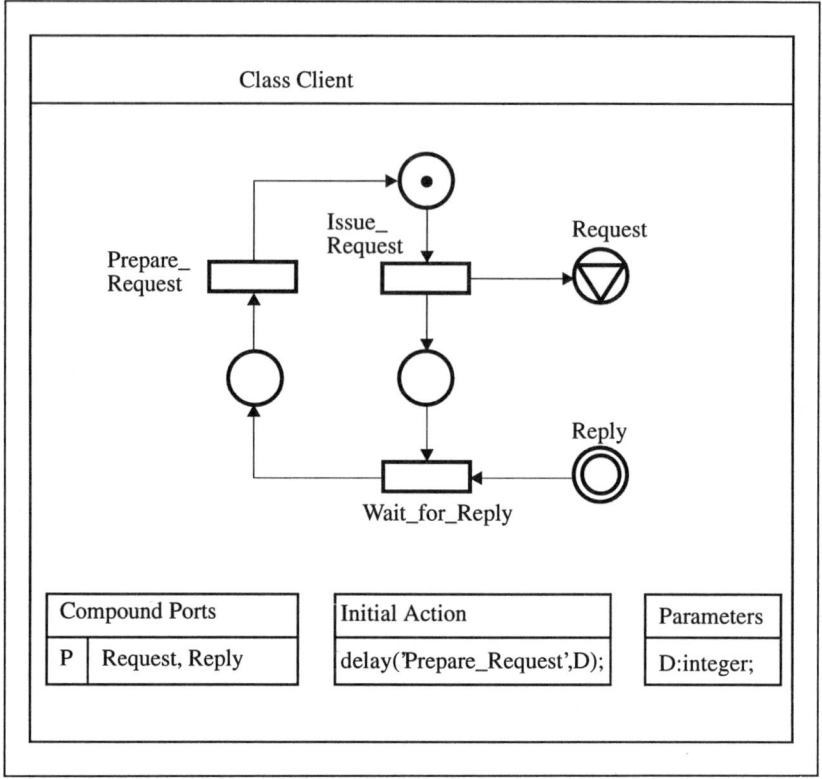

Figure 6.8 *The Protob net describing client actors*

transition Register_Server uses primitive **get_address** to read the address of the server.

When a request is received from a client (at input place Client_Request) and there is a free server, transition Forward_Request_to_Server fires. It removes a token from place Free_Server and uses the server address contained in this token to stamp the token to be sent from output place Server_Request with the address of the destination server. At the same time, Forward_Request_to_Server puts a token into place Busy_Server in order to store the address of the server that will fulfill the request and the address of the client.

When a server notifies the completion of a service (i.e. a token is received at input place Server_Reply), transition Forward_Reply_to_Client fires. It has a predicate which selects the token corresponding to the server among those contained in place Busy_Server. The predicate is based on a primitive (**same_identity**), which has been introduced because the user has no access to the internal structure of addresses. Primitive **same_identity** is a

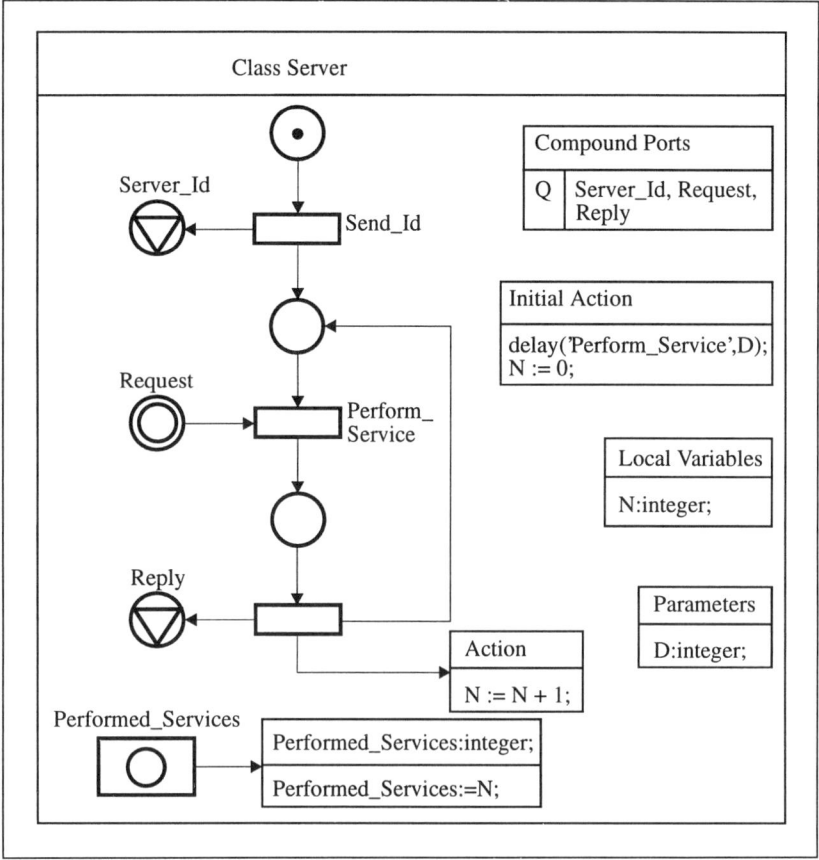

Figure 6.9 *The Protob net describing server actors*

two-parameter boolean function returning true only if the two addresses, passed by value to the function, are identical. The action of transition Forward_Reply_to_Client sends the reply to the right client, by using the client address contained in the token taken from place Busy_Server; further, it puts a token into place Free_Server so as to keep the address of the server that has notified the completion of the service.

Class Router has two compound ports, P and Q, which enable it to interface with classes Client and Server, respectively.

An actor model is included in a Protob class (as shown in Figure 6.11) which is in charge of generating actors and associations between actors as well as of performing navigations among actors.

Class System_Manager, given in Figure 6.11, includes an actor model, A, and this is indicated by a new graphical symbol, i.e. a double rectangle which contains two classes and one relationship. When a Quid model

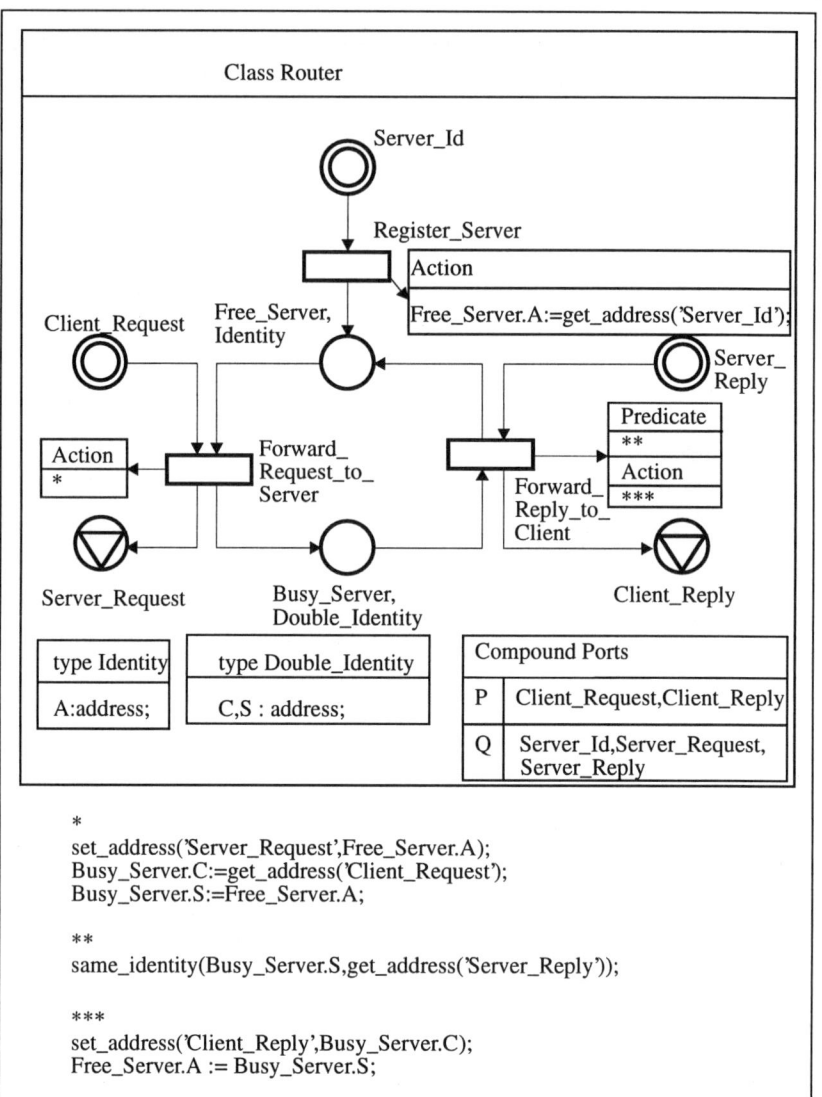

Figure 6.10 *The Protob net describing router actors*

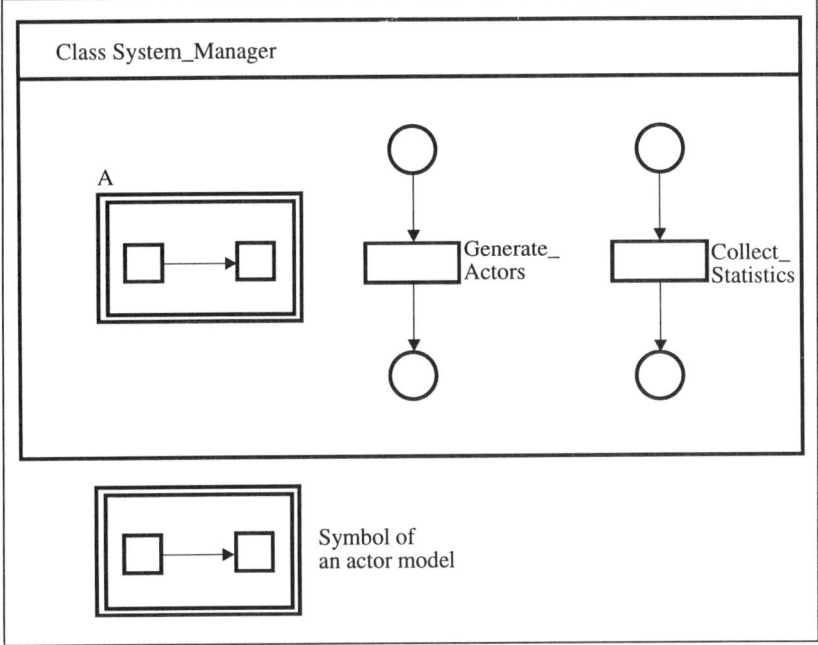

Figure 6.11 *A Protob class that includes an actor model*

represents a collection of (passive) objects, we use a single rectangle which contains two classes and one relationship.

For the sake of simplicity, only two transitions, Generate_Actors and Collect_Statistics, have been shown in class System_Manager. The former generates a structure with three clients, two servers and one router, the latter gives the number of services performed up to the instant it is invoked.

The action of transition Generate_Actors contains the declarations and the statements listed below.

```
var R: handle(Router); C: handle(Client);
    S: handle(Server);
...
Qd_new Router R (Name := 'R1');
Qd_new Client C (Name := 'C1', D := 10);
Qd_new Asks_Service C -> R;
Qd_new Client C (Name := 'C2', D := 15);
Qd_new Asks_Service C -> R;
Qd_new Client C (Name := 'C3', D := 20);
Qd_new Asks_Service C -> R;
Qd_new Server S (Name := 'S1', D := 12);
Qd_new Provides_Service S -> R;
```

```
Qd_new Server S (Name := 'S2', D := 18);
Qd_new Provides_Service S -> R;
start;
```

When actors are generated by means of Quid statements, they are put into an inactive state. When primitive **start** is called, the initial actions of the newly generated objects are performed and their execution is started.

The action of transition Collect_Statistics is shown below.

```
var R: handle(Router);
    Counter, N: integer;

Qd_apply Router R do
  {Counter := 0;
   writeln('Services managed by router ',R.Name);}
then do
  {writeln('Total number = ',Counter);}
//Server S do
  {N := S.Performed_Services;
   writeln(N,' performed by server ',S.Name);
   Counter := Counter+N;}
Qd_end;
```

For each router, R, the above navigational statement lists the number of services that each server has performed on behalf of R and prints the total number of services managed by R. Variable Counter counts the total number of services managed by each router.

During navigation it is possible to interact with actors by calling their services, as shown above.

6.3 Summary

This chapter has presented an operational language, Quid, which enables the analyst not only to build Class-Relationship models but also to generate objects and associations as well as to navigate among objects and to act on the objects reached during navigation.

Three kinds of models have been considered:

1. information models, in which classes are similar to the entities of the Entity-Relationship formalism;

2. object models, in which objects cannot be acted on directly but only through the services of the corresponding classes;

3. actor models, in which actors have their own dynamics expressed by Protob nets.

7

Building models

This chapter deals with two important topics: the architecture of models based on the Protob and Quid modeling languages, and the construction of complex behaviors through the combination of simple behaviors.

The building blocks of the models considered in this chapter are actors, i.e. active objects represented by Protob nets. The number of actors included in a model can be fixed or variable: in the latter case, the model is called an actor model and is based on a Quid model whose classes are Protob classes. An actor can act on a complex information structure (i.e. an actor model), which is represented by a Quid model whose classes are passive. As an example of a typical architecture, the cell supervisor presented in Chapters 2 and 3 is illustrated.

As regards the second topic, actors are subdivided into two classes: simple actors and compound ones. A simple actor has a behavior which is described by a Protob net similar to a state-transition diagram (presented in Chapter 2) as well as to a state machine (presented in Chapter 4). Simple actors can be combined according to certain standard forms of interaction and thus give rise to a compound actor: the resulting net is a fully fledged Protob net.

7.1 Model architecture

The architecture of a model depends on the complexity and characteristics of the system (or subsystem) being considered. There are three typical situations:

1. The system is thought of as a statical collection of interacting components, each component having its own thread of control. Then, it is best represented by a statical collection of actors.

2. The system is made up of interacting components whose number is not known a priori. In such a case, an actor model is appropriate.

3. The system must act on a complex information structure and its actions
   depend on external events (including the user's commands). Then, that
   information structure is described by an object model, while the handling
   of external events as well as the actions on the information structure are
   performed by an actor which includes the object model. The specific
   actions that a Protob net can perform by taking advantage of an object
   model will be described later in this section.

In general, an actor can contain other actors as well as actor models and
object models. The system being considered is always represented by one
actor, called the system actor; its class is called the system class.

Although, in general, several actor models and several object models
could be included in the same actor, we restrict our attention, for the sake
of simplicity, to the case in which an actor includes at most one actor model
and/or one object model. Further, although, in general, an object model
represents an information structure that can pertain to several actors, we
assume, for the sake of simplicity, that an object model is completely owned
by the actor which includes it.

The cell supervisor discussed in Chapters 2 and 3 gives the opportunity
of examining a fairly complex architecture which includes an actor model
and an object model.

The actor model (Manufacturing_System) shown in Figure 7.1 is a general and flexible schema which represents the management and control
systems of manufacturing plants.

A plant is governed by a plant supervisor and is made up of several cells.
A cell is managed by a (cell) supervisor and consists of one warehouse,
one cart and a variable number of workstations. Each device (warehouse,
cart or workstation) is made up of two components, i.e. the controller and
the machinery (which is controlled by the controller). Device controllers
interact with the supervisor and, further, the cart controller communicates
with both the workstation controller and the warehouse controller.

Actor model Manufacturing_System is included in system class System_-
Manager, as shown in Figure 7.2. This class contains transitions which
generate actors as well as associations between actors.

Actor model Manufacturing_System is very general, since it can represent a cell including a variable number of workstations. However, if it is
necessary to consider a cell that is made up of a given number, say four,
of workstations, a more specific representation which focuses on instances
rather than on classes is easier to manage and to understand.

When we want to build an instance-oriented model, we can define an
actor that includes as many actors as required. In the above-mentioned
case of a cell with four workstations, we can define a system actor that
includes four instances of class Workstation_Controller and four instances
of class Workstation_Machinery; then we connect these instances by means

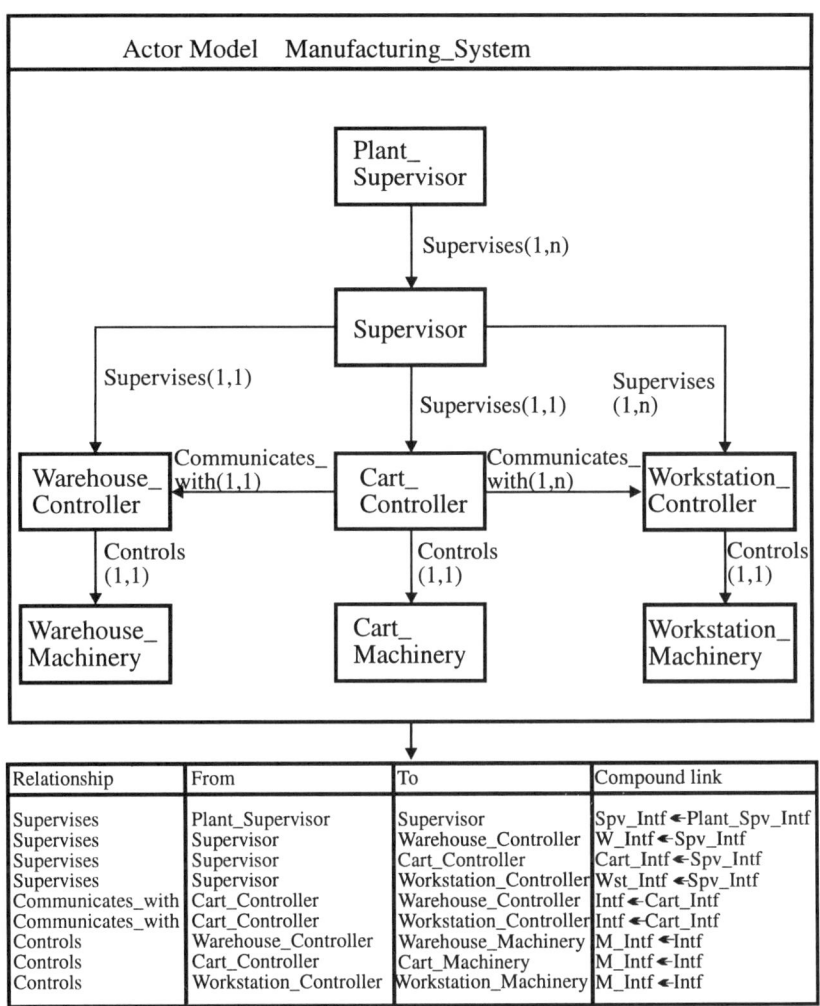

Figure 7.1 *The actor model of the manufacturing system*

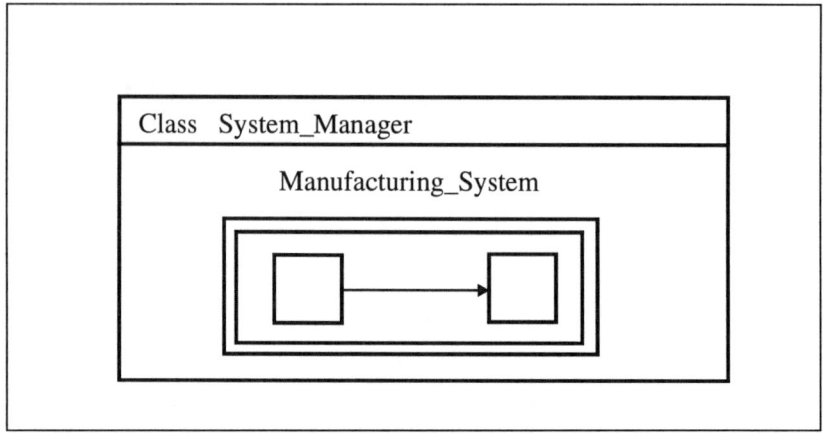

Figure 7.2 *A class that includes an actor model*

of appropriate compound links. However, doing it in such a way, we do not emphasize that what we are actually building is an instance (i.e. a particular case) of an actor model. On the other hand, if a statical collection of actors is acknowledged as an instance of an actor model, some checks can automatically be performed to ensure consistency and completeness: for example, the number of associations between actors can be checked against the relationships defined in the actor model. Further, an association between actors can be interpreted as a compound link because it is an instance of a relationship defined in the actor model and such relationships stand for compound links.

Therefore, we introduce a new representation, which is based on instances but implies the existence of an 'underlying' actor model; it is called an actor diagram and can directly be included in an actor, as shown in Figure 7.3.

The actor diagram shown in Figure 7.3 refers to a cell containing four workstations.

An actor diagram is an instance of an actor model, while each actor is an instance of a class defined in the actor model and each association between actors is an instance of a relationship defined in the actor model (thus each association is interpreted as a compound link). An association between actors is labeled with the name of the relationship of which it is an instance. If there is only one relationship in the actor model between a given pair of classes, then the labels of the corresponding associations in the actor diagram can be omitted, since the relationship implied by such associations can be identified unambiguously.

In the actor diagram given in Figure 7.3, for the sake of simplicity, only the names of the objects are shown. Their corresponding classes are provided in a separate table.

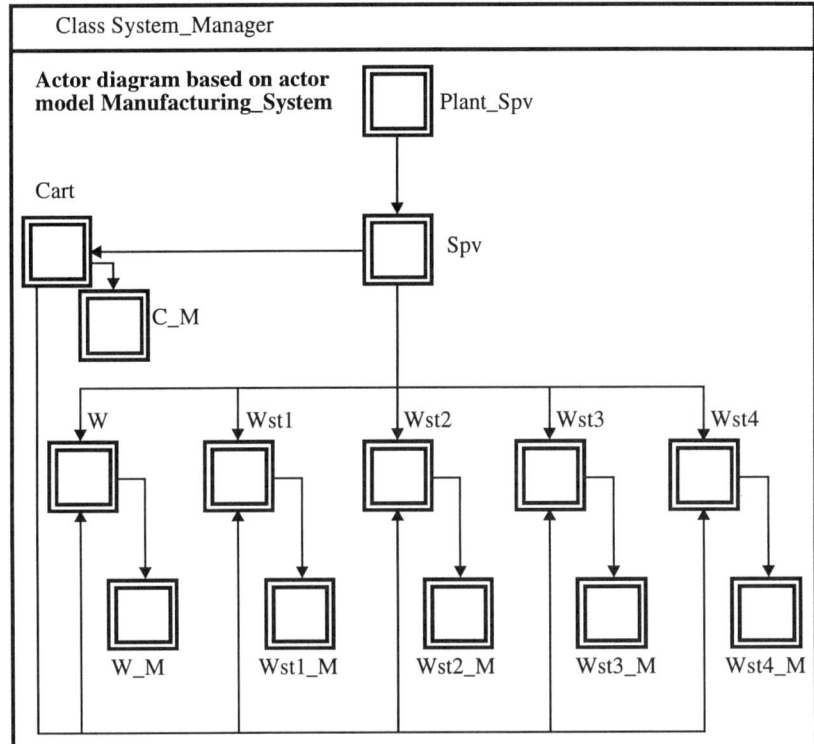

Actors	Classes
Plant_Spv	Plant_Supervisor
Spv	Supervisor
W	Warehouse_Controller
Cart	Cart_Controller
Wst1,Wst2,Wst3,Wst4	Workstation_Controller
W_M	Warehouse_Machinery
C_M	Cart_Machinery
Wst1_M,Wst2_M,Wst3_M,Wst4_M	Workstation_Machinery

Figure 7.3 *A class that includes an actor diagram*

7.1.1 Actors and object models

When an actor has to manage a complex information structure, it includes an object model, so the Protob net expresses the actor's behavior, while the object model represents a global information structure which is visible to all the transitions of the net.

The cell supervisor is an example of an actor that includes an object model, as shown in Figure 7.4.

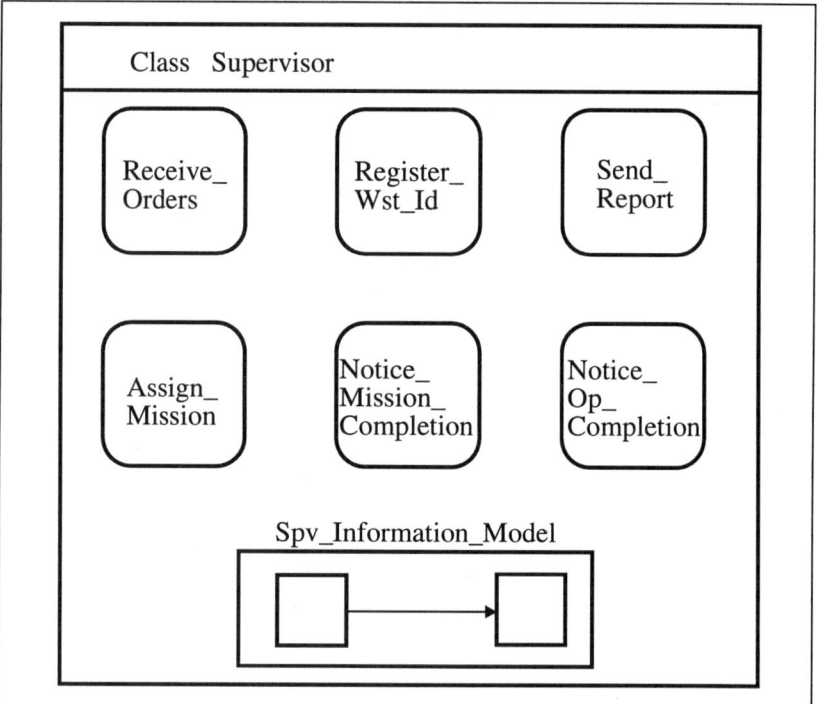

Figure 7.4 *The main view of class Supervisor*

An actor which includes an object model can take advantage of it in two ways:

1. Its transitions can include Quid statements in order to generate or cancel objects or associations as well as to navigate the underlying object graph. This will be illustrated later in this section.

2. Some tokens can be given the meaning of handles to objects in the object graph. This is done in the following way: if there are places in the net whose type name is identical to the name of a class defined in the object model, then the tokens contained in such places are assumed to be handles to objects belonging to that class. In many cases, the presence,

in a given place, of a token which is a handle to an object indicates that the object is in a particular state. Therefore, the states of objects can effectively be shown using places without it being necessary to add state attributes to the corresponding classes.

Object model Spv_Information_Model is presented in Figure 7.5; it is similar to the Entity-Relationship model illustrated in Figures 2.16 and 2.17.

The behavior of class Supervisor is described in six views, given in Figures 7.6 and 7.7, which contain all the features introduced in Chapters 2 and 3. However, for the sake of simplicity, many token types have been omitted.

Places Idle, Working and Finished contain tokens that are handles to the objects of class Workstation and indicate the states of these objects. Likewise, places M1, M2 and M3 contain tokens that are handles to objects of classes Mission_1, Mission_2 and Mission_3, respectively.

A short description of the views is given below.

View Receive_Orders

Initially, the cell supervisor waits for orders to be received from the plant supervisor. This is indicated by the initial token present in place Receiving_-Orders.

When the supervisor receives an order, i.e. it receives a token at input place Prod_Order, it generates an object of class Order and associates it with the corresponding part type. It is assumed that, initially, the object graph contains static information (the information that does not depend on production orders), such as part types, operations and workstations, as well as their appropriate associations.

After command Start has been received by the supervisor, missions can be performed, so a token is put into place Mission_Enabled. That token triggers the choice of the first mission to be performed.

View Register_Wst_Id

The supervisor needs to communicate with several workstations, whose addresses are not known in advance. Therefore, initially, each workstation informs the supervisor of its existence by sending it a token. When the supervisor receives such a token, at input place Wst_Id, it copies the address of the workstation into a field of the corresponding object in the object graph, then puts a token, which contains the handle to that object, into place Idle. In fact, all workstations are assumed to be initially idle.

View Notice_Op_Completion

When the supervisor receives a token at input place Op_Done, this means that a workstation has finished working on a part. Therefore, the token

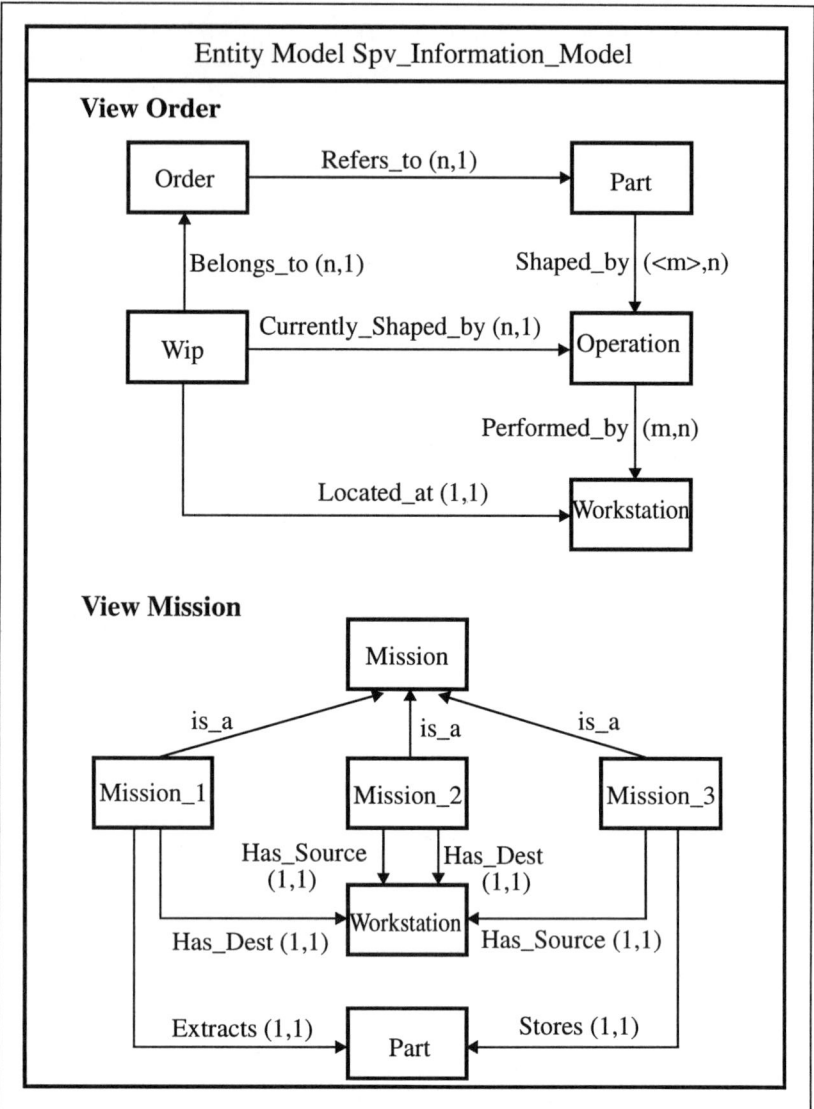

Figure 7.5 *The object model included in the supervisor*

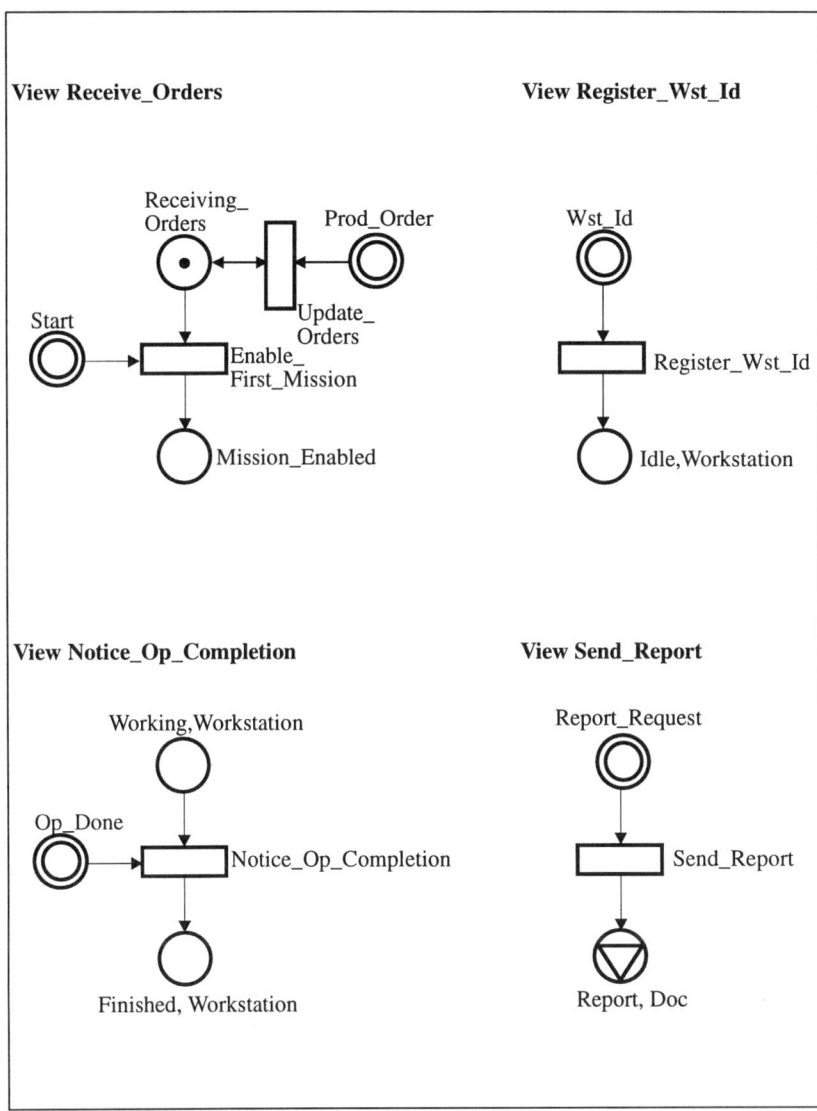

Figure 7.6 *The views of class Supervisor*

that contains the handle to the object corresponding to that workstation
is moved from place Working to place Finished.

View Send_Report

On receiving a request from the plant supervisor, the cell supervisor returns
a report. The action of transition Send_Report navigates the object graph in
order to collect information concerning the work in process, then prepares
the report and sends it to the plant supervisor.

View Assign_Mission

The supervisor manages three missions and they are started by the transitions contained in this view. These transitions send suitable commands
to the cart from output place Cart_Cmd, to workstations from derouting
place Wst_Cmd and to the warehouse from output places Out_Cmd and
In_Cmd.

In order to keep information on the current mission, the supervisor generates an object of the appropriate subclass of class Mission and puts a
token containing the handle to this object into one of three places, i.e. M1,
M2 or M3. The choice of the next mission to be performed is discussed
below.

1. Mission_1 consists in moving a raw part from the warehouse to a work-
    station that is able to perform the first operation on the part. It can
    be started if there is an order which has not yet been completed and if
    place Idle contains a token representing a workstation which is able to
    perform the first operation on a raw part belonging to that order.

2. Mission_2 consists in moving a part on completion from a workstation
    to another that is able to perform the next operation on the part. It
    can be started if there is a token in place Finished, which represents
    a workstation that has finished working on a part, p, and if place Idle
    contains a token representing an idle workstation that is able to perform
    the next operation on p. The predicate and the action of transition
    Issue_Mission_2 are illustrated later in this section.

3. Mission_3 consists in moving a finished part from the workstation that
    has performed the last operation on it to the warehouse. It can be started
    if there is a token in place Finished, denoting a workstation that has
    performed the last operation on a part.

The warehouse is assumed to put no additional constraints on the model,
therefore raw parts are available in the quantity that is needed to fulfill
production orders and there is enough room to contain all the finished
parts.

Transitions in this view have different priorities: Issue_Mission_2 has the
highest priority, while Issue_Mission_3 has the lowest one. The reason for

View Assign_Mission

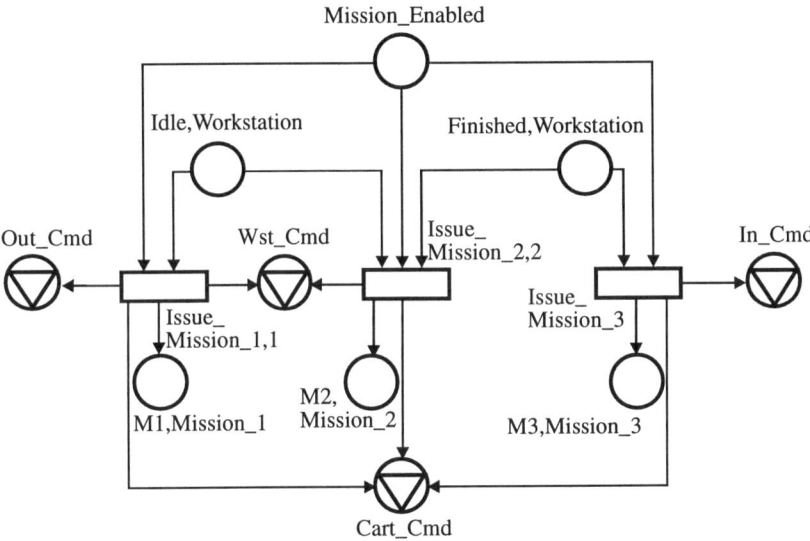

View Notice_Mission_Completion

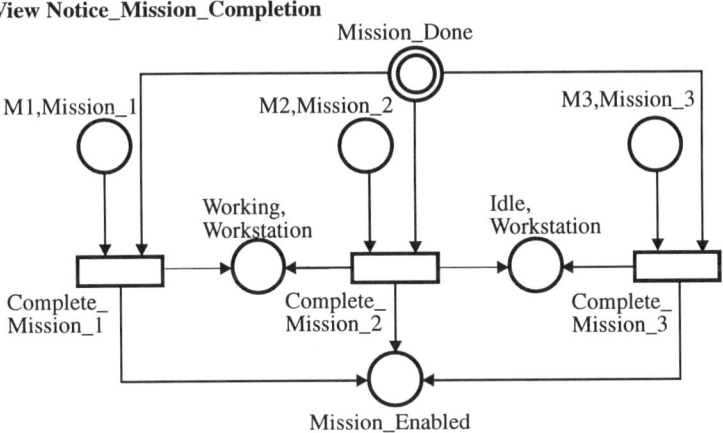

Figure 7.7 *The views of class Supervisor (continued)*

this is to maximize the utilization of workstations, thus the transitions that feed workstations are the most important ones.

View Notice_Mission_Completion

When the cart completes a mission, it informs the supervisor, which receives a token at input place Mission_Done. Then the supervisor updates the states of the objects (of class Workstation) that have been involved in the mission. The update depends on the type of the mission, which is indicated by the token being present in place M1, M2 or M3. Specifically,

1. transition Complete_Mission_1 puts the workstation that has received the raw part into state Working;

2. transition Complete_Mission_2 puts the workstations that were in states Finished and Idle when the mission was started into states Idle and Working, respectively;

3. transition Complete_Mission_3 puts the workstation that has performed the last operation on the finished part into state Idle.

Each of the above transitions puts a token into place Mission_Enabled so that a new mission can be started.

7.1.2 Navigational statements in transitions

Transitions, especially those whose input or output tokens contain handles to objects, can include Quid statements, so it is possible to navigate and act on the underlying object graph (represented by the object model).

As an example, attention is focused on transition Issue_Mission_2. At a certain instant, the object graph is assumed to be the one depicted in Figure 7.8.

At that time, places Finished and Idle contain one token each: the token in place Finished refers to workstation Wst4 and shows that Wst4 has finished working on a part, while the token in place Idle refers to workstation Wst1 and thus indicates that Wst1 is idle. Now, if a token is put into place Mission_Enabled, transition Issue_Mission_2 is allowed to fire only if Wst1 is able to perform the next operation on the part that is located at Wst4. How can this condition be checked?

A predicate that checks the condition by navigating the object graph can be associated with Issue_Mission_2; it is illustrated below.

```
var W: handle(Wip); O,Q: handle(Operation);
    B: handle(Workstation); P: handle(Part);
...
Predicate := false;
Qd_apply Workstation:Finished
//Wip W  do
```

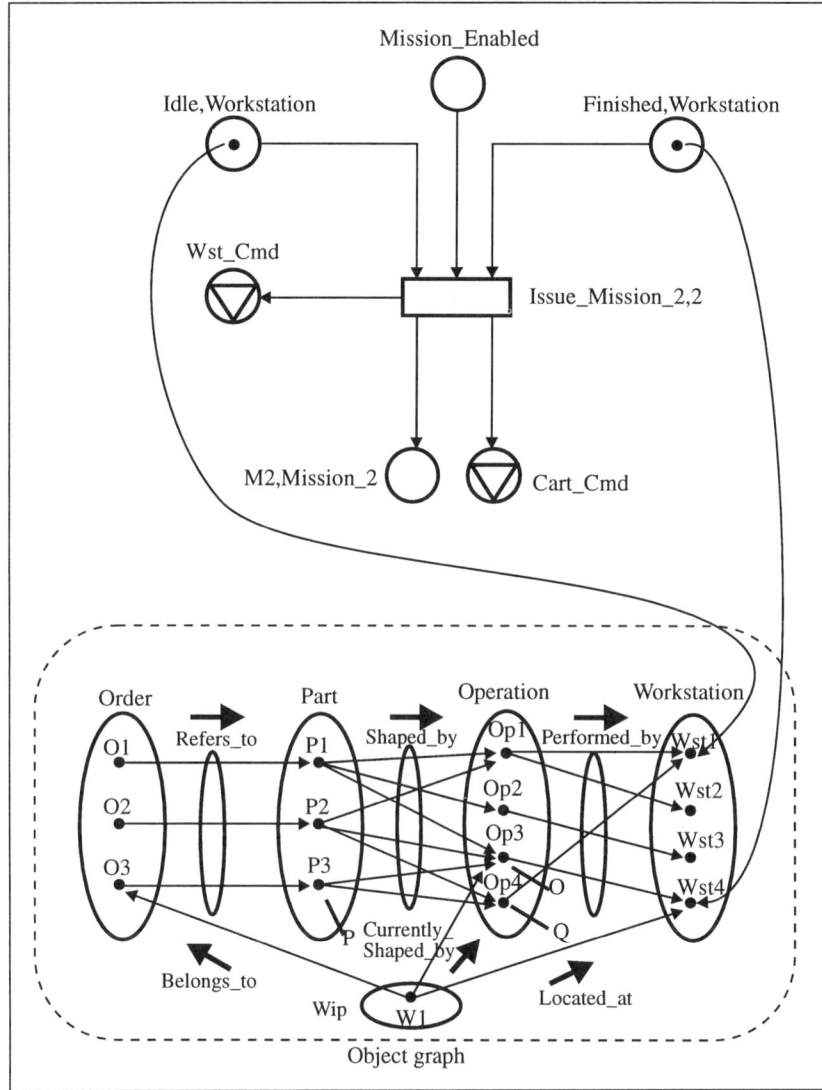

Figure 7.8 *A transition that acts on an object graph*

```
  Qd_apply Wip:W//Operation O Qd_end;
//Order//Part P
/Shaped_by next(O)
/Operation Q//Workstation B
where {B=Idle}
do {Predicate := true;}
Qd_end;
```

A special boolean variable (Predicate) must be used to determine the result of a predicate when it is not given, as in this case, by the evaluation of a logical expression, but it depends on the execution of an algorithm.

It should be noted that handles Finished and Idle correspond to the input tokens (located at the homonimous places) of the transition and, as such, they must not be declared. Navigation starts from the workstation that, being referred to by handle Finished, has finished working on a part. Then, the related object of class Wip, which will be referred to by handle W, is reached.

The internal navigational statement has the purpose of identifying the operation that has just been performed on the part denoted by W and of making a reference to this operation available for later use. Handle O keeps such a reference.

The path that starts from W and follows associations Belongs_to and Refers_to gives the handle (P) to the type of the part referred to by W. The paths that start from P and follow all the related Shaped_by associations identify all the operations to be performed on the part type denoted by P. However, interest is concentrated on the next operation for the particular part which is present at the workstation referred to by handle Finished. How can that operation be found? The question can easily be answered if the ordering constraint of relationship Shaped_by is exploited as follows: if operator **next** is applied to the Shaped_by association from P to O, the Shaped_by association, if there is one, that follows the one from P to O is obtained and, consequently, the operation that follows O can be obtained as well. Such an operation will be referred to by handle Q.

If navigation is continued from Q and all the Performed_by associations are followed, each workstation, B, that is able to perform the next operation on the part located at the workstation referred to by Finished can be reached. Handle B scans each such workstation and, if it turns out to be equal to handle Idle (i.e. handles B and Idle refer to the same object), then an idle workstation that can be given as the destination to mission 2 has been found.

The action of transition Issue_Mission_2 consists in sending suitable commands to both the cart and the destination workstation and in registering the information on the mission in an object of class Mission_2. Such an object will be referred to by the output token to be put into place M2 and is generated by the Quid statements:

```
Qd_new Mission_2 M2;
Qd_new Has_Source M2 -> Finished;
Qd_new Has_Dest   M2 -> Idle;
```

The first statement generates an object of class Mission_2 and returns a handle to it in the token delivered to output place M2. The other statements connect that object both to the workstation (referred to by handle Finished) which is the source of the mission and to the workstation (referred to by handle Idle) which is the destination of the mission.

7.2 Modeling simple behaviors

In this section, attention is focused on systems made up of components which can be represented by actors.

An actor can perform actions, take decisions and react to other actors on the basis of a behavior which is expressed by a Protob net.

Since the simplest behavioral form is the one based on the notions of state and state transition, we assume that simple actors have a behavior which can be described by a state-transition diagram or by a state machine. The former has been presented in Chapter 2, while the latter has been illustrated in Chapter 4.

Simple actors can be combined to form compound actors: such a combination, as will be shown in the next section, is based on standard patterns of interactions between actors.

The case study presented below will be used to illustrate and classify the behavior of simple actors.

Requirements of a logistic system

A logistic system has the responsibility of procuring, storing and transporting products or components. The system being considered includes a warehouse and 4 carts. The warehouse has 20 slots and 4 access points, each of which is assigned to a different cart. Slots are numbered from 1 to 20 and can be empty or full.

Carts perform missions repeatedly. During a mission, a cart moves from its rest point to its access point near the warehouse, then requests to be loaded or to be unloaded, indicating the slot, say s, which is involved in the operation. In the case of load, the part contained in s will be moved onto the cart and this slot will become empty. In the case of unload, the part carried by the cart will be moved into s and this slot will become full. For the sake of simplicity, it is assumed that the cart is empty when it requests to be loaded and that it is full when it requests to be unloaded. After issuing the request, the cart waits for the reply.

The warehouse performs the operation requested by a cart, but a failure can occur. In fact, if the cart tries either to get a part from an empty slot or to deliver a part to a full slot, the warehouse signals an error to the cart; otherwise, the warehouse returns a confirmation.

If the operation has been performed successfully, the cart goes back to the rest point and, after some time, it will start a new mission. Otherwise, the cart repeats the same request, indicating a different slot. Retrying is allowed until three consecutive failures occur, then the cart goes back to its rest point.

Each cart takes 10 time units to move from its rest point to the warehouse or vice versa.

For the sake of simplicity, a cart selects the slot and the operation (load or unload) to be performed by calling two random functions (respectively F1 and F2). Counters of successful and unsuccessful missions must be kept for each cart.

The warehouse is served by one robot, which carries out one operation at a time and, in the case of several pending requests, carts asking to be unloaded have priority over the others. Requests of the same kind are processed on a FCFS basis. The time to extract a part from a slot and to load the cart with the part as well as the time to unload a cart and to store the part into a slot are random values provided by a random function (G1).

Initially, some slots of the warehouse are empty and the others are full: the initial state of each slot is determined by calling a random function (F3). The carts are located at their rest points.

Building simple actors

It is easy to recognize that the warehouse and the carts are the actors of the above case study, since they are the only elements of the problem domain that exhibit a behavior. Slots are features of the warehouse, while requests and replies are communication items between the carts and the warehouse.

Each cart is a simple actor as it exhibits a state-based behavior which is expressed by the state-transition diagram shown in Figure 7.9. The cart has five states: Idle, Ready, Waiting, W2 and W3. The formalism is similar to the one presented in Chapter 2, except for states which are drawn as circles.

The initial state of a cart is Idle, because, initially, each cart is idle at its rest point. Then, the cart moves to its access point near the warehouse and, when it arrives there, it is ready to issue a request. Therefore, the state that follows Idle is Ready. The transition from Idle to Ready is unconditional, because there is no event that triggers it. The action of that transition is called Move_to_Access_Point to show that it involves moving the cart to its access point near the warehouse.

When the cart is ready, it issues a request and waits for a reply. Two

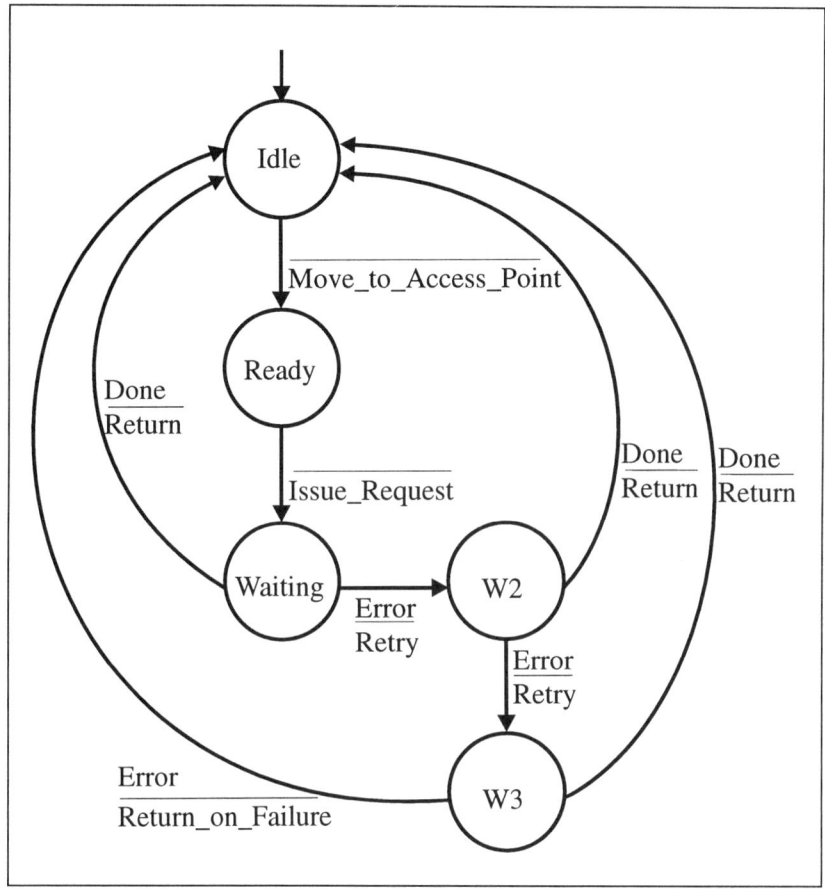

Figure 7.9 *The state-transition diagram of the cart*

possible replies can be received from the warehouse: Done, if the operation has been successful, Error, otherwise. In the first case, the cart goes back to its rest point, as shown by action Return (which is triggered by event Done). Action Return involves moving the cart as well as incrementing the counter of successful missions.

If the first request fails, another request is issued, as shown by the transition from state Waiting to state W2. This transition is triggered by event Error and its action is called Retry to indicate that a new request is sent to the warehouse.

If the second request fails, too, the third request is issued and the new state is W3. Should the third request fail too, the whole mission fails, thus the cart goes back to its rest point, as indicated by the transition (triggered by event Error) from state W3 to state Idle. Its action, Return_on_Failure, involves moving the cart as well as incrementing the counter of unsuccessful missions.

The actions that move the cart, i.e. Move_to_Access_Point, Return and Return_on_Failure, have a non-negligible duration (equal to 10 time units, as indicated in the requirements), while the others are assumed to be immediate, as, basically, they are computer communications between the cart control computer and the warehouse control computer.

The state-transition diagram given in Figure 7.9 can be represented by the Protob net shown in Figure 7.10, which contains all the details mentioned in the requirements.

The major difference between these models is the number of states, which is reduced to three in the Protob net. In fact, on receiving an error from the warehouse, the cart uses the counter of unsuccessful requests (i.e. local variable E_Counter) to select which transition, Retry or Return_on_Failure, has to fire. This counter is incremented at each retrial.

The Protob net includes three local variables: the counter of failed requests (E_Counter), the counter of failed missions (Failures), and the counter of successful missions (M_Done).

A request contains two fields, Dep_Flag and Slot. The former contains a boolean value indicating whether the cart has to be unloaded or loaded (true stands for unloading), while the latter denotes the slot involved in the operation.

The features of a Protob net which describes the behavior of a simple actor are illustrated below.

1. There are some places, e.g. Ready, Waiting and Idle, which represent the states of the actor. Such places are called state places and the tokens contained in them are called state tokens.

2. The transitions of the net that correspond to the state transitions of the equivalent state-transition diagram are called state transitions. Usually they have exactly one state place among their input places and exactly one state place among their output places; however, in some cases, either the input state place or the output state place (but not both) can be missing.

3. A place that is not a state place can be classified as follows:

   (a) It is an input-event place if its tokens represent input events, and, for this reason, they cause state transitions. Input-event places, e.g. Done and Error, have only outgoing arcs (at least one), which are directed to state transitions.

   (b) It is an output-event place if its tokens represent output events, and thus they are produced by state transitions. Output-event places, e.g. Request, have only incoming arcs (at least one), which originate from state transitions.

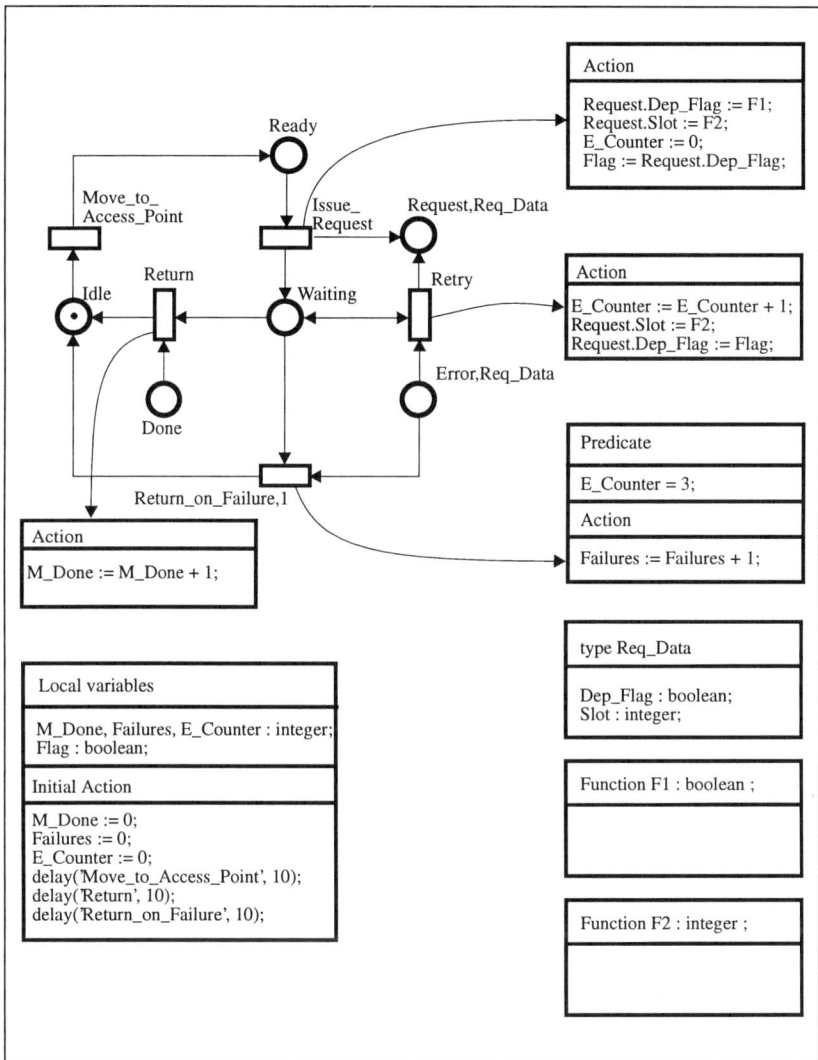

Figure 7.10 *The state net of a single cart*

(c) It is a resource place if its tokens represent resources: a resource is an item that a state transition takes from a place, p, possibly modifies and then returns to p. A resource place, e.g. Slots in Figure 7.12, is an output place for a state transition as well as an input place for the same transition.

4. In addition to state transitions, there are transitions that consume input events. Such transitions, which are called event-consuming transitions,

have the purpose of consuming events which cannot or must not cause state transitions. An event-consuming transition must have exactly one input-event place; further, it can be connected to resource places and can deliver tokens to output-event places.

A Protob net exhibiting the above features is called a state net. If all the places that are not state places and all the event-consuming transitions as well as all the outgoing and incoming arcs of such places and transitions are dropped, then a state net can be reduced to a state machine (defined in Chapter 4).

A state net can easily be transformed into an object (and, by extension, into a class), if the input-event and output-event places are converted into input ports and output ports, respectively.

When several actors exhibiting the same state-based behavior have to be modeled, two different approaches can be followed.

1. A class that models only one actor can be built and then as many actors of this class as required by the system being considered will be generated. A state net is called a single-state net if, in every marking, all state places but one, which contains exactly one token, are empty.

2. A class, called a group class, which is able to model a group of similar actors, can be built. Such a class is described by a state net which is called a multiple-state net. In a multiple-state net, several tokens can be contained in state places, each token denoting the current state of one of several similar actors. Further, the number of state tokens and, consequently, the number of actors is constant, so actors are neither created nor destroyed.

A multiple-state net is shown in Figure 7.11.

Four tokens circulate in the net, each of them representing a cart. Type Cart defines the information associated with these tokens. It has four fields: Id, M_Done, Failures and E_Counter. Field Id identifies the cart, thus it contains an integer number ranging from 1 to 4. The other fields correspond to the local variables used in the net shown in Figure 7.10: in fact, the net given in Figure 7.11 manages several carts at a time, therefore such pieces of information must be associated with tokens.

The warehouse is modeled by the actor shown in Figure 7.12, which performs three actions: it fills a slot with the part taken from a cart, it loads a cart with the part taken from a slot, or it signals an error when the request is not feasible. Such actions are serialized because there is only one robot and, further, the action of filling a slot has priority over the one of loading a cart.

The net presented in Figure 7.12 is a state net, but, unlike the cart model that has a unique interpretation, it can be given three different interpretations, which are listed below.

1. Place Robot is the only place state, while place Slots is a resource place

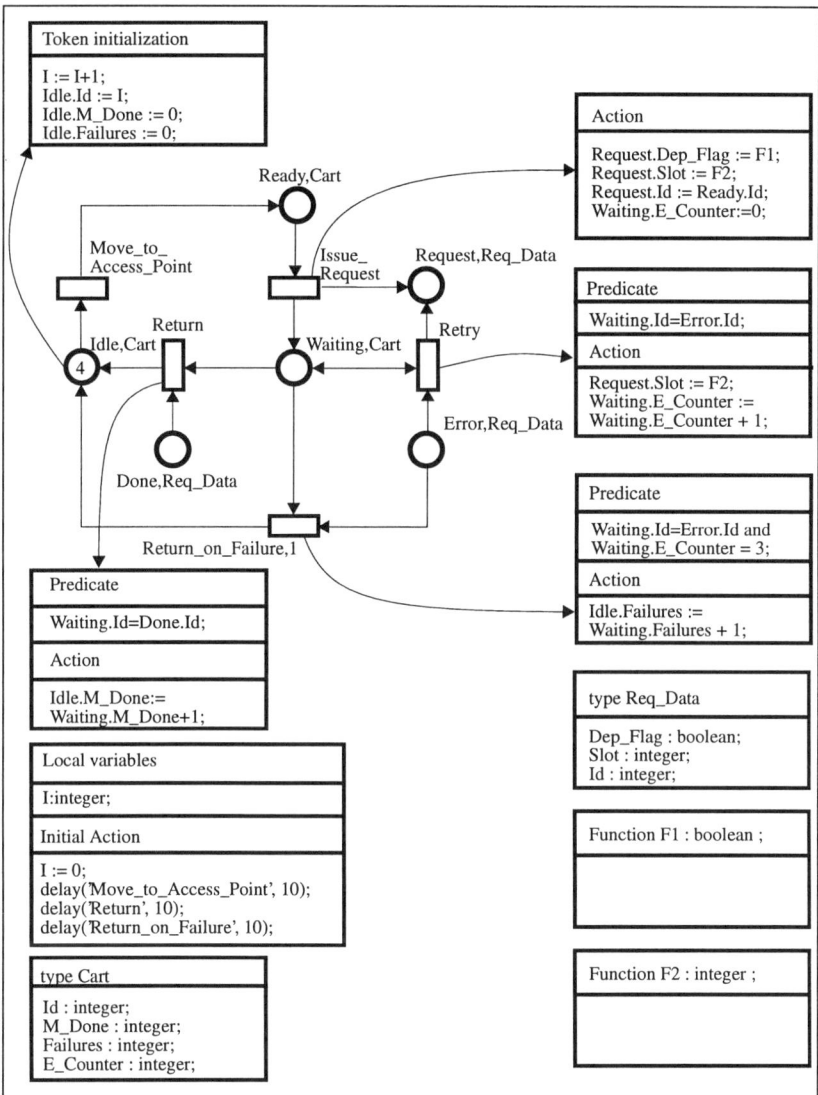

Figure 7.11 *The multiple-state net that handles four carts*

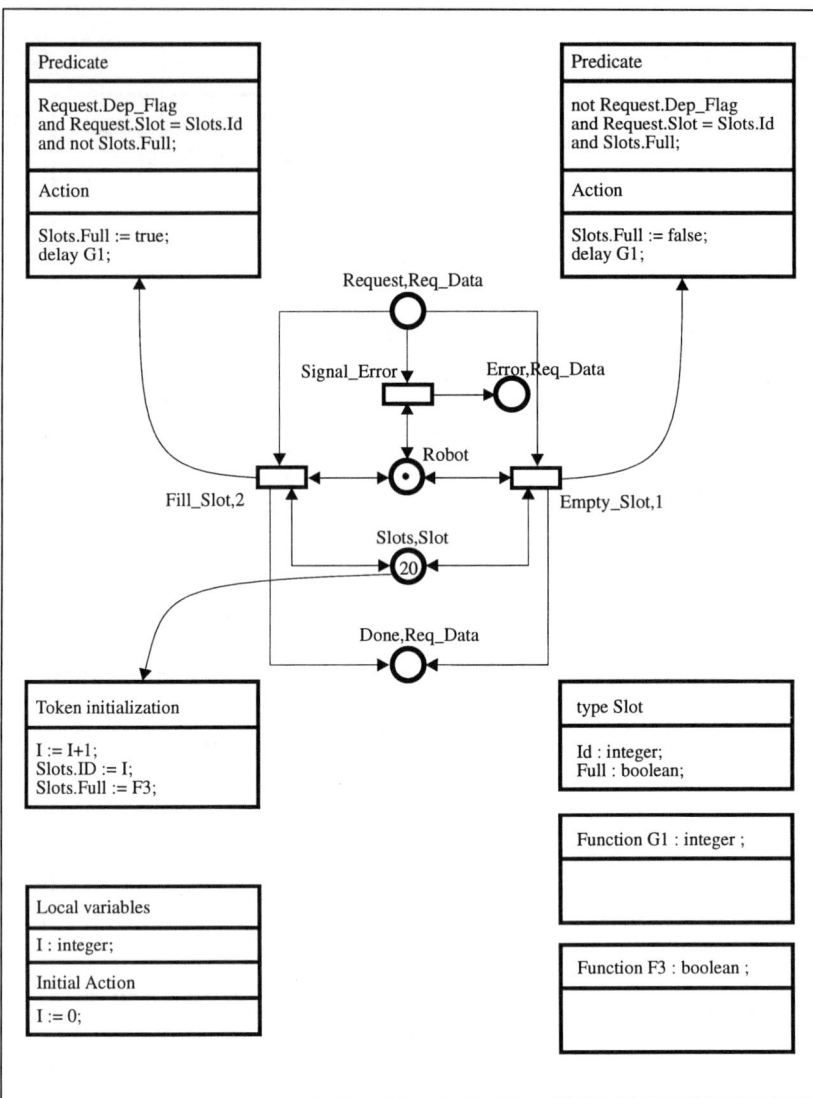

Figure 7.12 *The state net of the warehouse*

and the other places are event places. There is only one state token, which indicates that the actor is idle when it is in place Robot. When the state token is not in place Robot, one of three transitions is firing.

(a) Transition Fill_Slot fires when the request asks for a deposit and the slot indicated by the cart is empty; its action changes the slot state from empty to full. Each token in place Slots has two attributes: the identifier of the slot (field Id) and the state of the slot (field Full). Field Id contains an integer number in the range from 1 to 20, field Full is boolean. Fill_Slot has a higher priority than the two transitions considered below, according to the requirements.

(b) Transition Empty_Slot fires when a part must be delivered to a cart and the slot indicated by the cart is full; its action changes the slot state from full to empty, i.e. it changes the value of field Full from true to false.

(c) Transition Signal_Error fires when the request cannot be satisfied; it has no predicate, because it is executed only when no other transition can fire.

Transitions Fill_Slot and Empty_Slot have a non-negligible duration, which is determined by a random function (G1) according to the requirements.

2. Place Slots is the only state place, while place Robot is a resource place and the other places are event places. Transition Signal_Error is an event-consuming transition, while the other transitions are state transitions. In this case, the net is a multiple-state one, because place Slots contains 20 tokens.

3. Places Request, Done and Error are state places, while places Robot and Slots are resource places. In this case, the number of tokens in state places is not constant; a state net with this feature is called a variable-state net. In a variable-state net, there is generally only one state place, called the initial-state place, which receives tokens from the outside, while there can be several state places, called final-state places, which send tokens to the outside. If a variable-state net is turned into an object, the initial-state place is transformed into an input port, while the final-state places are converted into output ports. State tokens in Figure 7.12 represent requests from the instant they enter the actor (at place Request) to the instant they exit the actor (at place Done or at place Error). A variable-state net is equivalent to the network approach (Fishman, 1973) adopted in discrete event simulation languages.

The actors modeling the carts and the warehouse can be put together to give rise to different Protob models, as discussed below.

1. They can be combined to form one Protob class. Then, the nets shown

in Figures 7.11 and 7.12 become the views of this class; places Request, Done and Error are common to both views. The resulting Protob model consists of one object belonging to that class.

2. They can be turned into separate classes (e.g. Carts and Warehouse) and places Request, Done and Error become the interface places of these classes. The resulting Protob model consists of two objects, one belonging to class Carts (whose behavior is depicted in Figure 7.11) and the other to class Warehouse, and of three links between them.

3. If each cart is modeled by a different actor on the basis of the state net shown in Figure 7.10, then the actors presented in Figures 7.10 and 7.12 give rise to two classes (e.g. Cart and Warehouse) with the same interface ports as the classes in the case considered above. However, the resulting Protob model is made up of four objects belonging to class Cart (one for each cart) and one object belonging to class Warehouse. In this case, a client-server form of interaction, as shown in Chapter 5, takes place between the cart objects and the warehouse object, so the model of the warehouse has to be extended in order to handle the addresses of the cart objects.

7.3 Combining behaviors

Simple actors are described by (single, multiple or variable) state nets. Two or more simple actors can be combined to give rise to a compound actor and the resulting net is no longer a state net. Compound actors can be combined as well, in the same way as simple actors can.

The composition of actors is based on some standard forms of interaction, which are illustrated in Figure 7.13. They involve either pairs of places or pairs of transitions; a dashed arc indicates the components of a pair.

1. **One-way communication.** There are two actors, A1 and A2, and two places, P and Q, that belong to A1 and A2, respectively. A1 puts tokens into P, while A2 gets tokens from Q and the tokens that A1 puts into P are those that A2 gets from Q. P is an output-event place or a final-state place of A1, while Q is an input-event place or the initial-state place of A2.

2. **Two-way communication.** It is given by two one-way communications in opposite directions. There are two actors, A1 and A2, and two pairs of places, P1 and P2 which belong to A1 and Q1 and Q2 which belong to A2. A1 puts tokens into P1, then waits for replies to be received at P2. A2 gets tokens from Q1, processes them and then replies by putting tokens into Q2. The tokens that A1 puts into P1 are those that A2 gets from Q1, while the tokens that A2 puts into Q2 are those that A1 gets from P2. A client-server interaction is an example of a two-way communication. The

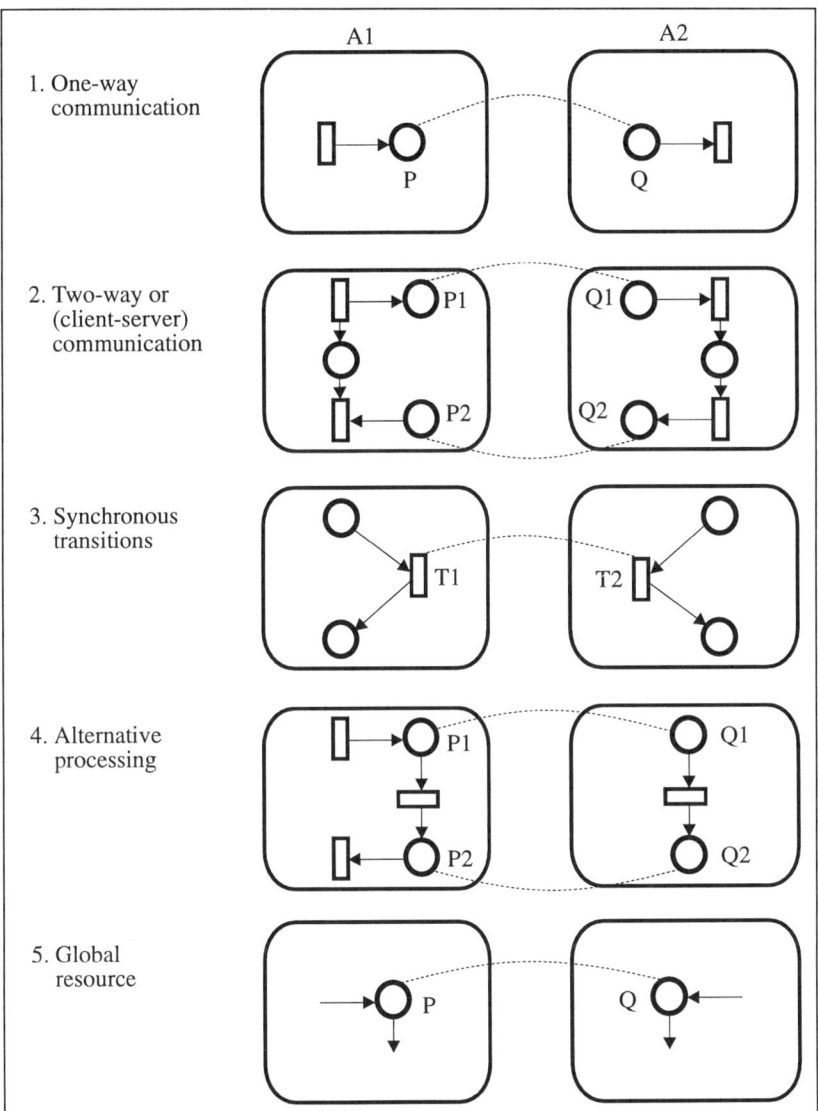

Figure 7.13 *The standard forms of interaction between actors*

interaction between a cart and the warehouse, in the example presented in the previous section, is a two-way communication.

3. **Synchronous transitions**. Two actors change state simultaneously when they have two *synchronous* state-transitions. Two transitions, T1 and T2, belonging to different actors are called synchronous if they are allowed to fire only when both are enabled. Therefore, when T1 and T2 fire, they fire simultaneously.

4. **Alternative processing**. There are two actors, A1 and A2, and two pairs of places, P1 and P2 which belong to A1 and Q1 and Q2 which belong to A2. When a state token reaches P1 in A1, it can either continue to follow a path (that includes P2) in A1 or it can start a new path from Q1 in A2. Eventually, a one-way communication from A2 to A1 puts the token back into P2, where the path that was previously interrupted at P1 is resumed. For example, this interaction takes place when A1 represents the normal operation of a subsystem and A2 models the handling of some failure which can happen when the state of the subsystem is P1.

5. **Global resource**. There are two actors, A1 and A2, and two resource places, P and Q, that belong to A1 and A2, respectively. The tokens in P and Q are common to both actors, so P and Q are actually the same place.

When two simple actors are merged into one compound actor, the resulting Protob class has two views which correspond to the nets of the component actors. If the interaction between the component actors involves a pair of places, such places become the same logical place which is common to both views; however, if the interaction involves a pair of synchronous transitions, they are merged into one transition which appears in only one view.

All interactions are allowed when actors are views of the same Protob class. Only the first two, namely one-way communication and two-way communication, are allowed when actors give rise to separate classes; in this case, the places involved in the communication are turned into ports.

The actors presented in Figure 7.14 correspond to the views of the cell supervisor given in Figures 7.4, 7.6 and 7.7 (except for view Send_Report, which, for the sake of simplicity, has been omitted), and all the common places are shown. All the interactions between these actors are one-way communications.

Some of the simple actors corresponding to those views are considered briefly below.

In actor (or view) Receive_Orders, Receiving_Orders is the only state place, while Prod_Order and Start are input-event places and Mission_-Enabled is an output-event place.

In actor (or view) Register_Wst_Id, Wst_Id acts as the initial-state place and Idle is a final-state place.

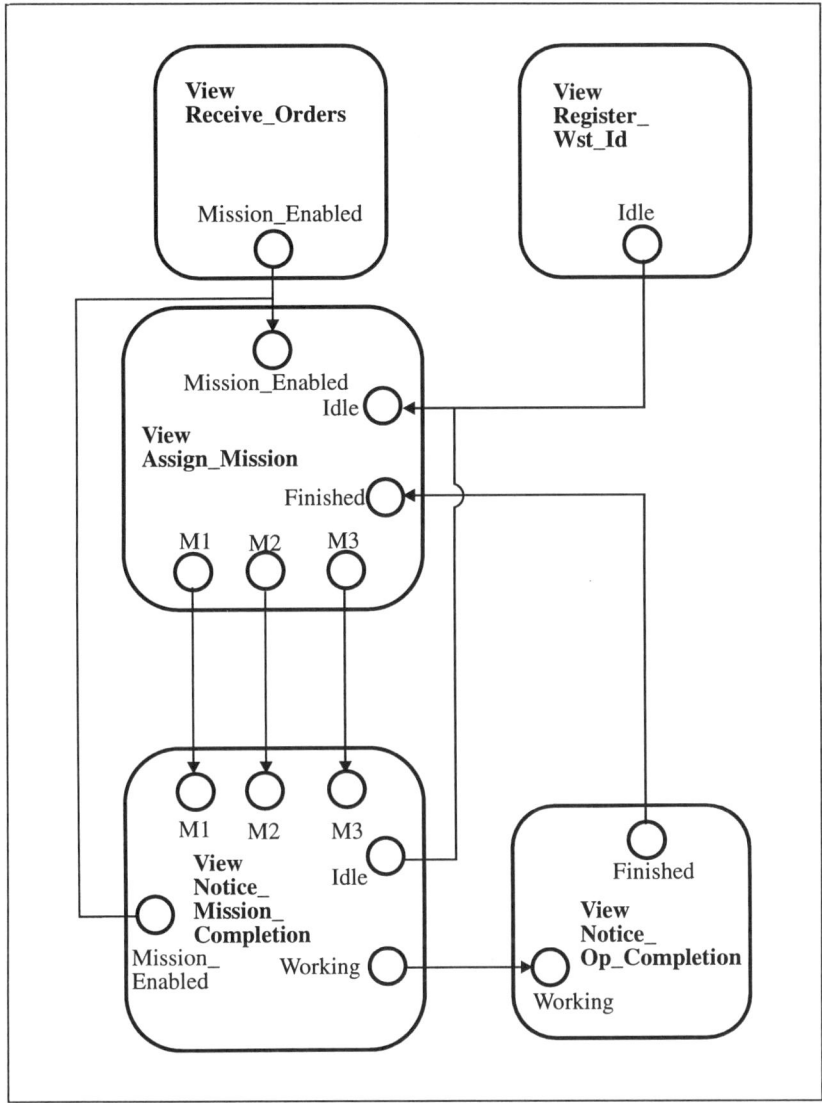

Figure 7.14 *The actors forming the cell supervisor*

In actor (or view) Assign_Mission, Mission_Enabled is the initial-state place and M1, M2 and M3 are final-state places, while Idle and Finished are input-event places and Out_Cmd, In_Cmd and Wst_Cmd are output-event places.

In actor (or view) Notice_Mission_Completion, Mission_Done is the initial-state place and Mission_Enabled is the final-state place, while M1, M2 and M3 are input-event places and Working and Idle are output-event places.

7.3.1 An example of synchronous transitions

The example presented below illustrates the interaction based on synchronous transitions.

Requirements of a production system

A production system includes two workstations, A and B, a test site, T, a repair site, R, and a cart, C. All the machines, A, B, T and R, process only one part at a time. A and B perform some kind of machining; parts flow from A to B through T. There is no intermediate buffer between A and T, nor between T and B, so the part that has been machined by A waits at A until T is free and then it is moved to T. T performs a thorough testing on the part: if it is good it is sent to B (if B is not free, T holds the part until B is free), otherwise it is sent to R.

In front of R, a large buffer holds the parts to be repaired. After repairing a part, R puts it into a bin (X) which contains at most 40 parts; when X is full, R blocks.

A can take parts from two bins, X and IN; parts in X have priority over those in IN. IN contains raw parts; its capacity is 20 parts. When IN is empty, it is automatically replaced.

After machining a part, B delivers it to the cart (C). In fact, when there is a finished part in B and C is ready (i.e. it is near B), the part is moved onto C. Then, C goes to a warehouse, where the part is stored; after that, C comes back to B to take another part.

Initially, A, B, T, R and X are empty, IN is full and C is near B.

Model of the production system

It is easy to identify five major actors in the above-mentioned system, which correspond to the machines and to the cart. They have a state-based behavior, as shown in Figure 7.15.

A sixth actor (F) has been added: it has a very simple behavior, since it is in charge of replacing bin IN, when it is empty.

For the sake of simplicity, the place types as well as the predicates and actions of transitions have been omitted.

Actor A has three state places, Idle, Ready and Done, and Idle is the

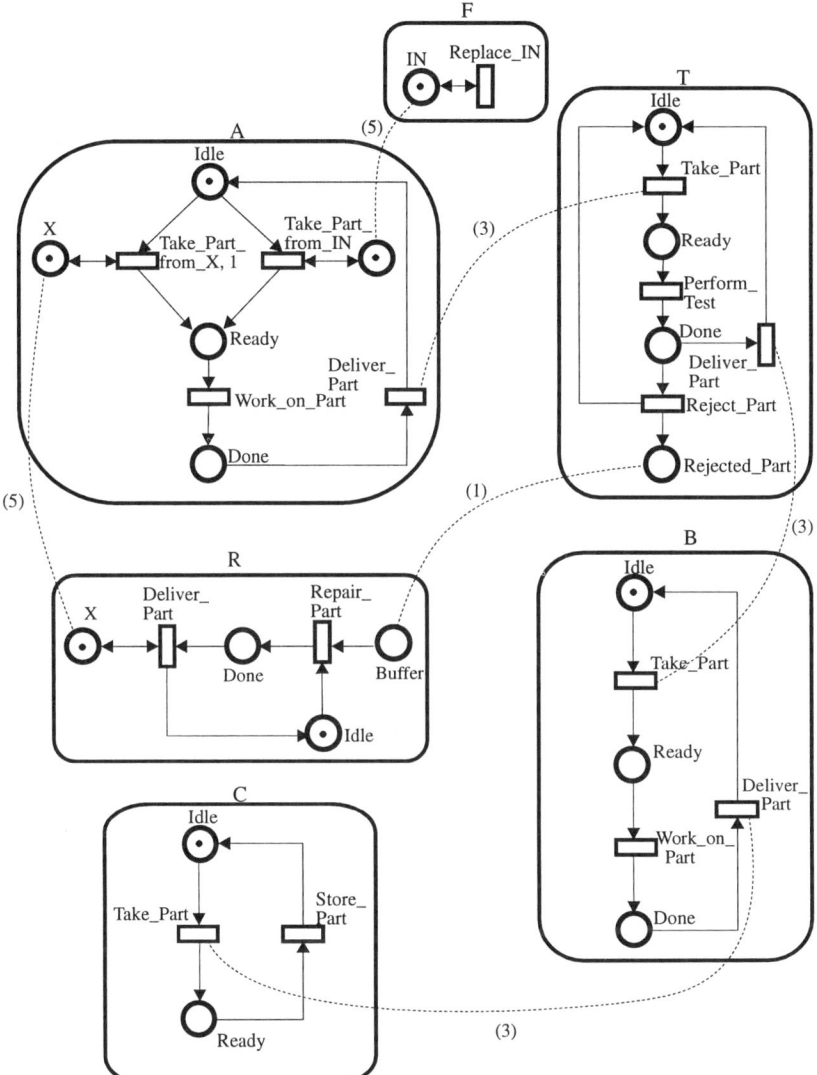

Figure 7.15 *The actors of the production system*

initial-state place. It becomes Ready after taking a part either from X or from IN; transition Take_Part_from_X has priority over transition Take_-Part_from_IN, according to the requirements. When the state is Ready, A starts machining the part, so transition Work_on_Part fires. The next state is Done: at this point, transition Deliver_Part fires only when transition Take_Part in actor T can fire as well, since these transitions are synchronous, as shown by the dashed arc in Figure 7.15. In fact, A goes back into state Idle only when T becomes ready, as the part processed by A must be carried to T before A can take the next part.

Actor T has three state places, just as A. When T is in state Done, either transition Deliver_Part or transition Reject_Part fires depending on the result of the test, which is represented by transition Perform_Test. It is assumed that the token in Done contains a boolean value, set by Perform_-Test, which indicates whether the test was successful or not. In the negative case, T becomes idle immediately, because the part is moved to a large buffer (there is no capacity constraint) in front of R. If the part is good, T becomes idle only when B becomes Ready. In fact, transition Deliver_Part of T and transition Take_Part of B are synchronous, as the part tested by T must be carried to B before T can accept a new part.

Actors B, C and R behave in a similar way, so they are not described. Transition Deliver_Part of R has a predicate that checks the number of parts contained in bin X, so that if X is full, Deliver_Part cannot fire and R blocks.

The token in place X has an integer value which represents the number of parts currently contained in bin X. Initially, that number is zero, then it is incremented by transition Deliver_Part of actor R and decremented by transition Take_Part_from_X of actor A.

Actor F consists of one transition, Replace_IN, which models the replacement of the bin of raw parts, when it is empty. The token in place IN, like the one contained in place X, has an integer value which represents the number of parts currently contained in bin IN. Initially, that number is 20, then it is decremented by transition Take_Part_from_IN of actor A. When it reaches 0, transition Replace_IN fires and sets the value to 20. In order to make the net associated with F a state net, it is necessary to introduce a state place that is both an input place and an output place of transition Replace_IN, since IN is a resource place for actor F. For the sake of simplicity, such a place has been omitted.

As regards the interactions between the actors shown in Figure 7.15, place X is a global resource between A and R and place IN is a global resource between A and F, while places Rejected_Part and Buffer implement a one-way communication between T and R. The other interactions are based on synchronous transitions. The number that appears on a dashed arc in Figure 7.15 indicates which kind of interaction takes place according to the classification given in Figure 7.13.

An example of a compound actor, which is obtained by merging actors B and C, is shown in Figure 7.16.

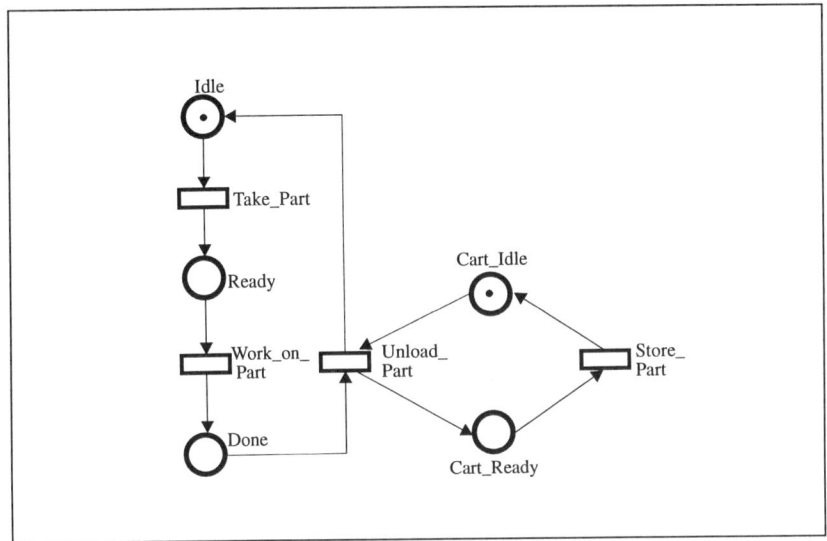

Figure 7.16 *A compound actor obtained by merging two simple actors*

Its behavior is thus described by a Protob net which is no longer a state net (in this case, it is a marked graph). When actors are merged, conflicts between the names of elements that come from different actors must be avoided. For example, the name (Idle) of the initial-state place of actor C has been changed to Cart_Idle in the compound actor in order to avoid the conflict with the name (Idle) of the initial-state place of actor B.

7.4 Summary

This chapter addressed the architecture of models that are made up of actors and information structures. The issues dealt with are general, although the examples are based on the Protob and Quid modeling languages. Protob is used to define the behavior of actors, while Quid is used to represent dynamic structures of actors as well as dynamic structures of passive objects.

Attention has also been focused on the architecture of complex actors and a technique based on combining simple behaviors (corresponding to state machines) has been presented. Simple behaviors are represented by restricted Protob nets called state nets. State nets can be subdivided into three classes: single-state nets, multiple-state nets and variable-state nets.

The modeling process is not necessarily a bottom-up one. In most cases, the behavior of an actor turns out to be described by a state net, but, in other cases the analyst may work out a fully fledged Protob net directly. However, in such cases, it is still useful to identify the component actors, even if this is only done conceptually, in order to make the model easier to understand.

8

Model-based software engineering

This chapter illustrates an operational software life cycle based on the Protob and Quid modeling languages, and emphasizes two processes, i.e. the validation and performance evaluation of models through simulation and the production of distributed applications using program generation tools. Such processes are supported by two environments, which are called simulation workbench and application workbench, respectively.

The production of programs from Protob models is illustrated in detail and several cases are discussed: in the simplest case, a Protob model is translated into a passive object implementing a token engine, while in the most complex case a Protob model is transformed into a collection of distributed processes.

The Protob and Quid support tools have been implemented in this way, so a fragment of the model of the Protob editor is described as an example of a tool that exhibits, as well as a complex information structure, an interesting dialogue with the user which takes place through graphical objects based on Motif (Open Software Foundation, 1990).

Recent research has focused attention on the formal description of the software processes (Feiler and Humphrey, 1993) with the aim of making them easier to understand and control. This effort is boosted by the fact that as the development process is improved so the quality of the products obtained becomes higher.

Several high-level formalisms and languages have been proposed to specify software processes (Curtis, Kellner and Over, 1992). However, since the models of software processes have many aspects in common with the models of event-driven systems, which are addressed by the modeling languages presented in this book, these languages will be used in this chapter to outline software processes as well.

8.1 Basic development chain

The basic development chain depicted in Figure 8.1 is a simple process consisting of two sequential activities, namely Formalize_Requirements and Generate_Code.

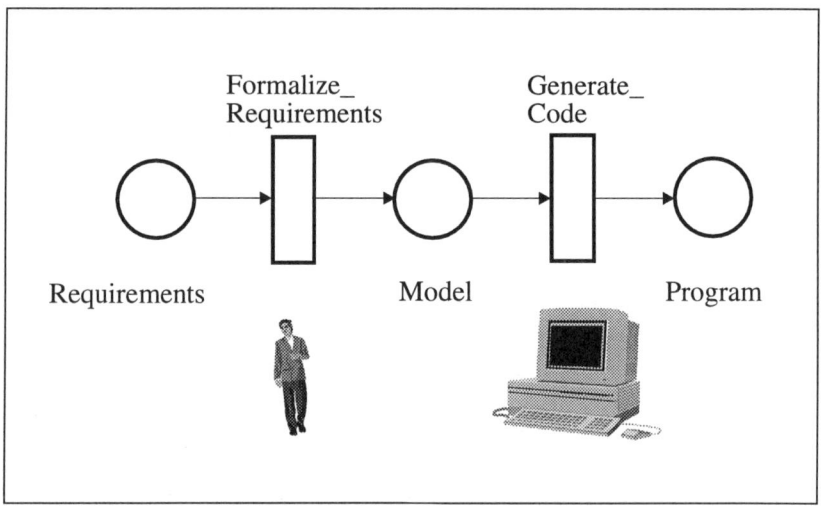

Figure 8.1 *The basic development chain*

The need to build a new system or to improve an existing one, which is expressed in the requirements document, sets off an activity of modeling (where modeling encompasses both analysis and design). Modeling, which is represented by transition Formalize_Requirements in Figure 8.1, is a human activity that is guided by a methodology and is supported by a modeling language: it yields a model, i.e. an abstract representation of the desired system, which is based on that modeling language.

The power of such a process depends on the power of the modeling language and we strongly believe that expressivity and executability are essential features of the modeling language. In fact, besides expressing all the features of the system, i.e. behavior, information structure and user-interface, in a scalable way, the modeling language must exhibit well-defined and operational semantics, so that models can be translated into executable programs automatically. Transition Generate_Code represents that computer-based and technology-driven activity.

The basic development chain is scalable. On the one hand, it represents conventional program development, if the Model is interpreted as the source program and the Program is taken as the corresponding object code. On the other hand, the Model can be a complex hierarchical Protob actor and the Program can be a distributed system made up of several C processes running on a network of heterogeneous computers.

The basic development chain can be enriched in order to give rise to more sophisticated development processes, two of which, namely the simulation process and the application generation process, are presented in the next sections together with their associated environments.

8.2 Simulation process

The simulation process, depicted in Figure 8.2, enables the user to make a model evolve over simulated time and to observe its behavioral traces.

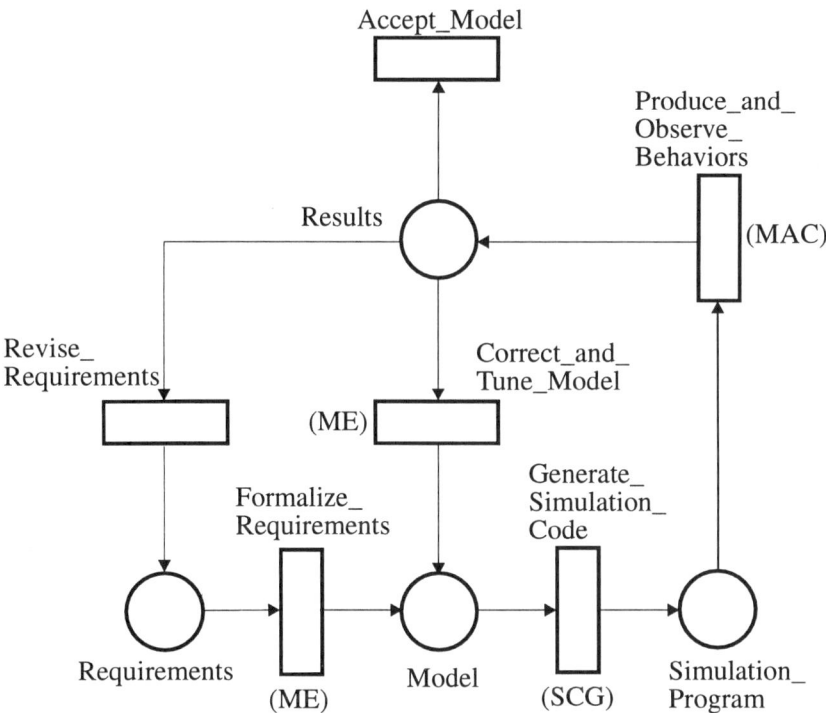

Figure 8.2 *The simulation process*

It is supported by a simulation environment (called simulation work-bench) that consists of three major tools:

1. ME (Model Editor) is a graphical editor of Protob and Quid models.
2. SCG (Simulation Code Generator) is a program generation tool which produces the simulation program from the model automatically. This

program manages time and events according to techniques that are well-known in the domain of discrete event simulation languages (Fishman, 1973).

3. MAC (Model Animator and Controller) is a tool that enables the user to control the execution of the simulation program. It shows results directly on the model: this feature, i.e. the capability of displaying, on the model, the information that is produced by the execution of the program (generated from the model), is referred to as the *animation* of the model.

Often we say that the model is executed, meaning that the program generated from the model is executed.

The simulation process, illustrated in Figure 8.2, shows that the analysis of the behavioral traces produced during simulation leads to the acceptance of the model or to its revision. In fact, simulation results can involve either a revision of the model or a revision of the requirements. The latter situation occurs when the execution of the model shows that the requirements are inconsistent or incomplete. Each transition in Figure 8.2 represents an activity; if the activity is performed using a tool, the name of the tool is written between round brackets near the transition.

8.2.1 Animation of models

When a Protob model is being simulated and its animation is being observed, some information is displayed for each symbol of the net, as shown in Figure 8.3.

The model given in Figure 8.3 refers to a simple production system which is made up of two machines and one cart. Machines behave as follows:

1. When a machine is idle, it requests a raw part and waits for it. The request is represented by a token in place In_Req and is generated by transition Issue_In_Req. A token in place W indicates that a machine is waiting for a raw part.

2. When the cart carries the part to a machine, the machine takes the part, then informs the cart that it has been unloaded and starts machining the part. Transition Input_Part fires when a machine is waiting and a raw part is available. A token in place Part_Ready indicates that the cart has carried a raw part to a machine which issued a request. Input_Part puts a token into place Unloaded to inform the cart that it has been unloaded and also puts a token into place W_Enabled to start the machining of the part.

3. When the work is done, the machine puts the finished part into a bin and becomes idle. Transition Work_on_Part represents the actual machining of the part.

The cart services requests coming from machines in the following way:

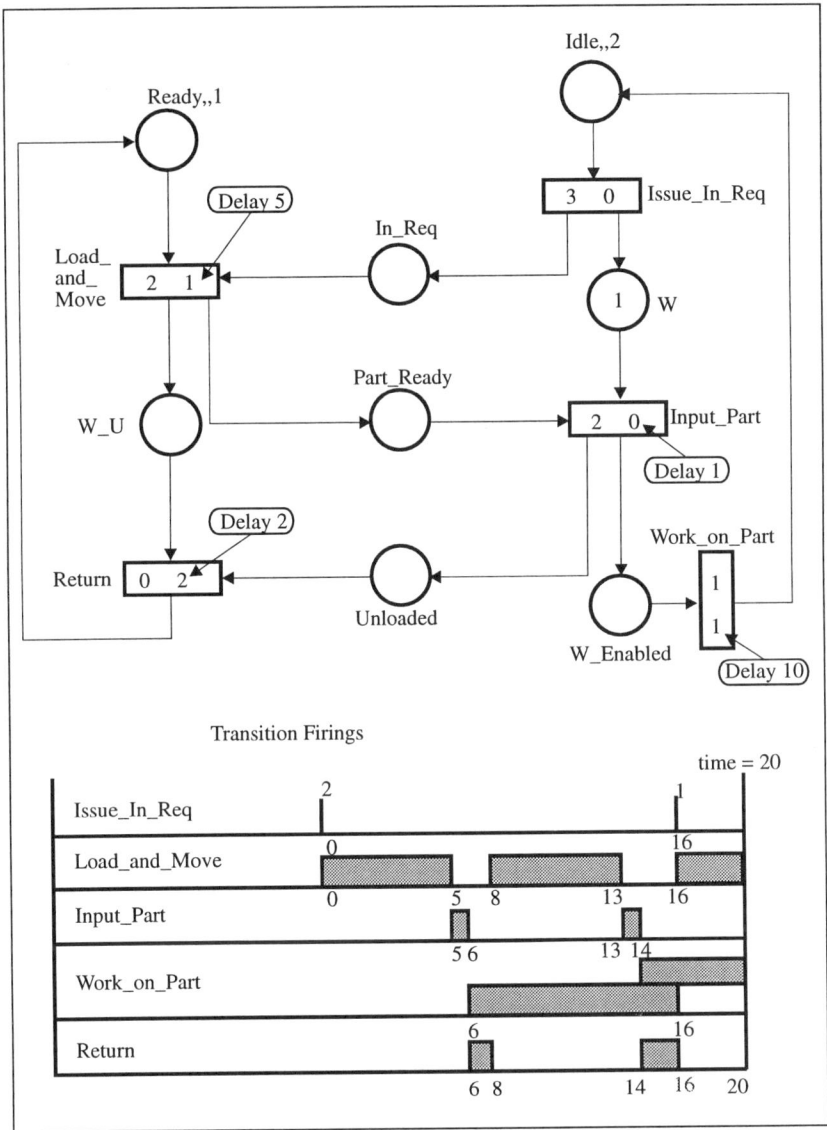

Figure 8.3 *The animation of a net during simulation*

1. When the cart is ready, it services the first pending request, so it takes a raw part from a warehouse and carries it to the machine that issued the request. This activity is represented by transition Load_and_Move. A token in place W_U shows that the cart is waiting to be unloaded.

2. When the cart has been unloaded, it goes back to its rest position. Transition Return models this action.

Initially, machines are idle and the cart is ready at its rest position.

It is assumed that activities have a fixed duration: the cart takes 5 time units to service the request of a machine and 2 time units to go back to its rest position, while a machine takes 1 time unit to unload the cart and 10 time units to machine a part. The action of requesting a raw part is assumed to take negligible time compared with the other activities, so transition Issue_In_Req is immediate.

The initial marking of the model given in Figure 8.3 is made up of two tokens in place Idle and one token in place Ready. Tokens have no attributes, so the type of all places is nul.

When the model is being simulated, both instantaneous and historical information is collected. Instantaneous data refers to the current time and includes:

1. the number of tokens in each place, such numbers being shown inside places;

2. the number of firings that each transition has completed so far and the number of firings that each transition has started but has not yet completed, such numbers being shown inside transitions: the former on the left and the latter on the right if the transition is a horizontal rectangle, and the former above and the latter below if the transition is a vertical rectangle.

Historical data shows, over a given period of time, the firing sequences for the transitions on which attention is being focused. The diagram presented in Figure 8.3 shows how transitions fire in the interval from 0 to 20 time units.

At the beginning, i.e. when the current time is 0, only transition Issue_In_Req is enabled, because it has only one input place and this contains two tokens. Issue_In_Req fires instantaneously; after its firing, the current time is still 0 and there are two enabled transitions: Issue_In_Req (as there is one token left in place Idle) and Load_and_Move. Since these transitions are not in conflict, they start firing simultaneously. Issue_In_Req is immediate, so its second firing ends when time is still 0.

Instantaneous firings are indicated in the diagram using a bar; the number near a bar shows how many instantaneous firings take place at the same instant.

Transition Load_and_Move ends firing at time 5, because it has a deterministic release delay of 5 time units.

At the end of the given period, i.e. when time is 20, there are two ongoing firings, one related to transition Work_on_Part, the other related to transition Load_and_Move. In fact, at that instant, one machine is machining a part, while the other is waiting for a new part.

Other historical data shows, over a given period of time, the number of tokens in the places on which attention is being focused. Two examples of such diagrams were given in Figures 4.22 and 4.23 in Chapter 4.

When tokens are not null, it is possible to show their contents at the current time. In fact, if a place is selected with the mouse, the contents of all the tokens contained in it are displayed on the screen.

The case in which tokens are handles to objects belonging to an object graph managed by Quid is more interesting, since it is possible to browse the object graph starting from such tokens. An example is given in Figure 8.4; it refers to the cell supervisor described in Chapter 7 and, specifically, to the fragment shown in Figure 7.8.

The token in place Idle identifies an object of class Workstation whose code is Wst1, while the token in place Finished identifies another object of class Workstation whose code is Wst4. For the sake of simplicity, the former object will be referred to as Wst1, while the latter will be referred to as Wst4.

In general, we can browse an object graph interactively by acting on the corresponding Quid model; first, we have to select the object from which we want to start navigating the object graph. In this case, since we are observing tokens that are handles to objects, it is among such objects that we must select the one from which navigation will be started. In fact, we select Wst4.

When we are focusing our attention on a particular object of a given class, we can examine the other objects that are associated with it by following the relationships in which its class is involved. In Figure 8.4, an arrow near a relationship indicates that this relationship has been followed during navigation.

Therefore, if we start from Wst4 and follow relationship Located_at, we obtain the object of class Wip that represents the part located at Wst4. Then, following relationship Order, we reach order O3, which caused the production of that part, and, following relationship Currently_Shaped_by, we obtain operation Op3, which has been performed on that part. If we follow relationship Refers_to from order O3, we reach part type P3 to which the part located at Wst4 belongs.

Of course, there is an association belonging to relationship Shaped_by between part type P3 and operation Op3. A suitable command (Show_Association) enables us to emphasize this association; further, since relationship Shaped_by is ordered, we can invoke another command (Next) to obtain the association that follows the above-mentioned one as well as the opera-

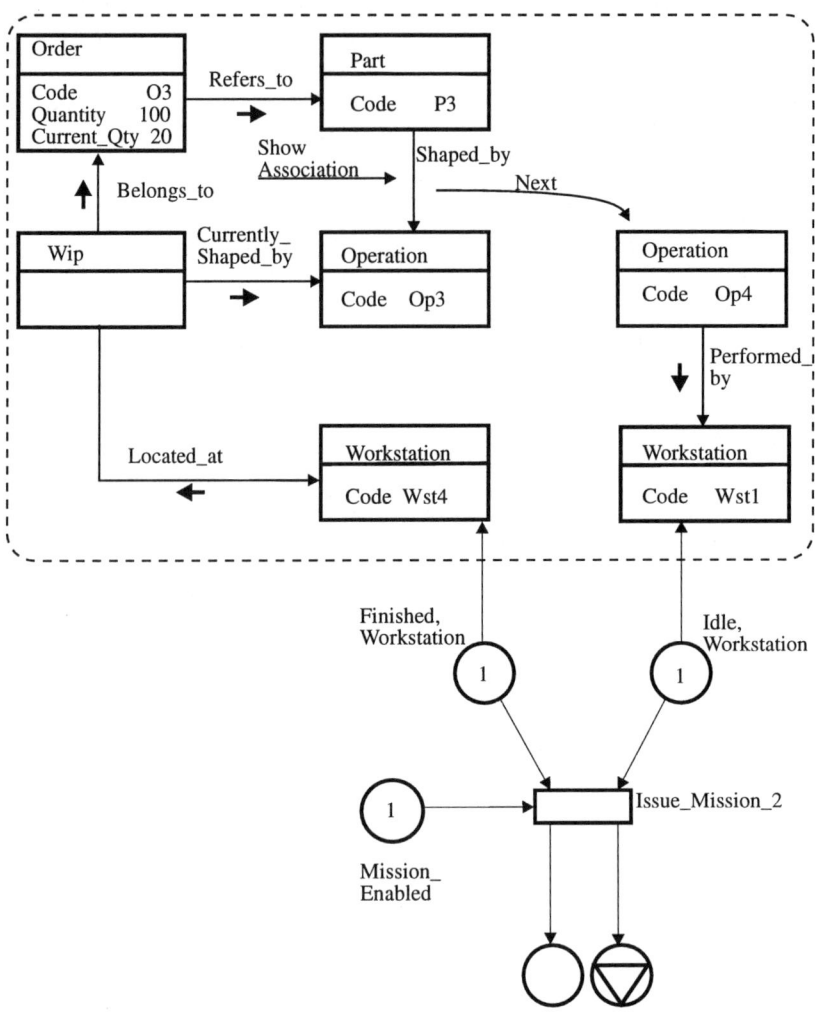

Figure 8.4 *Browsing an information structure during simulation*

tion associated with it. This operation is Op4 and it is the next operation
to be performed on the part located at Wst4.

If we follow relationship Performed_by starting from operation Op4, we
can observe all the workstations that are able to perform Op4. Among
them, we find Wst1 which is the object referred to by the token contained
in place Idle. Thus, by browsing the object graph, we have checked that
the predicate of transition Issue_Mission_2 is satisfied.

8.3 Application generation process

The application generation process, depicted in Figure 8.5, enables the
user to generate a distributed program and to observe its behavioral traces
during its execution in real time.

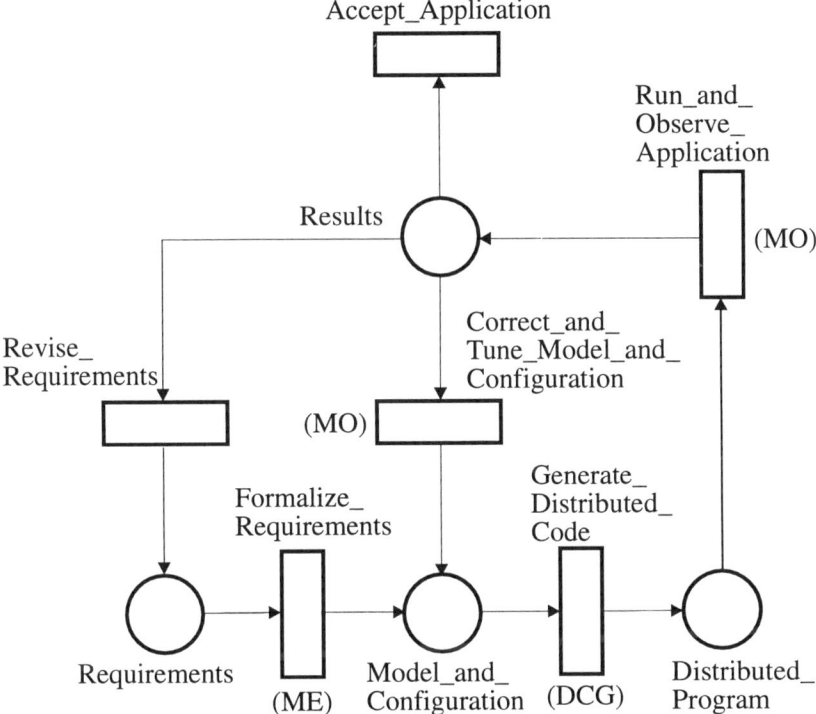

Figure 8.5 *The application generation process*

The application generation environment (called application workbench)
includes two major tools:

1. DCG (Distributed Code Generator) is a program generation tool which
   produces the distributed program from the model automatically.

2. MO (Model Observer) is a tool that animates the model during its execution. It interacts with the distributed program and provides the user with commands to control its execution as well as to display information.

For the sake of simplicity, the application generation process given in Figure 8.5 directly takes the requirements as its input; actually, it is subsequent to the simulation process, so that the model is already available.

The design activity, which is represented by transition Formalize_Requirements, yields a model and a configuration. The term configuration denotes the mapping of the model's components, i.e. the actors, into distributed processes and this mapping has to be supplied by the user. If the resulting program is to be run on a network of computers, each process must be identified by the name of the node it will reside on and by the name of the process itself.

When the application is being executed, it can be observed and some measurements can be collected. The application might need to be tuned, for example to improve its performance. In this case, the model and/or the configuration are modified, as indicated by transition Correct_and_Tune_Model_and_Configuration, and new tests will then be performed. If, instead, the execution reveals problems pertaining to the requirements, a revision must be carried out as indicated by transition Revise_Requirements.

A complete model, one which integrates the simulation process and the application generation process, is given in Figure 8.6.

The simulation process contains two loops to manage changes in the model and changes in the requirements. After the model has been tested in simulation, the mapping of actors onto processes, i.e. the configuration, is defined. The distributed program is then tested: changes in the configuration are managed internally, while changes in the model are submitted back to the simulation process.

The animation of the distributed program can be performed at different levels of granularity, depending on the average firing frequency, which is related to the execution speed of the actual system. In fact, if the firing frequency is not too high, e.g. at most a few firings per second, it makes sense to observe real-time information regarding the number of tokens in places as well as the number of transition firings. Otherwise, if the system is too fast for real-time observations, it is possible to take a snapshot to see such numbers at a given instant; snapshots can also be taken automatically after a given period has elapsed.

8.4 Operational life cycle

In this section, a software development process that is based on operational models is outlined.

It is an incremental process consisting of four major phases: system modeling, software modeling, software production and software maintenance.

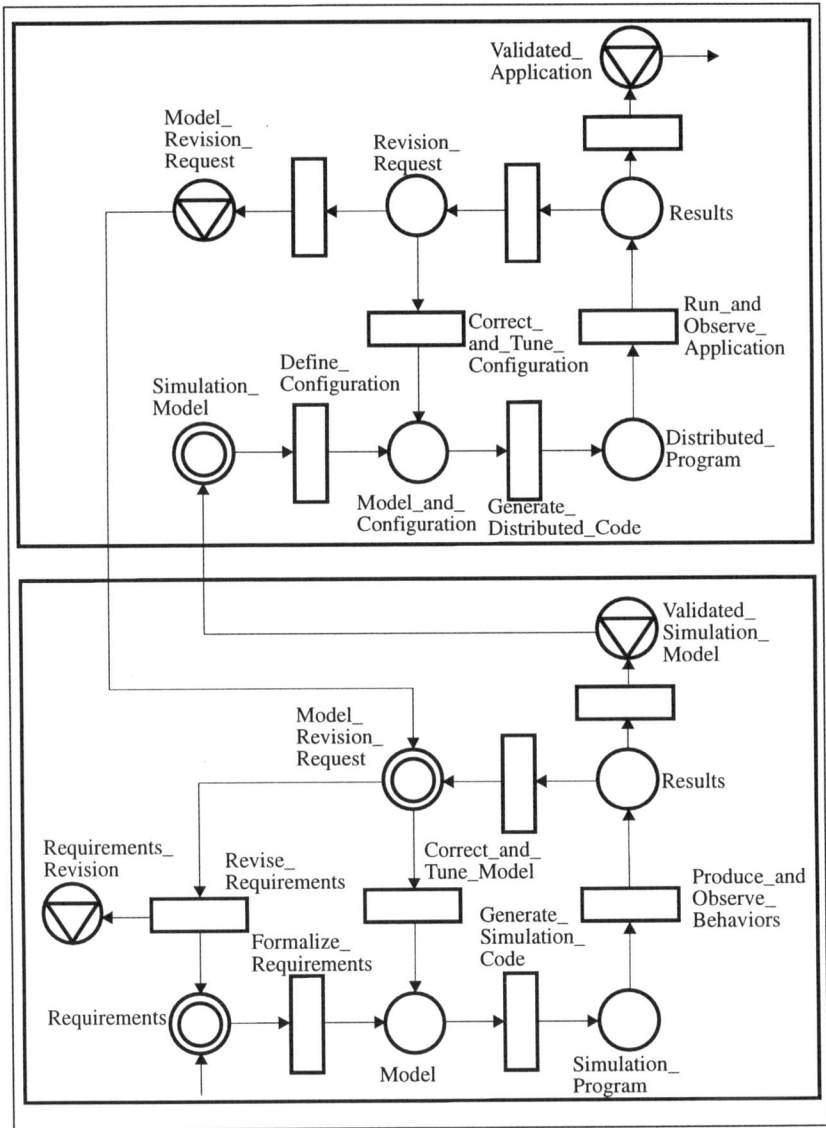

Figure 8.6 *The simulation and application generation processes integrated*

8.4.1 System modeling

System modeling aims at providing an abstract, expressive and rigorous representation (called a system model) of the system being considered so as to improve understanding, to validate behavior and to evaluate performance. The term system is used here in a broad sense, as it can encompass mechanical hardware, computer hardware and software (including networks), as well as the organization of people.

In this phase, it is important to get an insight into the system as a whole and to understand how the different subsystems have to cooperate to achieve the common goal.

The simulation process is used in this phase to produce and check behavioral traces.

Since system modeling and analysis are often carried out with the help of traditional simulation environments, it is worth saying a few words on the differences between the approaches based on such environments and the approach proposed in this book. Two major differences must be emphasized.

1. Most simulation environments are highly tailored to specific application domains, such as production systems and communication systems. They provide plenty of specific parameterized building blocks which the user can combine and specialize depending on his or her needs. However, it is difficult to add a new building block, because the internal language with which building blocks are carried out is not available to the user or it is difficult to understand for non-software specialists.

2. Traditional simulation environments are not able to address software modeling, because the building block technique they are based on is not suitable for representing software issues. Consequently, reusing portions of system models directly when software models have to be built is impossible.

8.4.2 Software modeling

At the end of the system modeling phase, software requirements are issued. Then the software system has to be designed, developed and tested.

This phase is called software modeling because its goal is to produce an effective model of the software system. In general, it is necessary to split this phase into two sequential phases, namely analysis and design.

The specification model produced during the analysis phase captures the high-level behavior of the software system and fulfills the same general purposes as the system model, namely improving understanding, validating behavior and evaluating performance.

In this phase, actors modeling the external environment (with respect to the software system) are introduced. They have their own dynamics and provide the actors representing the software system with the appropriate external stimuli. Such actors often turn out to be the same as the ones developed during the system modeling phase (so those can be fully reused) or can be built on top of them.

During the design phase, the specification model is enriched with details and its architecture progressively reaches the final shape.

Design models can still be tested just as specification models, by means of simulation; however, in this phase, more is needed, i.e. it is necessary to test the model on the target architecture with the emulation of the environment. Therefore, the application generation process is extensively used in this phase.

The design model is tested in a controlled environment, where the computing platform is the target one but the external devices are not connected to it; they are represented, instead, by suitable actors, called emulation actors, that interact with the design model on behalf of the actual devices. Emulation actors might be too complicated, in some cases more complicated than the software model, so the level of refinement up to which they have to be developed is left to the designer's judgment.

An important benefit of this approach is the assessment of performance. The response times to external stimuli as well as the processing times of complex activities can be measured in a realistic setting easily and carefully. However, only rough performance figures can be obtained from the simulation model, because the scheduling of processes and the performance of the underlying operating system cannot be taken into account.

If bottlenecks are detected, a new configuration can be tried or the model can be changed. In the latter case, before the updated distributed program is generated, a simulation cycle is performed for the updated model.

The difference between analysis and design is mainly a matter of detail, since the approach and the modeling language are the same.

8.4.3 Software production and maintenance

The purpose of the software production phase is to provide a deliverable software system.

At the end of the design phase, the model of the software system will have been thoroughly checked, so, if the design model is modified by replacing the actors emulating physical devices with suitable interfaces, the final model (called the application model), from which the deliverable software system can be generated automatically, is obtained.

The transition from the design model to the application one consists in simple actions that can be repeated automatically; therefore, at this point, the design model can be considered as the conceptual image of the final software system. Then maintenance will be performed on the design model and the updated software will be generated from the updated design model.

In general, the application model is strongly related to the design model, because either many classes are the same in both models or a class of the application model is an extension, by means of inheritance, of a class of the design model. Therefore, when some classes of the design model are modified during maintenance, the application model turns out to have been changed automatically. The application model does not add any real value, but it allows the design model to interface with the actual devices.

8.4.4 Comparison with other life cycles

The software life cycle notion expresses the need to organize work for people who develop software systems. Since this industrial sector is relatively new, its specific issues are not yet completely understood, hence the software life cycle is not yet a mature topic and current research is dedicating increasing attention to it.

The study of the software life cycle is highly challenging, because organizational and technical issues are strongly intertwined in a rapidly changing technological scenario and, moreover, because both the production process and the final product have a common origin, i.e. the computer-based technology.

The most widely known life cycle is the one called waterfall life cycle (Royce, 1970), which consists of a sequence of phases. It draws heavily on Taylor's principles, as work is split into rather rigid phases which are expected to be carried out by specialized people: specifically, system modeling by system analysts, software requirements specification by sofware analysts, software design by designers and software implementation by programmers. Communication between these phases mainly takes place through appropriate documentation.

This approach is suitable for the development of sequential systems, such as traditional data processing systems, but fails when other systems, such as event-driven systems, have to be tackled. Event-driven systems are difficult to understand because they are not sequential but consist of several autonomous entities that interact with each other and with the external world, often with severe timing constraints. In many cases, an in-depth understanding of the system can be achieved only if an executable model is built and simulated.

The benefits that can be obtained from experimenting on a suitable representation of the system being considered have been emphasized by research on rapid prototyping (Davis, 1992). However, the idea of a prototype is often that of a quick and dirty realization to play with and then to throw away. In this sense, prototyping is a more fashionable remake of the old code-and-fix development approach, as has been pointed out by Boehm (1988). On the contrary, although the model, as conceived here, is still a sort of prototype, for it enables the user to observe how the system will react to certain stimuli, nevertheless it is built according to a methodology that is able to guide its evolution up to the final application.

The operational life cycle is a technical approach, and as such it may still lack sound management principles, which merits further investigation. Its aim is to enable the analyst and the designer to work on a conceptual and abstract level as far as possible, the gap between the model and the underlying technology being bridged by sophisticated tools, which exploit state-of-the-art software engineering techniques.

8.5 Program generation

The key feature of the operational life cycle illustrated in the previous section is the capability of producing programs from models automatically. In particular, the term *program generation* denotes the production of an executable program from a Protob model; it is performed automatically by means of program generation tools.

Since program generation can be given several objectives and the complexity of the software produced can be high, it is convenient to represent the software produced in an abstract way by means of a model, which is called an implementation model.

The implementation model has a lower level of abstraction than the corresponding conceptual model (i.e. the model of the system being considered), but it has a more concrete operational meaning. In fact, while the conceptual model is made up of abstract entities, such as nets and token-based communications, the implementation model is based on technological entities, such as passive objects, concurrent processes and inter-process communication and synchronization mechanisms. The implementation model makes the program generation process more transparent, since it reduces the number of assumptions that are hidden in the program generation tools.

It is now time to comment on the major results of program generation, which are shown in Figures 8.7, 8.8 and 8.9.

The conceptual model in Figure 8.7 is a Protob actor, as indicated by the double square icon. According to the principle of composition, an actor can include other actors, so the overall structure is an actor tree. For the sake of simplicity, only fixed composition is considered here.

The simplest case of program generation is shown in Figure 8.7(a) and consists in converting a Protob actor, together with all the actors that it includes directly or indirectly, into one token engine which manages all of them. The term *token engine* basically indicates a piece of code that is able to accept (input) tokens from the outside, to execute transitions (i.e. their predicates and actions) according to the logic expressed in the conceptual model and to deliver (output) tokens to the outside. As a matter of fact, the token engine is a passive object that provides services suitable for entering input tokens and for controlling the operation of the engine. It keeps an

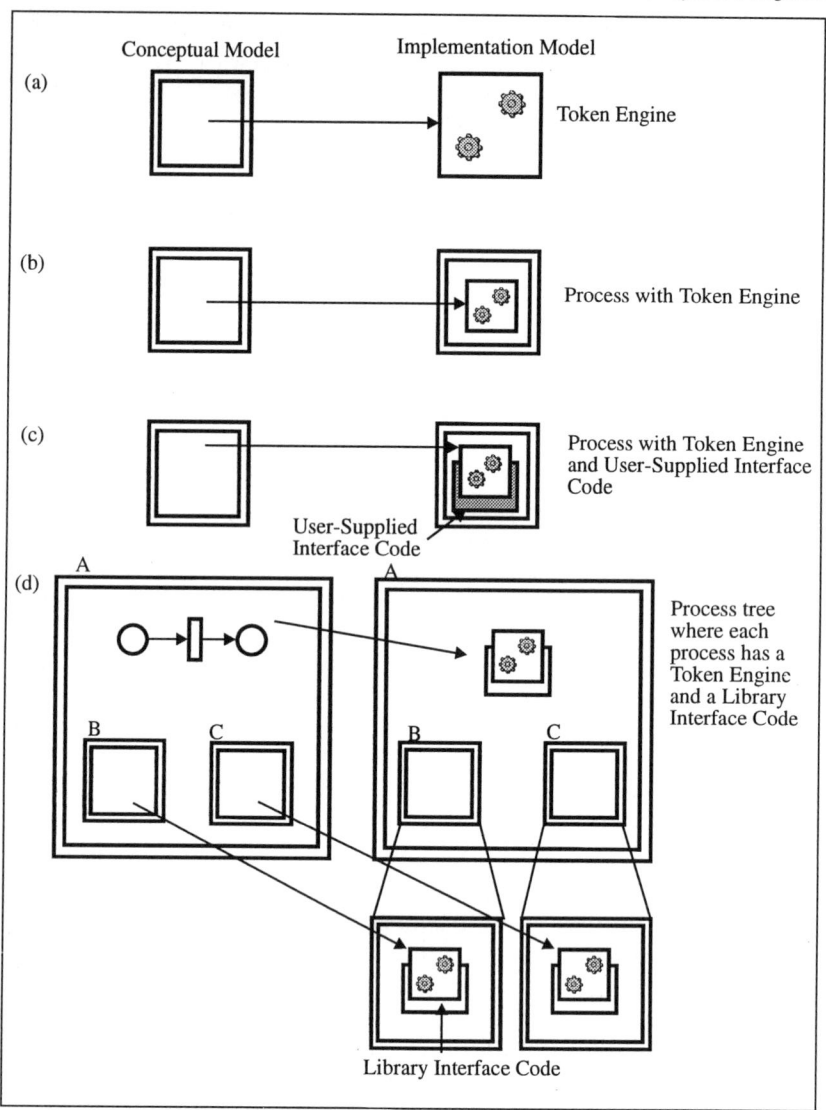

Figure 8.7 *Implementation models*

event list, such as the one described in Chapter 4, and it can also be given callbacks so that specific actions (called output actions) can be performed whenever output tokens are released.

The token engine is the basis of more complex implementation models; however, it can also be used directly by the user, who then has to provide both a main program in order to control the operation of the token engine and an interface code in order to enter input tokens and perform output actions. In other cases, which will be illustrated later, such an interface code is a parametric library code and it is automatically linked to the token engine code by the program generation tool.

In many cases, the conceptual model represents activities that have to be executed within a single thread of control. Then, the implementation model will be a single process; such a process (called an implementation process) will generally be started by the underlying operating system on behalf of the user. In other cases, an implementation process will be started by another implementation process. Implementation processes are depicted as double squares.

There are two cases, as shown in Figures 8.7(b) and 8.7(c), in which a single implementation process is used.

1. The applications of this category neither receive tokens from the outside nor send tokens to the outside or, alternatively, they receive tokens in a well-defined way (e.g. through a graphical user interface). An application featuring window-based interactions with the user receives tokens that correspond to the user's inputs; however, such interactions can be managed automatically by a library code provided by the program generation tool. As an example, a fragment of the Protob editor will be illustrated in the next section; such an application is event-driven (as events correspond to user's inputs), but it has to be executed within a single thread of control.

   The most relevant part of the contents of the implementation process is given in this case by its token engine, as shown in Figure 8.7(b). The implementation process also includes a main program which controls the operation of the token engine; such a main program is provided by the program generation tool.

2. In this case the applications, such as real-time controllers, receive and/or send tokens from/to the outside. Therefore, the implementation process will include, besides the token engine, a main program and an interface code, both of which must be supplied by the user. Such an interface code contains interrupt routines (or services) which enter tokens into the token engine as well as output services which implement the token engine callbacks. This case is shown in Figure 8.7(c), where the user-supplied interface code is depicted as a black box.

   The most interesting situation occurs when the conceptual model represents a distributed application. Then, Protob actors are transformed into distributed processes according to configuration directives which are expressed by means of a suitable configuration language. The structure of the implementation model is a process tree.

The term *distributed application* denotes a collection of cooperating concurrent processes which can be assigned to different processing units interconnected by a communication network (Sloman and Kramer, 1987); for the sake of simplicity, the case in which processes reside on the same processor is included as well.

The transformation of Protob actors into processes can be carried out in several ways. The most common way is to transform the top-level actor as well as all the actors that it includes directly (i.e. the first-level actors) into distinct processes. In this case, a first-level actor together with all the actors it includes directly or indirectly are converted into a single process. In other cases, actors which are different from first-level ones can be converted into processes, too; however, if such an actor is mapped onto a process, its ancestor actor (i.e. the actor which contains it), A, as well as all the other actors that A contains must be mapped onto processes, too.

For example, the conceptual model shown in Figure 8.7(d) consists of a top-level actor (A) which includes two other actors (B and C); it is transformed into a process tree, where process A is the root and processes B and C are its descendants. Process A is called the ancestor process of B and C.

The meaning of the process tree is related to the activation of processes: each process, except for the root (which is started by the user), is started by its ancestor process.

Each implementation process contains a token engine derived from the corresponding actor in the conceptual model. Further, each process contains a main program and an interface code which performs three groups of functions:

1. **input functions**, which receive messages from other processes, convert them into input tokens and enter such tokens into the token engine;

2. **output functions**, which convert output tokens (released by the token engine) into messages and deliver them to the destination processes;

3. **management functions**, which activate descendant processes and establish the appropriate connections between them as well as between each of them and the current process (i.e. their ancestor process).

The interface code is depicted as a white box, because it is a standard parametric code, provided by the program generation tool. Tokens sent by one process to another located on the same processor are transmitted by means of local inter-process communication facilities. When processes are remote, tokens are packaged into messages which are transmitted by means of network facilities. The subdivision of large tokens into smaller packets and the conversion of data structures when there are heterogeneous processors are performed by the library code.

The simulation workbench and the application workbench, which respectively support the simulation process and the application generation process illustrated earlier in this chapter, are special cases of distributed applications.

The simulation workbench model is shown in Figure 8.8. It enables the user to simulate the model and to observe its animation.

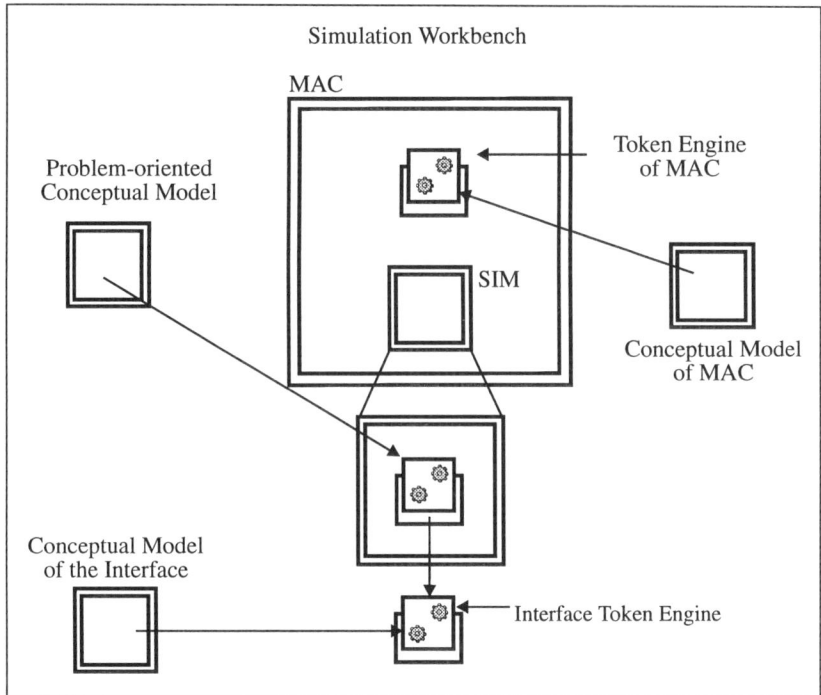

Figure 8.8 *The model of the simulation workbench*

The simulation workbench is made up of two processes, MAC and SIM, which are described below.

1. MAC, the Model Animator and Controller, is a library process because it is independent of the problem-oriented conceptual model. MAC has its own conceptual model from which its token engine is derived. It includes the process (SIM) that actually performs the simulation of the problem-oriented model; the MAC interface code enables the MAC token engine to start SIM as well as to communicate with it and to control its execution.

2. SIM, the SIMulator, contains a token engine that is derived from the

problem model. The interface code of the SIM token engine features a non-trivial behavior because it must manage the interactions with MAC. Not modeling the interface of SIM would make it very difficult to understand how it works, thus causing unacceptable maintenance troubles. For this reason, the interface behavior is described using a suitable Protob model. Of course, this conceptual model, which is called an interface conceptual model, has a lower level of abstraction than the problem-oriented conceptual model; nevertheless it makes implementation mechanisms more transparent and easy to maintain. It is mapped, in turn, into an (interface) implementation model which consists of a token engine, called an interface token engine, and of a simpler interface code. In this way, token engines turn out to be structured hierarchically; further, the model-based token engine is driven by the interface token engine.

The application workbench is shown in Figure 8.9. It enables the user to control the execution of a distributed application and to observe the real-time animation of the model.

The conceptual model is the same as the one shown in Figure 8.7(d). The implementation model is more complicated than the one given in Figure 8.7(d), because there are two additional processes, namely Monitor and MO (the animator process).

Monitor is a library process which starts and controls both the process (A) that is derived from the model and MO. MO is a library process, too, and performs the real-time animation of the model. For the sake of clarity, those processes which are derived from the actors of the conceptual model will be called model-based processes. In this case again, just as in the simulation workbench described above, the interfaces of model-based processes are derived from an interface model because they feature a complex behavior aimed at managing the interactions with MO and with the other model-based processes.

8.6 Tools

This section shows how the tools that form the support environment of Protob and Quid have been designed and developed according to the operational life cycle presented in this chapter. In particular, the model of the Protob editor, which gives rise to a single implementation process, is illustrated. The Protob editor must manage the dialogue with the user through a Motif-based interface as well as handle an in-memory database containing logical and graphical information regarding the elements of the model.

A fragment of the interaction with the user is given in Figure 8.10.

The model given in Figure 8.10 also shows some graphical objects. Graphical objects are similar to the service-based Protob objects described in Chapter 5, with the difference that some of their services are invoked di-

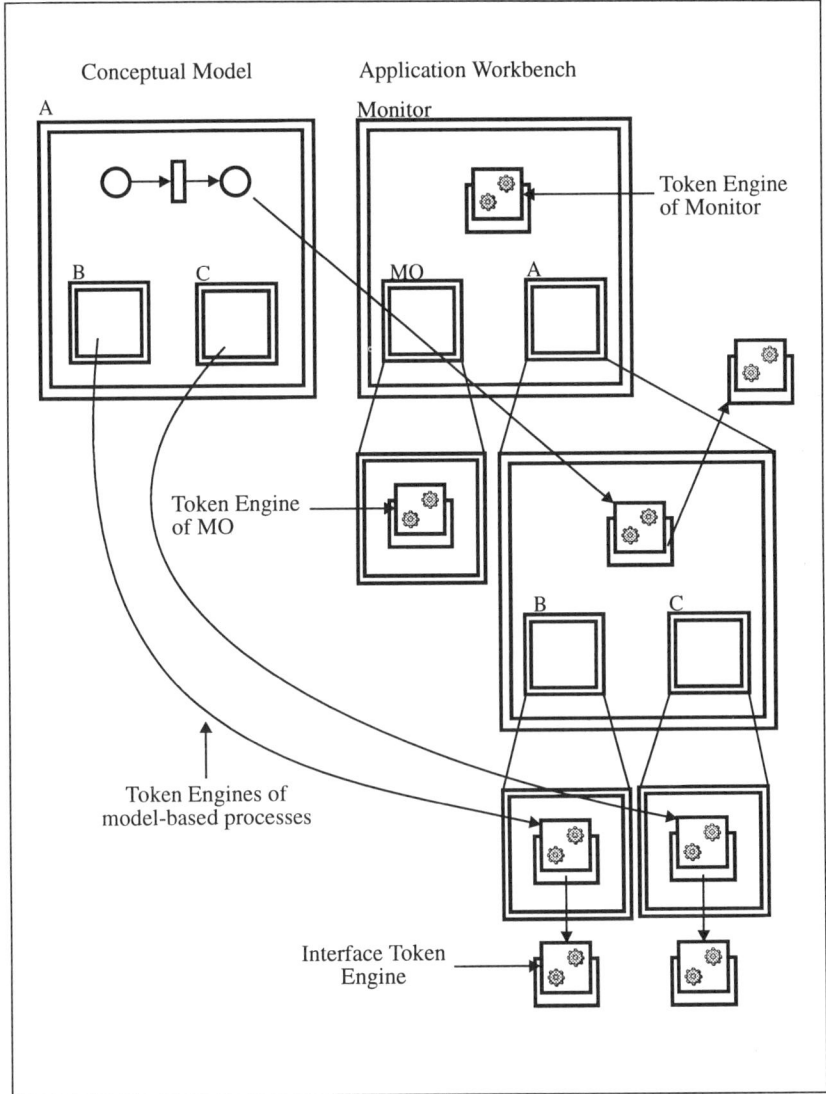

Figure 8.9 *The model of the application workbench*

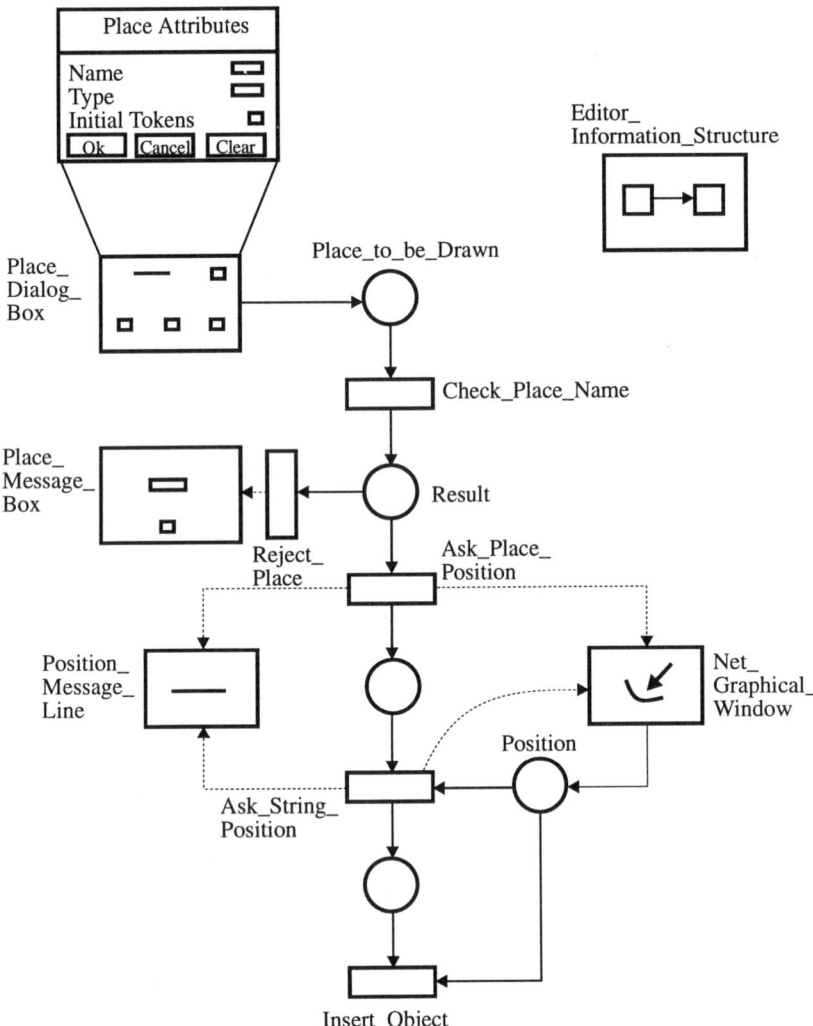

Figure 8.10 *A fragment of the behavior of the Protob editor*

rectly by the user, when he or she interacts with the tool using the mouse or entering data.

Graphical objects have special icons denoting their interaction styles. Each graphical object has a name which is shown nearby. In the model given in Figure 8.10, four classes of graphical objects are used: dialog boxes, message boxes, message lines and graphical windows. Hix and Rex Hartson (1993) present an interesting survey on interaction styles and an in-depth analysis of user interfaces.

A dialog box contains labeled fields to be filled in by the user as well as other interaction objects, such as lists and buttons.

Dialog box Place_Dialog_Box has a title, Place Attributes, and contains three labeled fields and a bank of three push-buttons. The labeled fields, Name, Type and Initial Tokens, must be filled in with a string denoting the place name, a string denoting the place type and a positive integer number indicating the number of initial tokens contained in the place. As regards the three push-buttons, when Ok is pressed the dialog box is closed and then a token containing the information entered through the dialog box is generated and put into place Place_to_be_Drawn; when cancel is pressed the dialog box disappears and no action is taken; when clear is pressed the fields are cleared.

A message box presents a message to the user and keeps his or her attention, because it does not disappear until he or she presses a push-button in the box. Message box Place_Message_Box shows a message which explains why the introduction of the place requested by the user is rejected.

A message line shows a short message without waiting for any confirmation. Message line Position_Message_Line asks the user to select where the place icon has to be positioned on the screen.

A graphical window allows figures to be drawn. It is made up of addressable points, which the user can select by moving the mouse. Graphical window Net_Graphical_Window displays a Protob model.

A complex user interaction involves several steps, which can conveniently be represented by means of a net. As an example, in Figure 8.10 it can be seen how the introduction of a place is managed by the Protob editor.

When the user asks the editor to add a place to the model, dialog box Place_Dialog_Box appears on the screen. After filling in the fields, the user presses the Ok push-button. At that point, a token containing the information about the place is generated and introduced into the model at place Place_to_be_Drawn.

The information entered by the user is checked by transition Check_-Place_Name. If there is another place in the same view with the same name, the new place is not accepted, so transition Reject_Place fires and notifies the user of the rejection by activating message box Place_Message_Box. If the new place is accepted, the user is enabled to position the place on the screen. In fact, transition Ask_Place_Position invites the user to choose the place position (by activating message line Position_Message_Line) and also informs graphical window Net_Graphical_Window that the cursor has to assume the place shape, i.e. a circle. Then, the user can freely move the cursor; when he or she selects the position of the place, the graphical window generates a token containing the coordinates of the center of the place and delivers it to place Position. Next, the user is asked to select the position of the string associated with the place: transition Ask_String_-Position acts in the same way as Ask_Place_Position did before (the shape of the cursor is changed to a rectangle which fits the string). Finally, transition Insert_Object fires and adds a new object to the editor database.

The editor database is defined and managed by means of a Quid model, a fragment of which is given in Figure 8.11.

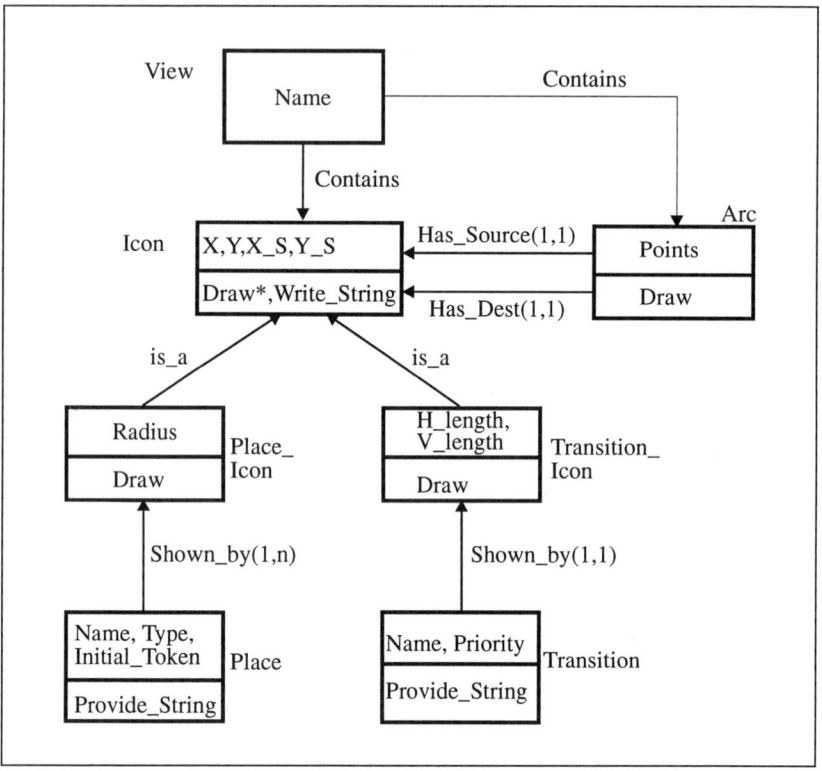

Figure 8.11 *Part of the information model of the Protob editor*

For the sake of simplicity, the object model shown in Figure 8.11 represents only simple Protob classes, i.e. classes including no objects. A simple Protob class can be made up of several views and each view contains places, transitions and arcs.

The object model given in Figure 8.11 contains fully-fledged classes and shows their visible attributes and services. Class Icon is a superclass that collects the features common to all the icons of the model, i.e. the coordinates, X and Y, of the center of the icon, the coordinates, X_S and Y_S, of the lower left corner of the rectangle in which the string associated with the icon will be displayed, the service (Draw) which draws the icon and the service (Write_String) which displays the string associated with the icon.

Service Draw is not implemented by class Icon (as indicated by the *), because it depends on the shape of the specific icon. Such knowledge resides in the subclasses, Place_Icon and Transition_Icon, which have specific attributes: the length of the radius of the circle, Radius, pertains to the former, while the lengths of the sides of the rectangle, H_Length and V_Length, pertain to the latter.

Since the same place can appear in several views, class Place has been introduced to keep the logical information pertaining to a place (i.e. its name, its type and the number of its initial tokens) separate from its physical data which can be contained in several objects of class Place_Icon.

Although class Transition is not strictly necessary as every transition appears in only one view, it has been introduced for the sake of uniformity.

Services Provide_String in classes Place and Transition return the string (built from the logical attributes of the icon) which has to be displayed next to the icon.

Class Arc represents the arcs between places and transitions. It features an attribute, Points, which is a list of the main points of the arc, and a service, Draw, which draws the arc. Each object of class Arc is connected to the source icon and to the destination icon of the corresponding arc.

When transition Insert_Object, shown in Figure 8.10, fires, an object of class Place is added to the internal database of the editor only if another object of class Place that refers to the same place does not already exist; then, an object of class Place_Icon is added and it is linked to the corresponding object of class Place.

The Quid navigational constructs shown below display the contents of a given view, which is referred to by handle V.

```
var
  V: handle(View);
  I: handle(Icon); A: handle(Arc);
  P: handle(Place_Icon);
  T: handle(Transition_Icon);
...
Qd_apply View:V//Icon I do
  {I.Draw;}
case of
when Place_Icon//Place P do
```

```
  {I.Write_String(P.Provide_String);}
when Transition_Icon//Transition T do
  {I.Write_String(T.Provide_String);}
end case;
Qd_end;
Qd_apply View:V//Arc A do
   {A.Draw;}
Qd_end;
```

The first navigational construct starts from a particular view, the one selected by handle V, and reaches all the icons contained in that view. For each icon, I, the actions described below are performed.

1. I is drawn on the screen.

2. The icon's label is displayed on the screen next to the icon. If I is a place (transition), the label is built using the logical information contained in the place (transition) element associated with I. Function Provide_String returns that label and procedure Write_String displays it.

The second navigational construct draws all the arcs contained in that view.

8.7 Summary

This chapter has presented a model-based operational life cycle, which is based on Protob and Quid. Its major benefits consist in enabling the user to effectively check the model's qualitative and quantitative features by means of simulation, and in cutting down development and testing costs thanks to the automatic program generation capability.

Effective quality control is intrinsic to the operational life cycle described in this chapter, since extensive testing can be performed at each stage of development by simulating or executing models.

The integration testing of a control system, such as the supervisor of a production plant or the supervisor of a railway network, can be performed very effectively by building a model of the external environment. Such a model, called an emulator, is connected to the control system model and provides it with the necessary stimuli under the appropriate timing constraints. Therefore, a realistic setting can be reproduced in the laboratory without the actual devices. This approach to integration testing (called testing by emulation) involves an additional cost in building the emulator, but it enables system integrators to cut installation costs dramatically, since response times and all the other critical issues, such as how exceptional events are handled, can be checked in the laboratory.

9

Applications

This chapter describes two case studies regarding the development of large-scale software systems, according to the operational life cycle presented in Chapter 8, in the domains of computer-integrated manufacturing (CIM) and telecommunications systems. These case studies are taken from actual projects.

9.1 CIM systems

The ideal of CIM is to enhance productivity and quality, while reducing lead times and improving flexibility. To achieve such a goal, one necessary step is to integrate all corporate functions and processes on a common computer-based platform.

In this section, we focus our attention on highly automated production processes because they present challenging issues from a software point of view.

Production takes place in plants and a plant consists of two major subsystems, the shop-floor and the management system. The term shop-floor denotes all the devices and physical subsystems which are used to machine, assemble, store and transport parts in the plant. Shop-floor components are equipped with computerized controllers, such as PLCs (Programmable Logical Controllers) and DNCs (Direct Numerical Controllers), which manage their operation.

The management system has to coordinate the activities of the shop-floor so as to ensure that the target production rate and mix is met. It is usually organized on levels which denote specific management functions, as shown below for the common case of four levels.

1. Conventionally, level 1 refers to the control function and this is performed by the controllers that manage shop-floor devices and subsystems. Often, the notion of shop-floor includes the level 1 controllers.

2. Shop-floor devices are usually grouped into production units, called pro-

duction cells. Level 2 refers to the local supervision function, i.e. the management of the interactions between shop-floor devices within a production cell. There is a specific processing unit, called the cell supervisor, which has the responsibility of routing parts and of monitoring production within the cell.

3. A plant is normally made up of several production cells, so a specific processing unit, called the plant supervisor, is needed to coordinate the operation of the cells, to schedule production and to report on the productivity of the plant. Level 3 denotes such a global supervision function.

4. Level 4 refers to central functions, such as production planning and logistics, which coordinate production when several plants are involved.

In the next subsections, we will illustrate the important role played by operational models during the design of the shop-floor, the design of the supervisors and the development and testing of the supervisors. Attention is focused on supervisors because they present the most critical software issues, such as the handling of real-time events and the management of a distributed system.

For further details on production management systems, the reader is referred to the book by Browne, Harhen and Shivnan (1988).

9.1.1 Shop-floor design

Since most shop-floor components have been standardized, plant engineers design the shop-floor of a new plant by putting standard building blocks together and by tuning their performance factors so as to achieve the desired production rate. The throughput of a manufacturing line (i.e. the number of parts produced per time unit) and the size of intermediate buffers are examples of performance factors. The decisions to be taken mainly refer to:

1. the type and the number of building blocks to be used (e.g. what kinds of workstation and of intermediate buffer are needed and how many instances of each kind);

2. their interconnection (e.g. which transportation system, how many carts and pallets);

3. their grouping into functional units (e.g. fully automated lines, semi-automated lines, manual areas).

As it is not easy to predict the effects of such decisions, plant engineers often need to experiment on a computer-based model of the shop-floor. The shop-floor model enables them to describe and understand the flow of parts. Further, by analysing the behavioral traces and the statistical data obtained from the simulation of the model, they can validate their architectural choices, e.g. they can check whether the desired production rate is met and whether synchronizations between shop-floor components are properly managed, and they can study the effects of the failures of some component and decide the right size of intermediate buffers.

In the shop-floor model, no sharp distinction is made between hardware and software activities, as attention is directed to the flow of parts.

The plant considered in this section is a gearbox assembly plant (Bruno *et al.*, 1991), a simplified layout of which is shown in Figure 9.1.

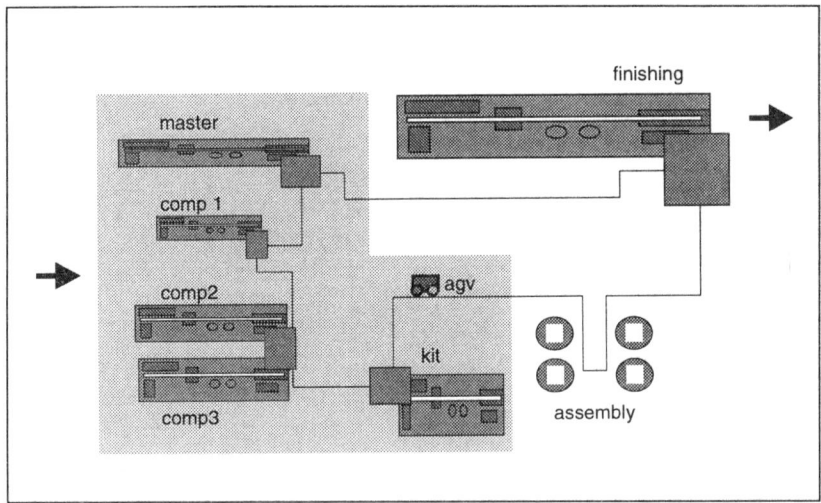

Figure 9.1 *The simplified layout of a gearbox assembly plant*

It includes five automated lines, called master, comp1, comp2, comp3 and kit, which perform machining and subassembly operations on the components of a gearbox. As a matter of fact, a gearbox is made up of five major components: the gearcase, the main shaft, the transmission shaft, the differential unit and the auxiliary kit. Each line is dedicated to a different component and receives raw parts from a warehouse through an input supply subsystem, which is not shown in Figure 9.1, but is represented by the arrow pointing to the lines.

The parts produced by the lines are delivered to a transportation system based on AGVs (automated guided vehicles). AGVs visit lines in sequence, taking one component from each line, then carry the set of five components to an assembly area where manual assembly takes place. After that, the gearbox is moved to a finishing area, where some final operations are performed. The gearbox is then ready for the final testing, which is carried out in another area not shown in Figure 9.1. The testing area is represented by the arrow leaving the finishing area.

The plant is able to produce concurrently different types of gearboxes which are organized in small lots. Parts are mounted on pallets; every part is identified by a tag attached to its pallet. A tag is a retentive memory which can be read and written by the main workstations of the plant.

Additional information concerning this application can be found in the paper by Bruno *et al.* (1991).

The main synchronization issues in the plant are raised by the transit of parts from lines to AGVs, as described below.

Every AGV carries a master pallet whose tag indicates which components it has to collect in order to form the desired gearbox. When the AGV reaches the bottom of a line, the unloading station of the line reads the tag of the pallet carried by the AGV; then it delivers the right component to the AGV if it has one, or, if it cannot deliver the right component to the AGV within a given interval of time, it informs the AGV so that the AGV, after visiting the lines, will go to a manual completion area where the missing components are added.

The Protob model of the shop-floor shown in Figure 9.2 mirrors the plant layout.

Since all the lines are conceptually similar, they are represented by actors of the same class, called Line. As will be explained later, the connections appearing in Figure 9.2 are compound links and represent physical interactions related to the flow of parts.

A line is composed of five workstations in cascade, as shown in Figure 9.3.

The new graphical symbol, i.e. the double circle with a triangle inscribed, which appears in Figure 9.3, denotes a compound port and can be used by an object when it has to pass tokens from the objects it includes to the objects to which it is connected and vice versa. Such a symbol, called a compound port icon, has been introduced to reduce the number of links that must be drawn between the I/O places of the object being considered and those of an object included in it.

An actor of class Line is merely a logical grouping of other actors that represent actual devices, i.e. a load station (L), a marking station (M), a transfer line (T), a release station (R) and an unload station (U). Line actors have no existence, hence they have no behavior.

The first and last components of a line, i.e. its load and unload stations, have to interact with actors outside the line: therefore, the I/O places of the two components should be duplicated in class Line and links should be drawn between such I/O places of class Line and the corresponding I/O places of the two components. Assuming that the load station and the unload station have five I/O places each, then ten I/O places should be put into class Line and ten links should be drawn between such I/O places of class Line and the corresponding I/O places of actors L and U (belonging to classes Load_Station and Unload_Station, respectively).

Using compound port icons as shown in Figure 9.3, we can avoid introducing I/O places that duplicate the I/O places of inner objects into a class as well as drawing all the related links. A compound port icon materializes

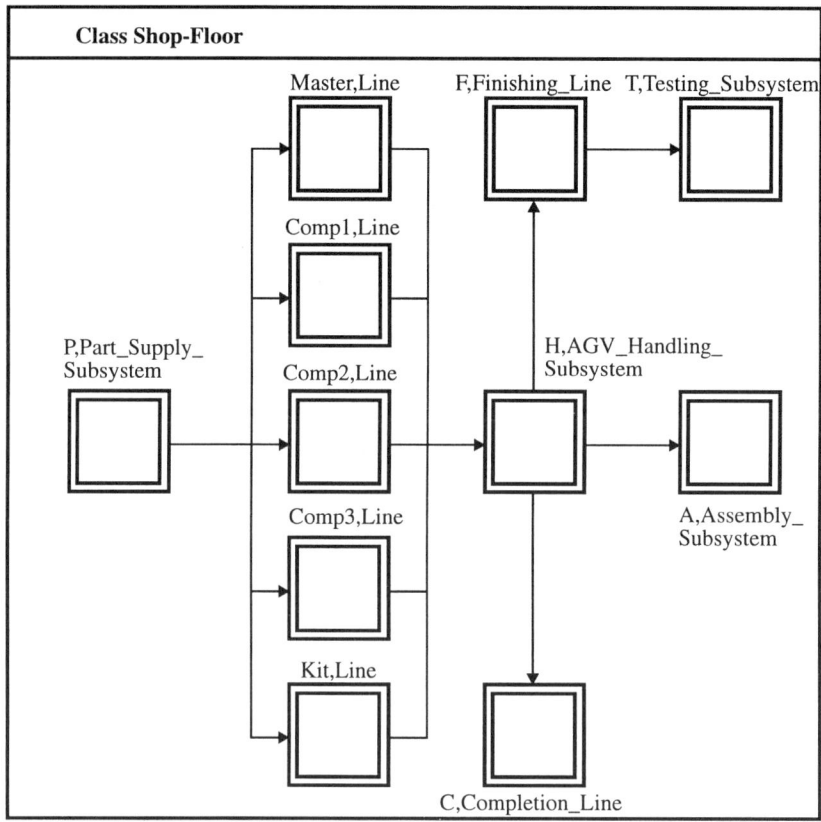

Figure 9.2 *The shop-floor model of the gearbox assembly plant*

the notion of compound port introduced in Chapter 5: it has a name and an inner attribute which contains the sequence of the names of the ports forming the compound port. Such an icon can be connected to an object by an arc (without any arrow) which is similar to a compound link since it connects a compound port of the class being considered to a congruent compound port of one of its component objects.

Compound port Load_Intf, shown in Figure 9.3, passes information between the supply subsystem (actor P in Figure 9.2) and the load station, while compound port Unload_Intf makes the unload station interact with the AGV handling subsystem (actor H in Figure 9.2).

The line components are briefly described below.

The load station receives a bin containing raw parts from the supply subsystem, then it takes one part at a time from the bin, mounts it onto

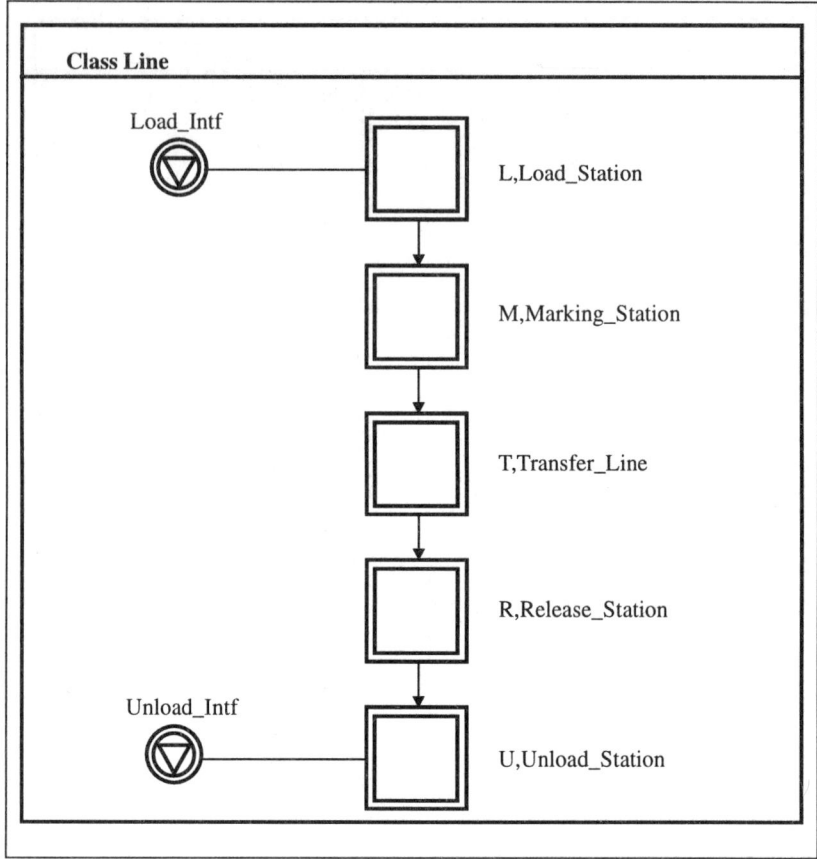

Figure 9.3 *The model of the line*

a pallet and forwards the pallet to the marking station; when the bin is empty, it requests a new one from the supply subsystem.

The marking station is illustrated in more detail, since it will interact with the plant management system, as shown in the next subsection. Its behavior is depicted in Figure 9.4.

The marking station processes one part at a time: when a part is received from the load station (at input place In_Part), transition Mark_Part writes the part type and other parameters that are extracted from an internal database onto the tag of the pallet on which the part is mounted. Such a database, which keeps a list of orders as well as the bill of materials, is represented by a Quid model (Production_Data). For simulation purposes, a delay representing the actual time taken to write the necessary information onto the tag is associated with transition Mark_Part.

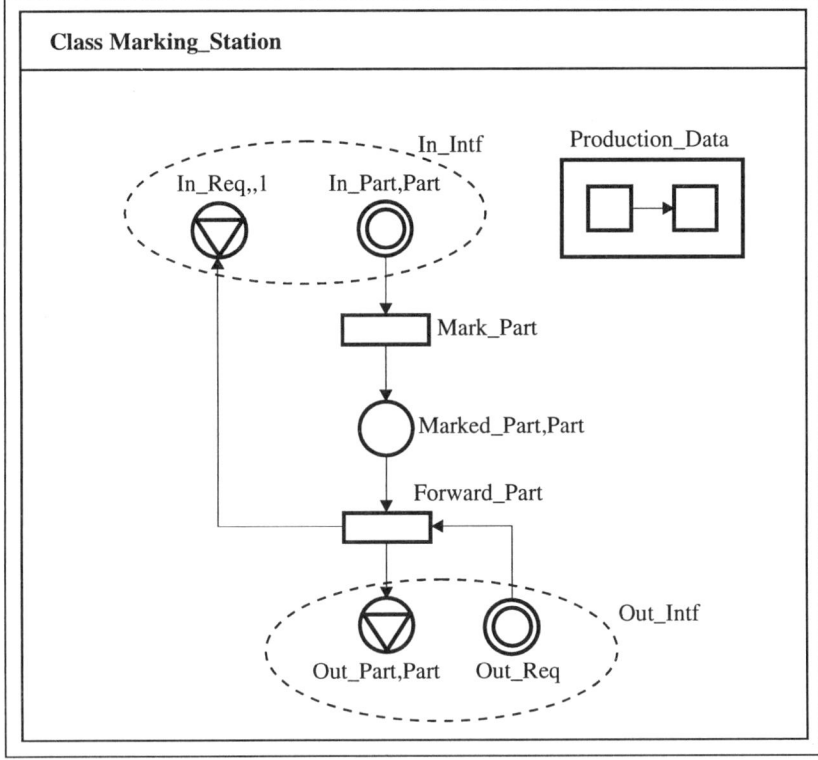

Figure 9.4 *The model of the marking station*

When the part has been marked, a token is put into place Marked_-Part. Then transition Forward_Part fires, provided that a request has been received (at input place Out_Req) from the downstream station (which is the transfer line): consequently, it sends the part to the transfer line from output place Out_Part and also sends a request for a new part from output place In_Req to the upstream station (which is the load station).

The interactions between pairs of adjacent workstations (with respect to the flow of parts, one is considered as the upstream station and the other as the downstream station) are governed by a pull logic: therefore, when the downstream station is ready to process a new part, it sends a request to the upstream station, which will deliver the part only after receiving a request.

The transfer station carries out a sequence of operations (simple machining and subassembly ones) on every part, depending on its type. The release station checks parts and discards defective ones. The unload station, when it receives a request from the AGV for the component to be collected for the current gearbox, delivers the right part, if there is one, to the AGV.

9.1.2 Supervisor design and development

The model of the shop-floor guides plant engineers and system integrators first in defining the features of the supervisor and then in validating them.

Supervisors, although they need to be tailored to their specific production processes, generally perform four major functions, which are described below, referring to the gearbox assembly plant.

Production management. The supervisor receives the master schedule (i.e. the sequence of lots of gearboxes to be produced) from the corporate planning system. Then it splits the master schedule into individual schedules for each line and sends appropriate production orders to each line, taking into account their relative production rates.

   The five lines have to produce lots of parts so that such parts can be assembled to give the desired gearboxes. However, if the production rates of the lines are not the same or when a breakdown occurs in a line, the supervisor has to take corrective action. Specifically, production orders have to be sent in advance to the lines that are slower (e.g. the line producing the gearcase). In addition, when a line is late because of internal failures, its pending orders have to be cancelled until the synchronization with the other lines is restored.

   Sometimes the overall bill of materials has to be updated and, consequently, the supervisor has the responsibility of sending new bills of materials to the marking station of each line.

Production monitoring. Each line notifies the supervisor whenever a part has been marked (by the marking station), accepted or discarded (by the release station) and also whenever a lot has been completed. The supervisor registers such information and sends periodical reports to the upper management level.

Materials procurement. On the basis of the line schedules, the supervisor issues appropriate material requests to the input warehouse and to the supply subsystem.

Line management. The supervisor issues start and restart commands to the lines and can also change, on behalf of the foreman, the state of a line from automatic to manual and vice versa.

A principle that, in many cases, proved to be very useful is to shape the supervisor to the plant and thus to decompose it into smaller supervisors, each one managing a different section of the plant. In the case of the gearbox assembly plant, each line is managed by its own supervisor and all line supervisors are coordinated by a central entity, called the real-time scheduler.

There are two major reasons for that choice.

1. A line, considered as an autonomous subsystem, can be used within different production processes, so its supervisor has to perform general

functions which are needed in all the contexts in which the line is supposed to operate.

2. All the control features that are related to the synchronization of multiple lines depend on the specific production process, thus they are committed to a special actor, i.e. the real-time scheduler, which incorporates specific knowledge.

Such a choice also facilitates the installation of the plant, which usually proceeds incrementally because each line is separately activated and tuned. Likewise, line supervisors can be activated without being connected to the real-time scheduler and, therefore, they can provide an intermediate management level before the final integration is completed.

The structure of the supervisor of the gearbox assembly plant is shown in Figure 9.5. For the sake of simplicity, only the supervision of the lines is considered.

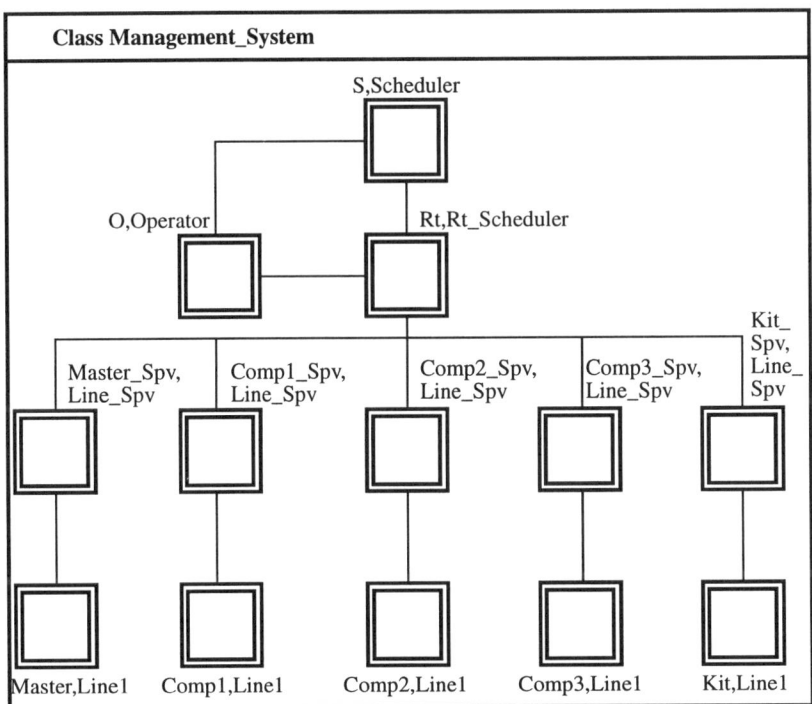

Figure 9.5 *The model of the plant management system*

Each line is directly managed by its own supervisor, which is an actor of class Line_Spv. The compound links that are drawn between the lines and their supervisors represent information flows, while the ones shown in Figure 9.2 represented part flows.

The external environment of the supervisor includes the shop-floor model, i.e. the actors modeling the lines, the operator interface (represented by actor O) and the module (corresponding to actor S) that schedules production for the plant being considered and for other related plants.

The shop-floor model presented earlier must be extended with the information flows needed by the supervisor. Therefore, the components of the shop-floor that have to interact with the supervisor must first be identified and suitable information flows have then to be introduced. For example, there are places in the gearbox assembly plant where raw parts have to be acknowledged and marked as units of a given lot (this takes place at marking stations) as well as places where parts have to be tested (at release stations). In such cases, the information flows between the shop-floor and the supervisor include the identification code of parts and the number of parts that have been marked, released and discarded.

The new model of the marking station, given by class Marking_Station1, is shown in Figure 9.6.

The new model inherits the one given in Figure 9.4 and extends it with two information flows, which are indicated by places Prod_Msg and Order_State, and one transition (Update_Production_Data). New orders and new bills of materials, sent by the supervisor, are received at place Prod_Msg and, when this occurs, the internal database is updated by Update_Production_Data. Whenever a part has been marked, the state of the current order as well as a flag indicating whether the part is the last of the current lot or not are sent to the supervisor.

The model of the line has to be modified, too; the new version, called class Line1, is given in Figure 9.7. The compound port (M_Intf) connected to the marking station in class Line1 corresponds to the pair of ports, Prod_Msg and Order_State, that have been introduced into class Marking_Station1.

Therefore, in the overall model shown in Figure 9.5 class Line1 has been used instead of class Line.

A portion of the line supervisor, that which manages the interactions with the marking station, is shown in Figure 9.8 and briefly described below.

On receiving a message from a marking station (i.e. a token at input place Order_State), transition Manage_Marking_Event updates the work in progress and propagates that token to place Completion_to_Check for further processing. If the event concerns the last part of a lot, transition Notify_Order_Completion sends a message to the real-time scheduler through output place Order_Completion and also puts a token into place Waiting_for_Order_Release. In fact, when a lot has been completed, the supervisor will send a new order to the marking station, but only after permission has

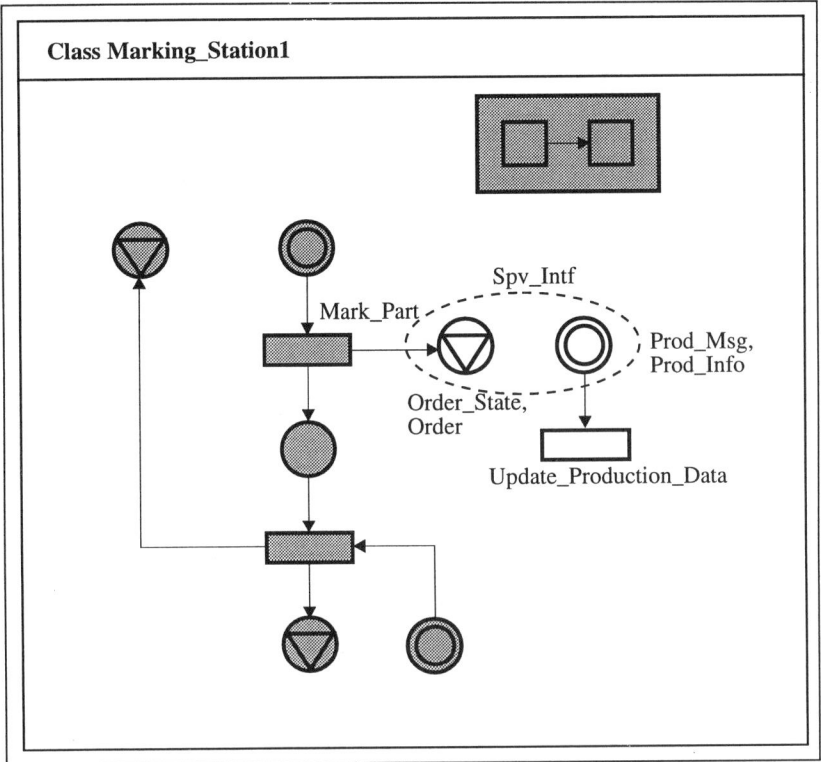

Figure 9.6 *The extended model of the marking station*

been given by the real-time scheduler (through input place Order_Release_-
Command).

Transition Down_Load_Order transmits a new order to the marking station through output place Line_Order and also issues a material request to
the supply subsystem through output place Req.

The management of orders and of data concerning the work in progress
requires complex information structures which could hardly be put in tokens. For this reason, an object model (Spv_Production_Data) has been
introduced into class Line_Spv. This object model is acted on by means of
Quid constructs which are contained in several transitions, e.g. Manage_-
Marking_Event and Down_Load_Order.

The real-time scheduler is responsible for synchronizing the lines; it also
enables the plant manager to modify the schedule and takes the appropriate
actions necessary to reorganize production. The interactions between the
real-time scheduler and the plant manager are carried out by actor Operator
which appears in Figure 9.5.

The model of the supervisor is the specification of a software system, but

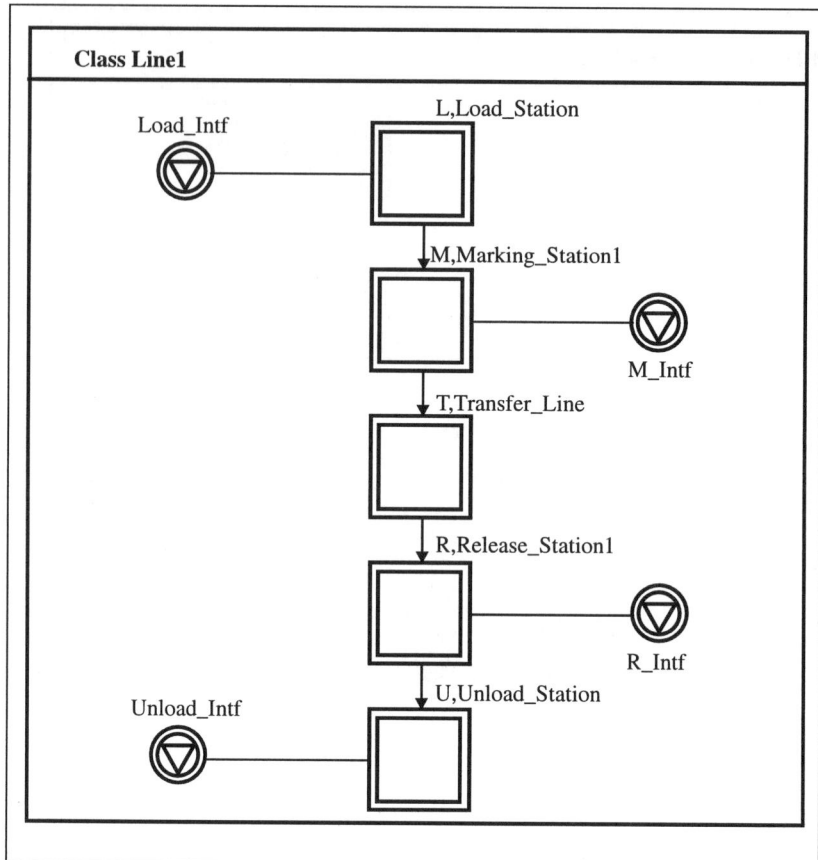

Figure 9.7 *The new model of the line*

the modeling languages are the same as those used to describe shop-floor behavior, so it is easy for a plant engineer to understand and validate the operation of the supervisor.

The supervisor model can be enriched until all the details have been included. Simulation allows the logic of the supervisor to be checked in advance in a friendly and controlled environment. The shop-floor model provides all the stimuli necessary to observe the supervisor's reactions.

According to the operational life cycle presented in Chapter 8, it is necessary to evaluate the actual performance of the supervisor before it is delivered. An example of a performance factor to be checked is the maximum delay elapsing between the arrival of a stimulus and the issue of the response. A thorough analysis of timing constraints has been performed by Dasarathy (1985) and is also described by Davis (1993).

To test performance factors, it is common practice to build an emulator

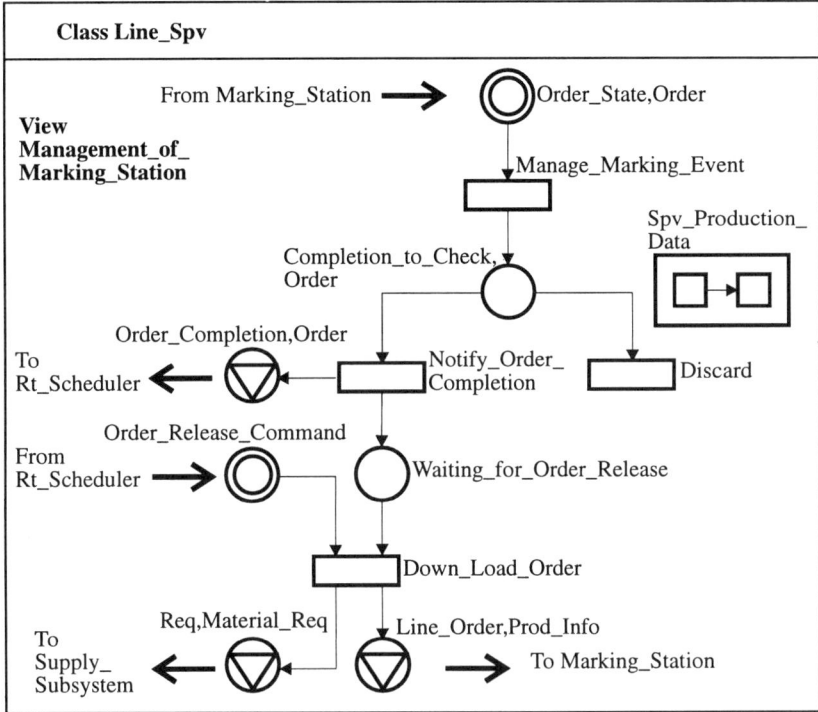

Figure 9.8 *Part of the model of the line supervisor*

of the environment of the system being considered: here, the emulator refers to the plant shop-floor.

The application workbench illustrated in Chapter 8 automatically generates a distributed program from the model, as shown in Figure 9.9.

Each actor shown in Figure 9.9 is transformed into a different process. The hardware platform consists of a local area network including five personal computers, each one running a line actor, and two minicomputers, one running all five line supervisors as well as the real-time scheduler and the user interface, the other running the plant scheduler.

Line actors emulate the actual shop-floor and send the supervisor processes the necessary stimuli with the appropriate timing constraints. After testing, they will be replaced by suitable interfaces to the device controllers. The supervisor is, therefore, observed in a realistic setting and its performance can be assessed; for example, it is possible to answer the following question: does the supervisor reply to the marking station within two seconds and what are the average and the worst-case response times?

During the execution of the distributed program, the related model can

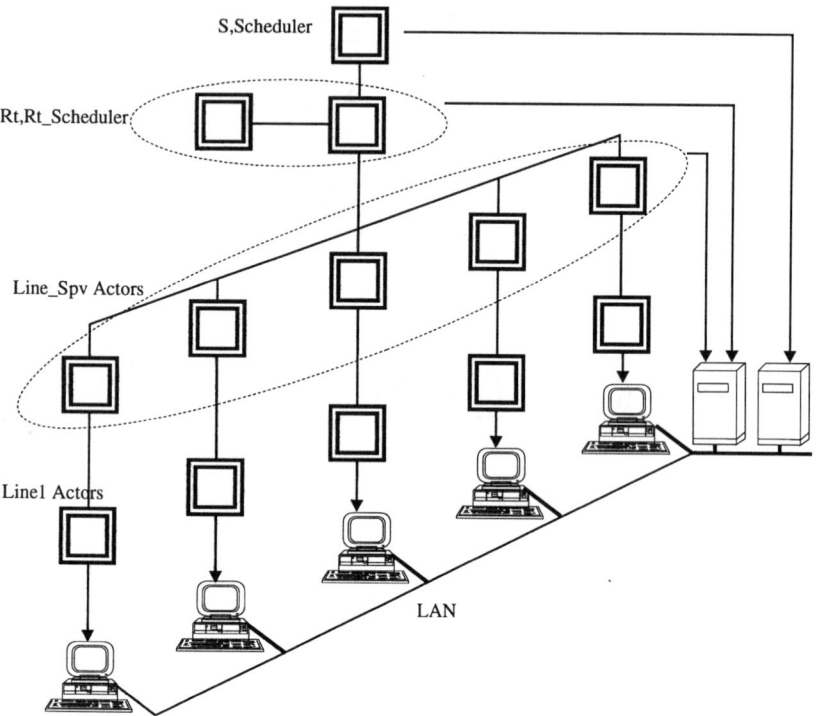

Figure 9.9 *Distributed code generation for the plant management system*

be animated; an example referring to the master line supervisor is shown in Figure 9.10.

Up to the instant (the current execution time) shown in the upper right corner, 270 parts have been marked. Orders consist of an average of 80 parts each, hence three orders have been completed.

The marking station has a buffer of pending orders which initially contains three orders; therefore, after the first order has been completed, the 4th order is down-loaded and so on.

There is a token in place Waiting_for_Order_Release: it indicates that the supervisor is waiting for a command from the real-time scheduler before sending the 6th order to the marking station.

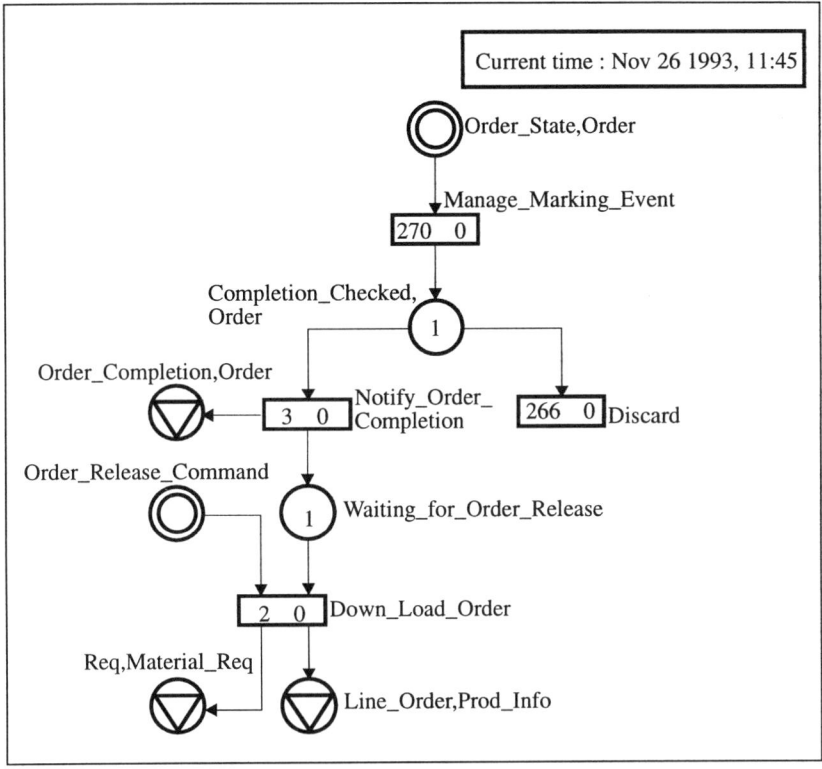

Figure 9.10 *An example of the animation of a line supervisor*

9.2 Telecommunications systems

Software for telecommunications systems consists of several concurrent activities which interact with each other and with external devices. Such activities have to respond to external events, e.g. calls, under timing constraints and in accordance with their internal state. They can have different priorities, e.g. an emergency call has priority over a call to give general information to passengers.

A conceptual model is needed to understand and define the system's behavior in all situations; further, it is essential that the model can be executed so that the system's reactions are validated and its performance assessed.

This section describes the use of Protob in the development of the supervisor of the communications system of an underground railway network. The system consists of several radio stations located along the railway network and of a control center; operators on trains are provided with mobile radio transmitters.

As an example, a call from a ground operator (i.e. an operator located at a ground station) to a train operator is modeled. For the sake of simplicity, only the main flow of operations is described, while failures as well as auxiliary activities are ignored.

Ground operators are supplied with personal computers including a radio transmitter. When a ground operator needs to get in touch with a train operator, he or she sends a request containing the identity code of the train to a ground processor, which collects requests from several ground operators.

Then the ground processor asks the radio processor (in the control center) to send a call signal to the radio device located on the train. The radio processor, by invoking a service of the table processor (in the control center, too), obtains the radio frequency of the callee and thus can send the call signal to the train. After receiving a confirmation from the train, it replies to the ground processor. Then the ground processor informs both the caller and the callee that the connection is open. When both parties have picked up their telephones, the conversation can start. The conversation is closed when one party hangs up.

The above interaction is illustrated in the interaction schema given in Figure 9.11.

Such a schema shows each actor, operator or processor, as a vertical line and each event (interaction from one actor to another) as a segment directed from the sender to the receiver. Time increases from top to bottom. Actual instants might be associated with events, but, for the sake of simplicity, they have been omitted. In Figure 9.11, the conversation is ended by the ground operator.

A simplified Protob model of the call is shown in Figure 9.12, where, for the sake of simplicity, place types have been omitted.

When a ground processor actor receives a call request from a ground operator actor (i.e. a token is put into input place Call_Req), transition Issue_Signal_Req sends a signal request to the radio processor actor and also puts a token that waits for the reply into place W_Signal_Done.

On receiving a signal request (i.e. when a token is put into input place Signal_Req), the radio processor actor sends a request to the table processor actor in order to get the frequency to use so that it can signal to the target train. In fact, transition Issue_Freq_Req sends a token to the table processor actor through output place Freq_Req and also puts a token that waits for the reply into place W_Freq. When the frequency is received (i.e. a token is put into input place Freq), the radio processor actor sends a signal to the radio device located on the train; transition Signal_to_Train sends a token to the train operator through output place Signal and also puts a token that waits for an acknowledge from the train into place W_Ack. When the acknowledge is received (i.e. a token is put into input place Ack), transition

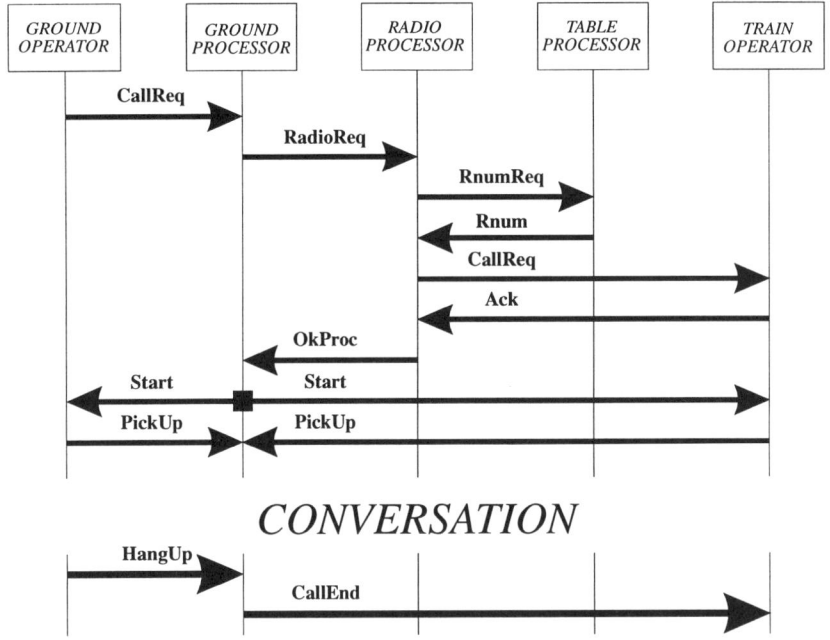

Figure 9.11 *A call from a ground operator to a train operator*

Send_Confirmation notifies the ground processor actor by sending it a token through output place Ok_To_Proceed.

The ground processor actor, when it receives the confirmation (i.e. a token is put into input place Signal_Done), informs both parties, the ground operator and the train operator, that the connection has been established; this is done by transition Notify_Connection which sends two tokens, through output places Opr_Connection_Ok and T_Connection_Ok, directed to the ground operator and to the train operator, respectively. In addition, transition Notify_Connection puts, into place W_Pick_Up, a token that waits for both parties to pick up their telephones. When this happens, the conversation starts; in fact, transition Start_Conversation is allowed to fire only when both parties have picked up their telephones, i.e. two tokens have been received, one at input place Opr_Pick_Up and the other at input place T_Pick_Up. Transition Start_Conversation puts a token into place W_End_Conversation so as to show that a conversation is taking place and to keep track of which parties are involved. When either party hangs up, the other is notified; in Figure 9.12 transition End_Conv_By_Opr ends the

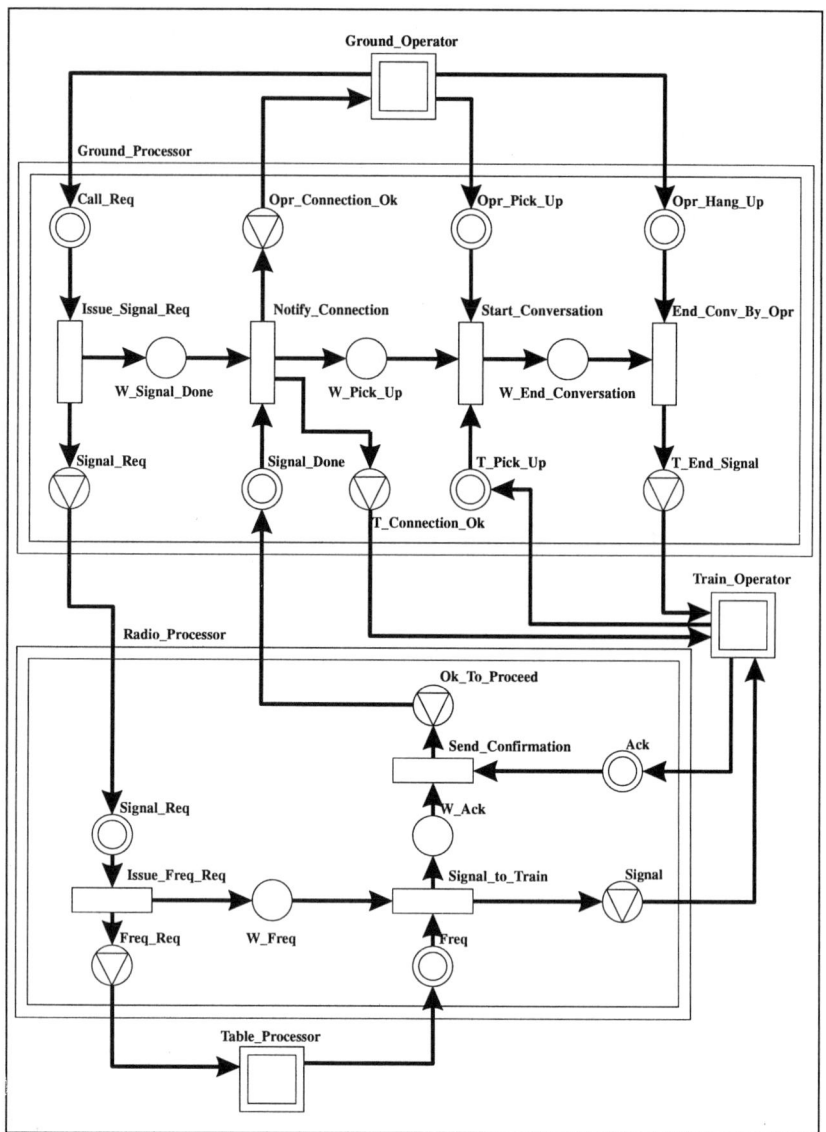

Figure 9.12 *A simplified model of the call*

conversation on receiving the signal that the ground operator has hung up (i.e. a token is put into input place Opr_Hang_Up) and then notifies the train operator by sending it a token through output place T_End_Signal.

The model allows multiple calls to be managed simultaneously; for each call the state is kept in a token that can be found in one of three places: W_-Signal_Done, W_Pick_Up and W_End_Conversation. Several tokens, which correspond to different ongoing calls, can be contained in those places at the same time.

The model can be animated during simulation as shown in Figure 9.13, where a fragment of a ground processor actor (GP1) is shown at a certain instant. There is one ongoing conversation, indicated by the token present in place W_End_Conversation, and one incoming call, indicated by the token in input place Call_Req. The contents of the latter token include the ground operator identifier and the train code.

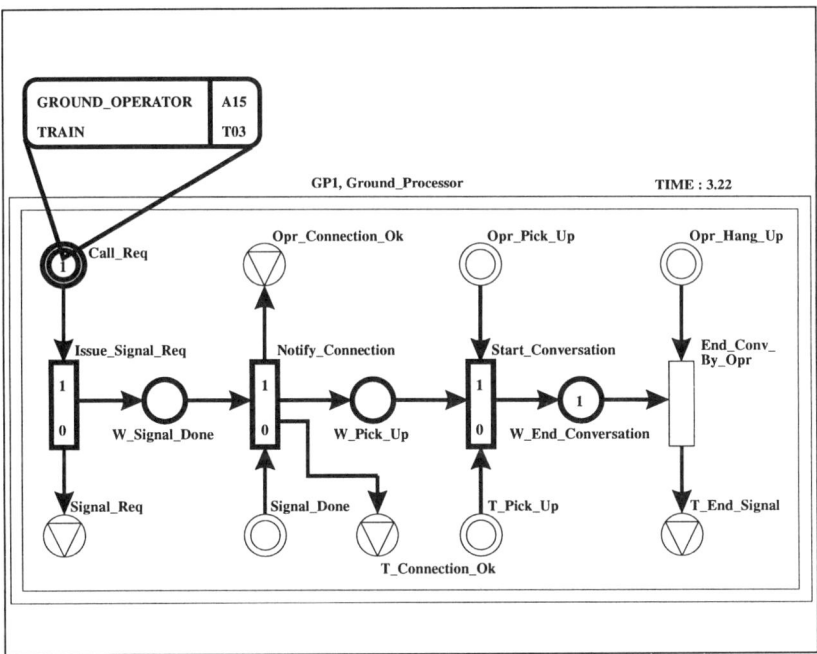

Figure 9.13 *An example of the animation of the model of the call*

9.3 Summary

The approach based on operational models that has been exemplified in this chapter offers several benefits, three of which are discussed below.

Modular composition. Plant/system engineers and system integrators (for the sake of simplicity, let's call them users), just as they design their systems by putting standard components together, can obtain the system model by picking submodels representing components from a library and then interconnecting them. The *software chip* metaphor followed in Protob leads to a very intuitive process of building models. In fact, Protob objects can be put together to form compound objects which, in turn, can be components of other larger objects. Objects have input and output pins, so that two objects can be put together simply by drawing a link from an output port of one object to an input port of the other object.

Transparent behavior. Protob, as a graphical language based on nets, provides an effective and rigorous representation of concurrency and synchronization, which are fundamental features of event-driven systems. Transparent behavior must not be interpreted from a static point of view only, but it must be considered from a dynamic point of view as well. In fact, when a model is so complex that mathematical proofs cannot be afforded, only by carefully examining its behavioral traces resulting from its simulation in well-understood scenarios can the user assess its correctness and effectiveness with reasonable confidence. By means of simulation, the user is able to study, on the model, how the logic of a component has to be modified and what the effects of the modification are.

Common language. Models are a common language for all the parties involved in a project: end-users, system engineers, system integrators, software analysts and developers, as well as subcontractors. Moreover, turnover time and cost are minimized when new people join an ongoing project, because the model is a conceptual representation of the system.

10

Epilogue

In this book, attention has been focused on operational models as a suitable means to overcome the chronic problems that bother the software industry: low quality and productivity, poor predictability and reusability.

This chapter presents the results of five years' work and discusses future trends.

10.1 Results of model-based software engineering

The effectiveness of *model-based software engineering* depends on the availability of sophisticated software tools that help users build models, study them through simulation and animation, and get efficient implementations from them. For this reason, several tools (Artis, 1992 and 1993) have been developed to promote the model-based approach.

The results of cooperation with clients on specific projects for five years, and the continuous improvement of the tools which are now available are summarized below.

Expressiveness. Protob models have a relevant graphical part (based on high-level nets) which represents concurrency and synchronization issues very effectively. They are particularly suitable for event-driven systems, in which the graphical part is far more important than the textual one. The textual part, which includes token types, predicates and actions associated with transitions, is written in a common programming language, such as C. Protob can also be used to represent the external environment of the software system, S, which is being developed: in fact, if the environment has its own dynamics, no matter how simplified it is, the behavior of S can be studied in a more realistic setting.

Management of complexity. The graphical techniques which put objects together (by peer-to-peer interconnection or by composition) enable designers easily to define and manage very complex architectures and also make it easier for them to experiment with different alternatives.

Understanding. By using models, all the parties involved in a complex project, such as end-users, plant engineers, system analysts, software analysts and developers, as well as subcontractors, are actually able to speak a common language, so that everyone can make a contribution in terms which can be understood and checked by all the other parties. Moreover, turnover time and costs are minimized, as new people can join an ongoing project with little initial training.

Integration. When a project is being developed by several teams, integration problems are minimized as each team can test its portion of the system using simplified models of the other teams' portions. Further, it is an open approach, which means that external software can be integrated with the program produced from the model, as was discussed in Chapter 8.

Quality control. Effective quality control is intrinsic to the operational life cycle, since extensive testing can be performed at each stage of development by simulating or executing models. The integration testing of a control system, such as the supervisor of a production plant or the supervisor of a railway network, can be performed very effectively by building a model of the external environment. Such a model, called an emulator, is connected to the control system model and provides it with the necessary stimuli under the appropriate timing constraints. Therefore, a realistic setting can be recreated in the laboratory without the actual devices. This approach to integration testing (called testing by emulation) involves an additional cost in building the emulator, but it enables system integrators to cut installation costs dramatically, since response times and all the other critical issues, such as exception handling, can be checked in the laboratory. Traditionally, a relevant part of integration testing is performed when the control system is directly connected to the plant, thus, software troubles are much more difficult and expensive to detect and to fix. The additional cost involved in the realization of the environment model is generally low, because the objects that have been developed during the system modeling phase are often extensively reused when the emulator is built.

Code inspection (in this case model inspection) has not to be suppressed; on the contrary, it can be performed more effectively, because it is done at a higher level, i.e. the level of the model rather than the level of the code.

Productivity. Since the model can be translated by program generation tools into the actual (also distributed) implementation, development and maintenance times are drastically reduced. The programmer can get rid of all the error-prone and time-wasting issues concerning process man-

agement and interprocess communication. He or she can even develop
and test the model on a given platform and, then, produce the implementation for another platform. Embedded systems are often developed
in this way: first, the model is developed and tested (in simulation or
emulation) on a host development system; then a program is generated
to be executed on a target platform whose operating system can be
different from the one of the host system.

Reusability. The model-based approach enables users to formalize knowledge about a particular domain in such a way that it can very easily
be shared. Practical results report reuse figures in similar projects of
up to 70%. Objects can easily be turned into parameterized building
blocks, so that a new application within a given domain can be developed
by picking objects from a domain library, giving them the appropriate
parameters and putting them together according to a set of domain
interconnection rules. For example, a dozen Protob classes are sufficient
to model the most common components of a production plant.

Human factors. The use of operational models raises the motivation of
developers, since they take the responsibility of well-defined portions of
the project, from design to testing, and their work results in tangible
and reusable objects (they deliver models, not only pieces of code).

Many event-driven applications have been developed so far, e.g. supervisors of production systems and logistic systems, supervisors of communications systems and measuring systems, and embedded systems for telephone
traffic monitoring and for toll collection on highways. The complexity of
such models ranges from few classes and few objects to dozens of classes
and thousands of objects, while some classes have up to two hundred transitions.

The applications that have been generated vary from a single-process
program to a distributed program running on a dozen nodes (each node
runs several processes). Heterogeneous architectures, e.g. those made up of
workstations and target systems, have been managed, too.

10.2 Future trends

The model-based approach is not a silver bullet, because as Brooks (1987)
said there is no magic solution to the problems of software development;
nevertheless, if it is used consciously, it can help the software developer
make substantial gains in quality and in productivity.

The model-based approach is dynamic owing to its very nature, hence it
will evolve over time, so that both problem-solving and process-management
capabilities are improved.

From our point of view, we envisage improvements in the following areas.

Extensions to the modeling language. As it took some time to understand which were the best constructs to put into third-generation programming languages, so the continual use of the modeling language in actual projects within a given application domain will indicate which specific features need to be incorporated in it in the future. For example, in process modeling, the notion of role, i.e. who does what, is fundamental: therefore, each Protob transition that represents a human activity must be supplemented with another attribute, the role, which specifies what competence is needed to perform the activity. A role, then, has to be mapped onto the specific resources that actually perform the activities in which the role is involved. A role can have a dynamic behavior that influences the execution of the activity. Further, a resource can play different roles, so rules must be defined in such a way that resource contention can be managed efficiently.

Development of building blocks and frameworks. Similar products require similar projects which can exploit similar models. While there is a high level of standardization for mechanical, electronic and computer hardware, the same is not true for software, hence a software components industry has never taken off, except for the libraries of mathematical routines.

However, using a modeling language, ready-to-use parameterized large-grain objects, such as a communication router or a warehouse supervisor, can easily be built and marketed. Since they address non-trivial problems, they offer great benefits to the purchaser, who, at the same time, feels confident that he or she can understand the product because it is a model. When the realization of a building block is too expensive, because there are too many variants to be taken into account, even the development of a framework, i.e. an abstract model, can be meaningful for novice users.

Improvements of the support tools. Support tools bridge the gap between the modeling language and the underlying technology, hence, as technology evolves over time, so do they. The novelty of *model-based software engineering* compared with the traditional approaches, such as the structured paradigm, is that the support tools are products of projects which are developed according to the operational life cycle; therefore, such tools originate from models and, consequently, they can be updated more easily.

Managing the process with the aid of suitable metrics. The use of models makes the software development process more transparent and easier to understand and to control; however, this possibility of controlling complexity very early in the development stage must be achieved by adopting suitable metrics. Empirical studies will enable the designer to indicate how models have to be structured so that they are easier to understand during both development and maintenance.

10.3 Conclusion

Model-based software engineering points out that software people can play several roles, e.g. users of predefined, parameterized building blocks, developers of building blocks and designers of methods for developing building blocks, as well as developers of support tools. In any case, each person does a job that produces visible results, i.e. models, on which he or she can easily judge his/her performance and identify the directions in which improvements can be made. More important, since tangible things, i.e. models, are produced, it is less difficult for everyone to learn from others.

References

Ajmone Marsan, M., Conte, G. and Balbo, G. (1984) A class of generalized stochastic Petri nets for the performance evaluation of multiprocessor systems. *ACM Trans. Comput. Syst.*, **2**, 93–122.

Artis (1992) *Artifex Reference Manual*, Torino, Italy.

Artis (1993) *Quid Reference Manual*, Torino, Italy.

Baldassari, M. and Bruno, G. (1991) PROTOB: an object oriented methodology for developing discrete event dynamic systems. *Comp. Lang.*, **16**, 39–63.

Batini, C., Ceri, S. and Navathe, S.B. (1992) *Conceptual Database Design: an Entity-Relationship Approach*, Benjamin/Cummings, Redwood City, California, USA.

Birtwistle, G. et al. (1979) *Simula Begin*, Studentlitteratur, Lund, Sweden.

Boehm, B.W. (1988) A spiral model of software development and enhancement. *IEEE Comp.*, **21**, 61–72.

Booch, G. (1986) Object-oriented development. *IEEE Trans. Softw. Eng.*, **12**, 211–221.

Booch, G. (1991) *Object Oriented Design with Applications*, Benjamin/Cummings, Redwood City, California, USA.

Brooks, F.P. (1987) No silver bullet: essence and accidents of software engineering. *IEEE Comp.*, **20**, 10–19.

Browne, J., Harhen, J. and Shivnan, J. (1988) *Production Management Systems: a CIM Perspective*, Addison-Wesley, Wokingham, England.

Bruno, G. et al. (1991) The impact of software engineering in the development of CIM systems, in *Proceedings of 7th CIM-Europe Conference, Torino, Italy, May 1991, (eds Vio, R. and Van Puymbroeck, W.)*, Springer-Verlag, London, pp.101–113.

Bruno, G., Castella, A., Pavesio, I. and Pescarmona, M. (1993) Temporal analysis of extended marked graphs for real-time applications, in *Proceedings of IEEE Workshop on Real-Time Applications, New York, May 1993*, IEEE Computer Society Press, pp.66–70.

Bruno, G., Grammatica, A. and Macario, G. (1992) Operational Entity-Relationship with Quid, in *Proceedings of 5th International Conference on Software Engineering and its Applications, Toulouse, December 1992*, EC2, Nanterre, France, pp.433–442.

Bruno, G. and Marchetto, G. (1986) Process-translatable Petri nets for the rapid prototyping of process control systems. *IEEE Trans. Softw. Eng.*, **12**, 346–357.

Chen, P. (1976) The Entity-Relationship model: toward a unified view of data. *ACM Trans. Database Syst.*, **1**, 9–36.

Coad, P. and Yourdon, E. (1991) *Object-Oriented Analysis*, Yourdon Press, Englewood Cliffs, New Jersey, USA.

Coleman, D. et al. (1994) *Object-Oriented Development: the Fusion Method*, Prentice-Hall International, London.

Cox, B.J. (1986) *Object-Oriented Programming*, Addison-Wesley, Reading, Massachusetts, USA.

Curtis, B., Kellner, M.I. and Over, J. (1992) Process modeling. *Commun. ACM*, **35**, 75–90.

Dasarathy, B. (1985) Timing constraints of real-time systems: constructs for expressing them, methods of validating them. *IEEE Trans. Softw. Eng.*, **11**, 80–86.

Davis, A.M. (1992) Operational prototyping: a new development approach. *IEEE Softw.*, pp.70–78.

Davis, A.M. (1993) *Software Requirements: Objects, Functions and States*, Prentice-Hall International, London.

De Marco, T. (1979) *Structured Analysis and System Specification*, Prentice-Hall, Englewood Cliffs, New Jersey, USA.

Edwards, K. (1993) *Real-Time Structured Methods*, John Wiley & Sons, Chichester, England.

Elmasri, R. and Navathe, S.B. (1989) *Fundamentals of Database Systems*, Benjamin/Cummings, Redwood City, California, USA.

Feiler, P.H. and Humphrey, W.S. (1993) Software process development and enactment: concepts and definitions, in *Proceedings of 2nd International Conference on Software Process (ICSP'2), (ed. Osterweil, L.)*, IEEE Computer Society Press, pp.28–40.

Fishman, G.S. (1973) *Concepts and methods in discrete event digital simulation*, John Wiley & Sons, New York, 1973.

Gane, C. and Sarson, T. (1979) *Structured Systems Analysis: Tools and Techniques*, Prentice-Hall, Englewood Cliffs, New Jersey, USA.

Genrich, H.J. and Lautenbach, K. (1981) System modelling with high-level Petri nets. *Theor. Comp. Sci.*, **13**, 109–136.

Goldberg, A. and Robson, D. (1983) *Smalltalk80: the Language and Its Implementation*, Addison-Wesley, Reading, Massachusetts, USA.

Harel, D. et al. (1990) Statemate: a working environment for the development of complex reactive systems. *IEEE Trans. Softw. Eng.*, **16**, 403–414.

Hatley, D. and Pirbhai, I. (1987) *Strategies for Real-Time System Specification*, Dorset House, New York.

Henderson-Sellers, B. and Edwards, J.M. (1990) The object-oriented systems life cycle. *Commun. ACM*, **33**, 143–159.

Hix, D. and Rex Hartson, H. (1993) *Developing User Interfaces*, John Wiley & Sons, New York.

Hopcroft, J.E. and Ullman, J.D. (1969) *Formal Languages and Their Relation to Automata*, Addison-Wesley, Reading, Massachusetts, USA.

Humphrey, W.S. (1989) *Managing the Software Process*, Addison-Wesley, Reading, Massachusetts, USA.

Jensen, K. (1981) Coloured Petri nets and the invariant method. *Theor. Comp. Sci.*, **14**, 317–336.

Jensen, K. (1991) Coloured Petri nets: a high level language for system design and analysis, in *High-Level Petri Nets: Theory and Applications, (eds Jensen, K. and Rozenberg, G.)*, Springer-Verlag, Berlin, pp.44–119.

Jensen, K. and Rozenberg, G. (eds) (1991) *High-Level Petri Nets: Theory and Applications*, Springer-Verlag, Berlin.

Korson, T. and McGregor, J.D. (1990) Understanding object-oriented: a unifying paradigm. *Commun. ACM*, **33**, 40–60.

Liskov, B. et al. (1977) Abstraction mechanisms in CLU. *Commun. ACM*, **20**, 564–576.

Merlin, P.M. and Farber, D.J. (1976) Recoverability of communication protocols: implications of a theoretical study. *IEEE Trans. Commun.*, **24**, 1036–1043.

Meyer, B. (1988) *Object-Oriented Software Construction*, Prentice-Hall International, London.

Molloy, M.K. (1982) Performance modeling using stochastic Petri nets. *IEEE Trans. Comput.*, **31**, 913–917.

Monarchi, D.E. and Puhr, G.I. (1992) A research typology for object-oriented analysis and design. *Commun. ACM*, **35**, 35–47.

Murata, T. (1989) Petri nets: properties, analysis and applications. *Proc. IEEE*, **77**, 541–580.

Open Software Foundation (1990) *OSF/Motif Style Guide*, Prentice-Hall, Englewood Cliffs, New Jersey, USA.

Parnas, D.L. (1972) On the criteria to be used in decomposing systems into modules. *Commun. ACM*, **15**, 1053–1058.

Peters, L. (1988) *Advanced Structured Analysis and Design*, Prentice-Hall International, London.

Peterson, J.L. (1981) *Petri Net Theory and the Modeling of Systems*, Prentice-Hall, Englewood Cliffs, New Jersey, USA.

Petri, C.A. (1962) Kommunikation mit Automaten. PhD thesis, Institut für Instrumentelle Mathematik, Bonn.

Ramamoorthy, C.V. and Ho, G.S. (1980) Performance evaluation of asynchronous concurrent systems using Petri nets. *IEEE Trans. Softw. Eng.*, **6**, 440–449.

Ramchandani, C. (1974) Analysis of asynchronous concurrent systems by timed Petri nets. PhD thesis, MIT, Cambridge, Massachusetts.

Royce, W.W. (1970) Managing the development of large software systems: concepts and techniques, in *WESCON*, August.

Rumbaugh, J. (1987) Relations as semantic constructs in an object-oriented language, in *Proceedings of OOPSLA'87, Orlando, October 1987*, ACM Press, New York, pp.466–481.

Rumbaugh, J. et al. (1991) *Object-Oriented Modeling and Design*, Prentice-Hall, Englewood Cliffs, New Jersey, USA.

Shlaer, S. and Mellor, S.J. (1988) *Object-Oriented Systems Analysis: Modeling the World in Data*, Yourdon Press, Englewood Cliffs, New Jersey, USA.

Shlaer, S. and Mellor, S.J. (1992) *Object Lifecycles: Modeling the World in States*,

Yourdon Press, Englewood Cliffs, New Jersey, USA.

Sloman, M. and Kramer, J. (1987) *Distributed Systems and Computer Networks*, Prentice-Hall International, London.

Stroustrup, B. (1986) *The C++ Programming Language*, Addison-Wesley, Reading, Massachusetts, USA.

US Dept. of Defense (1983) *Reference Manual for the Ada Programming Language*.

Ward, P.T. and Mellor, S.J. (1985) *Structured Development of Real-Time Systems*, Yourdon Press, Englewood Cliffs, New Jersey, USA.

Wegner, P. (1987) Dimensions of object-based language design, in *Proceedings of OOPSLA'87, Orlando, October 1987*, ACM Press, New York, pp.168–182.

Wirfs-Brock, R.J., Wilkerson, B. and Wiener, L. (1990) *Designing Object-Oriented Software*, Prentice-Hall, Englewood Cliffs, New Jersey, USA.

Wirfs-Brock, R.J. and Johnson, R.E. (1990) Surveying current research in object-oriented design. *Commun. ACM*, **33**, 104–124.

Yourdon, E. (1989) *Modern Structured Analysis*, Yourdon Press, Englewood Cliffs, New Jersey, USA.

Yourdon, E. and Constantine, L. (1978) *Structured Design*, Prentice-Hall, Englewood Cliffs, New Jersey, USA.

Zave, P. (1982) An operational approach to requirements specification for embedded systems. *IEEE Trans. Softw. Eng.*, **8**, 250–269.

Zave, P. (1984) The operational versus the conventional approach to software development. *Commun. ACM*, **27**, 104–118.

Index

Action, 24, 35, 153
  final, 155
  initial, 125
  output, 215
Actor, 35, 55, 160
  compound, 197
  emulation, 211
  first-level, 216
  simple, 181
  system, 168
  top-level, 216
Actor diagram, 170
Actor tree, 213
Address, 130
Agent, 11, 22
Alternative processing, 192
Animation, 202, 237, 243
Application workbench, 207, 218, 237
Arc, 64
  call, 137
  stimulus, 137
  view, 116
Artifex, 103
Association, 27, 56
Asymmetric-choice net, 84
Attribute, 26, 28, 148
  key, 27
  local, 48
  state, 173

Behavioral property, 74
Bill of materials, 30

Binding, 53
Bottom-up modeling, 22
Boundedness, 75
Branch node, 14
Broadcasting, 132

Call model, 240
Callback, 215
Cardinality, 28
Cell, 14, 56, 168, 226
Choice, 13
Class, 50, 121, 148
  active, 55
  ancestor, 52
  compound, 121
  descendant, 52
  group, 186
  passive, 55
  system, 168
  triggering, 153
Class-Relationship, 55, 147
Classification, 50
Classification of languages with
  respect to objects, 49
Client, 47
Color, 97
Command, 36
Communication property, 56
Communication protocol, 70
Completeness, 13
Composition, 30, 56, 120, 190, 243
Condition, 154

Condition/Event net, 96
Configuration, 208
Conflict, 66, 109, 113
Confusion, 85
    asymmetric, 85
    symmetric, 85
Consistency, 13
Context diagram, 18
Control flow, 40
    disable, 41
    enable, 41
    trigger, 41
Control store, 40
Coverability, 75
    strict, 75
Coverability graph, 79
Coverability tree, 77
Cycle, 94
Cycle time, 95

Data dictionary, 10
Dataflow, 10
    environment, 11
    external input, 21
    external output, 21
Dataflow diagram, 10
Datastore, 11
    local, 22
Deadlock, 75, 77
Delayed firing, 111
Delayed release, 109
Department, 26
Design, 211
Dialog box, 221
Directed circuit, 81
Directed path, 94
Dot notation, 51

Employee, 26
Emulation, 211
Emulator, 224, 237
Entity, 26
Entity-Relationship, 25, 147
Environment, 11
Event, 13, 35, 45, 115
Event list, 215
Event sequence, 36

Execution mode, 24
Extended dataflows, 40
Extended free-choice net, 84

Field, 26
Firing delay, 111
Firing rule, 64
Flow balancing, 21
Framework, 248
Free choice, 83
    extended, 84
Free-choice net, 83
Function, 9, 216
    input, 216
    management, 216
    output, 216

Generalization, 30
Generalization mapping, 157
Graph, 64
Graphical window, 221

Handle, 50, 150, 172
Hierarchical decomposition, 21
Home-state, 76

Identity, 50
Including set, 152
Information hiding, 49
Inheritance, 29, 49, 51, 56, 134, 157
    direct, 52
    indirect, 52
    multiple, 51
    single, 51
Inheritance graph, 52
Instance, 50
Instance graph, 31
Instantiation, 50
Interaction schema, 240
Interface, 118
    conceptual model of, 218
    implementation model of, 218
    provided, 137
    required, 137
    token engine of, 218
Interface code, 215

Life cycle, 212
  operational, 213
  waterfall, 212
Link, 122
  bottom-up, 122
  bottom-up service, 137
  compound, 123
  service, 137
  top-down, 122
  top-down service, 137
Liveness, 75
Local variable, 124
Logistic system, 181

Marked directed graph, 81
Marked graph, 81
  strongly connected, 94
  timed, 94
Marking, 64
  coverable, 75
  initial, 64
  reachable, 74
Merge node, 13
Message box, 221
Message line, 221
Metrics, 248
Mission, 13, 14, 176
Model, 2
  actor, 160, 168
  application, 211
  conceptual, 213
  control, 9, 35
  design, 211
  environment, 210
  functional, 9
  implementation, 213
  information, 9, 25, 166
  instance-oriented, 168
  object, 166, 173, 222, 235
  operational, 2
  specification, 210
  state, 55
  system, 210

Navigation, 32, 151
  example of, 180
  object-oriented, 158

Navigational statement, 153
Nul type, 105

Object, 47, 118
  active, 55
  component, 120
  compound, 120
  feature of, 48
  generic, 157
  graphical, 221
  interface of, 47
  operation of, 47
  passive, 55
  service of, 47
  specific, 157
  top-level, 120
Object graph, 149, 178
Object tree, 118
Object variable, 50
Object-oriented analysis, 54
One-way communication, 190, 196
Operation, 13
Operator Next, 29, 180
Operator Previous, 29
Optionality, 13
Order, 13, 15

Parameter, 125
Participation constraint, 148
Path, 151
  maximum, 152
  triggering, 153
Path expression, 151
  length of, 152
Petri net, 63
  colored, 97
  finite-capacity, 68
  ordinary, 80
  safe, 75
  structure of, 63
  timed, 90
  unbounded, 70
Place, 64, 104
  command, 142
  dataflow, 138
  datastore, 138
  derouting, 122, 130

event, 142
final-state, 189
initial-state, 189
input, 118
input-event, 184
interface, 118
internal, 118
output, 118
output-event, 184
resource, 185
self-loop, 89
state, 142, 184
unbounded, 70
Place/Transition net, 97
Plant, 14, 168
Polymorphism, 53
Port, 118
compound, 123, 228
input, 118
output, 118
Precondition, 24
Predicate, 108, 180
Primitive delay, 111
Primitive get_address, 132, 162
Primitive get_time, 116, 129
Primitive same_identity, 162
Primitive set_address, 132
Primitive set_parameter, 125
Primitive start, 166
Primitive time-out, 111
Priority, 25, 109
Process, 9, 237
ancestor, 216
application generation, 207
control, 37
controlled, 41
descendant, 216
enabled, 25
implementation, 215
model-based, 218
simulation, 201
transition, 142
uncontrolled, 41
Process tree, 216
Production system, 194
Program generation, 213
Project, 26

Property, 148
Protob, 103

Quid, 148

Rapid prototyping, 212
Reachability, 74
Reachability graph, 68, 75, 79
Reachability set, 74
Reachability tree, 77
Reactive system, 35
Regular expression, 10
Relationship, 27, 148
binary, 27
is-a, 29
is-part-of, 30
ordered, 29
recursive, 148
Release delay, 90, 111
Repetition, 12
Resource, 185
global, 192, 196
Reusability, 49
Reversibility, 76
Robustness, 49
Root, 149
internal, 149
primary, 150

Safeness, 75
Schema, 27, 31
Script, 103
Secondary item, 13
Selective routing, 132
Service, 47
abstract, 158
local, 137
provided, 137
required, 137
Service call, 159
Shop-floor, 225
Side effects, 49
Simulation workbench, 201, 217
Snapshot, 208
Software modeling, 210
Software production and maintenance,
211

Specialization, 29
Specialization mapping, 157
Specification, 210
State, 35
    initial, 35
State machine, 81
State net, 186
    multiple, 186
    single, 186
    variable, 189
State-transition diagram, 35, 81
Statechart, 60
Structural property, 74
Structured analysis, 9
Structured paradigm, 9
Subclass, 29
Subpath, 152
Superclass, 29
Supervisor, 14, 58, 173, 226
    line, 234
    plant, 226
Synchronous transitions, 192
Syphon, 83
System analysis and modeling, 210

Testing by emulation, 224
Token, 10, 64
    initial, 81, 104
    initialization code of, 105
    input, 66, 213
    output, 66, 213
    propagated, 106
    state, 184
Token engine, 213
Token routing protocol, 130
Top-down modeling, 22
Transition, 35, 64, 105
    delayed, 112
    delayed-firing, 111
    delayed-release, 112
    enabled, 65
    event-consuming, 186
    functional, 142
    immediate, 90, 112
    initial, 35
    input token of, 105
    output token of, 105

self-loop, 90
state, 184
time-out, 111
Transparent behavior, 244
Trap, 84
    marked, 84
Two-way communication, 190

Upward repartitioning, 23

View, 31, 57, 116
    control, 142
    functional, 142
View symbol, 116

Wip value, 15
Workstation, 13
    load, 229
    marking, 230, 234
    release, 231
    transfer, 231
    unload, 231